CARNEGIE
CORPORATION
of NEW YORK

In 1999, Carnegie Corporation of New York inaugurated an initiative on the contending norms of self-determination and the sanctity of existing international borders to encourage greater understanding of, and practical responses to, one of the most destabilizing and poorly comprehended phenomena of the post–Cold War era.

Coming to Terms: South Africa's Search for Truth traces the history of South Africa's Truth and Reconciliation Commission and the country's quest for self-determination in its transition from authoritarian rule to participatory democracy.

COMING TO TERMS

COMING
TO TERMS

South Africa's Search for Truth

MARTIN MEREDITH

WITH A FOREWORD AND AFTERWORD BY
TINA ROSENBERG

PublicAffairs

NEW YORK

Published in the United States by PublicAffairs™, a member of the Perseus Books Group.
All rights reserved.
Printed in the United States of America.

Book design by Jenny Dossin.

LIBRARY OF CONGRESS CATALOGING-IN-PUBLICATION DATA
Meredith, Martin.
Coming to terms : South Africa's search for truth / Martin Meredith :
with a foreword and afterword by Tina Rosenberg.
p.   cm
Includes index.
ISBN 1–891620–33–9
1. South Africa. Truth and Reconciliation Commission.
2. Apartheid—South Africa.
3. Human rights—South Africa.
I. Rosenberg, Tina.   II. Title.
DT1945.M47   1999
968.06'5—dc21   99–40362
CIP

FIRST EDITION
1   3   5   7   9   10   8   6   4   2

CONTENTS

FOREWORD

In the past quarter-century, perhaps half the world's nations have undergone a transformation from dictatorship or war to democracy or peace. All have had to struggle with the crimes of a past regime, to decide whether and how to put repressive leaders on trial, uncover the truth about patterns and individual cases of crimes, keep the guilty from continuing in powerful posts, and give victims some redress. Their dilemmas have produced some of the great political, philosophical, and moral dramas of our time.

Should Argentina attempt to try military officers who committed forced disappearances in the Dirty War if it puts the new democracy at risk? Who is qualified to decide whether people on a list of secret-police informants in the Czech Republic should lose their government posts? What is the best way to dispel the myths of victimization that Serbs cling to, before they explode into yet another war? Can Polish General Wojciech Jaruzelski be convicted of treason for his political decision to crush Solidarity by calling martial law—if he believed it prevented a Soviet invasion? Are the efforts of Rwanda's justice system to prosecute 120,000 people for genocide themselves doing injustice? Does Spain, which chose to do nothing about the crimes of General Franco, now have the right to take that choice away from Chile? The line between whitewash and witch-hunt, amnesty and amnesia, justice and vengeance is not always clear.

Dealing with the past is often the first test of a new government after tyranny, and the choices made can set the course for whether real democracy will develop. The trial of Louis XVI and the Terror stemmed from the French Revolution's betrayal of its ideals and then made that betrayal worse. "No freedom for the enemies of freedom!" Saint-Just cried at Louis' trial. Saint-Just was later guillotined; his own process bit back, taking his head. The French Revolution, and many governments since then, have proven that too much justice is also injustice. But more often, the problem is not enough justice. The same factors that produce tyranny or war also block a nation's attempt to overcome them, allowing impunity for powerful criminals.

Several factors give the issue of dealing with the past the urgency and scope it has today. Whereas in times past, forms of fascism and communism competed with liberal democracy as political models, today the world has settled, at least in theory, on one model as best: liberal democracy, with respect for human rights. And expectations that countries are able to adopt these ideals are higher than ever before. Before World War II, democracy, human rights, and civil liberties were considered out of reach for all but a few nations. Until Greece, Portugal, and Spain shed their dictatorships in the late 1970s, the conventional wisdom was that southern Europe's political terrain—much less that of Africa, Asia, and Latin America—could never grow democracy. Today virtually every nation, no matter how despotic its history, is expected to at least aim for the trappings of democracy. When war or dictatorship ends anywhere, the world is now eager to help.

The expectation is also growing that people who commit particularly atrocious crimes will be tried for them. Fifty years ago, the Nuremberg and Far East tribunals gave rise to the hope that the world would develop permanent institutions to punish and deter serious crimes. But the cold war ended any possible cooperation between the United States and Soviet Union on the issue, and nothing happened—until communism fell. Now, in the last ten years, various new international attempts to punish crimes have sprung up. The best known attempts are the International Criminal Tribunals for the former Yugoslavia and Rwanda, Spain's attempt to prosecute Chile's General Augusto Pinochet, and the International Criminal Court, which was born with a treaty signed by 120 nations in 1998 and will become a reality when half of them ratify it.

One reason that hopes for human rights and democracy are rising is the stunning number of nations that have become democracies, or have at least ceased to be outright dictatorships, since the transition in southern Europe in the 1970s. In the 1980s, at least ten countries in Latin America and the Caribbean ended wars or dictatorships. In 1989, the Soviet satellites of eastern Europe were liberated, and in 1991 the fifteen nations of the Soviet Union followed. During the 1980s and 1990s, at least fifteen African countries also shed dictatorships, although some, like Congo, have already slipped back. Korea, Taiwan, and now perhaps Indonesia have become democracies. In western Europe, Northern Ireland and Spain have made progress towards ending ethnic wars. Genocidal wars ended in Rwanda and three different parts of the former Yugoslavia.

South Africa under apartheid stood alone. It had characteristics of all three kinds of repressive regimes: Like ethnic cleansing and genocide, apartheid divided South Africa not by politics but by identity. Like communism, apartheid was an ideology that built a top-to-bottom system, in which members of society from the prime minister to the local bus driver were part of the machine and many people were both its victim and perpetrator at the same time. Like the Latin American-style military dictatorships, apartheid enforced the rules with assassination, torture, and forced disappearance, and it spawned guerrilla movements that committed crimes of their own.

When apartheid finally gave way to full democracy in 1994, South Africa invested most of its hopes for dealing with the past in one institution: the Truth and Reconciliation Commission. The truth commission sought to hear and publicize the victims' accounts of their repression, to research and write an account of political crimes that took place on all sides, to make judgments about the responsibility and relative weight of those crimes, to hear the perpetrators' pleas for amnesty from prosecution and to decide whether they should receive it, and to provide reparations for those who had suffered the most. No institution for dealing with the past anywhere in the world has taken on as ambitious a portfolio.

The complexity of apartheid and the breadth of the truth commission's mission make the story of the commission not just significant in itself but a vivid illustration of the problems societies face worldwide when trying to come to terms with their past. Every country is different, of course, and so is each nation's task in dealing with its past, but the issues they must deal with are at bottom remarkably similar. How can a nation heal the rot in its political culture and create true democracy and tolerance, not just their formal structures? How much can society give the victims before it risks provoking the perpetrators to kidnap a nation and return it to the old ways? What does a mother who saw her son dragged out of her kitchen, never to be seen again, need to make herself whole again—or to make society whole again? How should a nation treat criminals who carried out the will of the state or were raised from birth in a system that indoctrinated them in evil? Should justice be done when widespread trials are so expensive that they take money from the things necessary for a different future, such as schools and hospitals? How can efforts to deal with the past avoid repeating the injustices they seek to expose? How can those who do evil be convinced to drop their justifications and see what they have done? And finally, how does a nation choose who will answer all these questions?

Drawing on decades of experience in the country and on his extensive coverage of the truth commission, Martin Meredith tells a vividly South African story. But the issues involved are also utterly universal, a point I will return to in my afterword, where I try to give context to South Africa's experience by comparing it with other nations' attempts to deal with the past.

Because of the differences in our perspectives, Meredith and I have very different opinions on the question of whether the truth commission accomplished its goals. In his view, for all the truth commission's dramatic achievements (and they were many), it left South Africa ultimately unsatisfied. The political parties condemned its report; whites largely ignored its work; and many victims felt that it robbed them of traditional justice.

All that is true, and yet, viewed in global context, the Truth and Reconciliation Commission was a huge achievement, and its impact may seem even greater as time goes on. The modern obsession of dealing with a repressive past dates back less than twenty-five years. In that time, countries have tried dozens of varieties of truth commissions, trials, purges, and other schemes. For all the limitations of South Africa's truth commission, it seems to have been more successful than anything else yet tried, in part because its designers could learn from the mistakes of nations that had come before. For the victims, it democratized the process of dealing with the past. Whereas in other nations, a few high-profile cases were the only ones to get any attention from the courts or the media, in South Africa, thousands of people could tell their stories for nationwide broadcast. South Africa's truth commission also provided the most convincing blow to the myths of apartheid that any truth commission could, as hundreds of perpetrators came forward to admit to their crimes. Finally, it granted all who came before it the due process of law.

These achievements did not fulfill the expectations of most people in South Africa. But one thing the truth commission's architects know, but society as a whole cannot easily understand, is that no one should expect too much. It is normal for victims to feel that true justice was not done. It is normal for those who sympathized with the perpetrators to feel that justice tipped over into injustice.

All this is normal in part because no effort at healing can restore what is taken when a nation is crushed by a system like apartheid. More important, people's disillusion with trials or truth commissions is part of their general disappointment with the fruits of democracy. After years spent dreaming of freedom or democracy, few people find that the real thing lives up to their expectations. The policeman on their street is often the same arrogant one as yesterday; politicians are still out for themselves; the poor are not suddenly rich—and most infuriating to many, the old rich do not suddenly get poor. Political systems are easier to change than a political culture, and new democracies are always crippled by the habits they inherit. Trials or truth commissions are designed in part to help change the practices of authoritarianism to those of democracy. But these attempts, too, are inevitably poisoned by the past.

TINA ROSENBERG

I

The Widows' Testimony

ONE BY ONE, the widows came forward to testify. They had lived with their suffering and grief for many years, but for South Africa this was the beginning of a journey that would lead ever deeper into the dark recesses of its violent past. Each widow had a different ordeal to tell. But their common hope was that at last they would find out what had happened to their husbands, how they had died, where their remains were buried.

The commissioners listened attentively, steeling themselves for the tales of torture, kidnapping, and murder that were to become their daily fare. At their center sat Archbishop Desmond Tutu—head of the Anglican Church—dressed in a purple cassock and seeking to imbue the search for truth and reconciliation with a Christian sense of mission. He opened the proceedings with prayers, a hymn, and the lighting of a tall white candle in remembrance of those who had died and disappeared during the struggle against apartheid; he spoke ardently of the need for cleansing, for bearing witness, for joining hands, for forgiveness.

"We are charged to unearth the truth about our dark past," he told the audience gathered in the city hall in East London in April 1996, "and to lay the ghosts of that past so that they will not return to haunt us; and that we will thereby contribute to the healing of the traumatized and wounded—for all of us in South Africa are wounded people."

Few people at the time believed that the new Truth and Reconciliation Commission would establish either truth or reconciliation, let alone help solve murders and disappearances that had occurred as far as back as ten or twenty years beforehand. The old security police network, the prime suspect in most cases, had long since covered its tracks and was determined to thwart any investigation; for their part the commissioners had no clear idea of how to proceed other than to listen to the testimony of witnesses.

Nor did Tutu realize how grueling the task of what he called "looking the beast in the eye" would be. At the end of the second day of testimony, he laid his head on the table and wept openly. "I don't know if I'm the right person to chair the commission," he said later, "because I'm weak. I thought I was tough. Until today."

Among the black community there was nevertheless avid interest in the commission's proceedings. Each day, the ornate Victorian hall was crowded with spectators, filling rows of wooden benches that stretched from wall to wall and lining the galleries above. Many there retained vivid memories of the years of conflict that had engulfed the streets of East London and other towns in the Eastern Cape and that had claimed so many lives. Now, at last, it was time for the victims to be heard.

The first witness was Nohle Mohapi, the widow of Mapetla Mohapi, a twenty-five-year-old activist teacher who had been detained frequently by security police and who died in police cells in Port Elizabeth in August 1976. "He was in and out of jail," she told the commission. "He used to say: 'Our time together is short; the police are after me. You must be strong. You must never show the Boers you are weak. They must not see you crying.'"

One night, a security policeman hammered on her door and told her bluntly that Mapetla had hanged himself with a pair of jeans. "My first response was, 'No! Not Mapetla! He never killed himself.'" On her way to identify the body at the mortuary, the police had laughed at her. "They said: 'They call themselves leaders and they can't take the pressure and kill themselves.'"

An inquest recorded a verdict of suicide; the Supreme Court decided no one else was to blame. But Nohle Mohapi remained convinced her husband had been murdered. She told the commission that she herself had been tortured while held in detention after her husband's death. She had come forward, she said, in the hope that the commission would uncover what had really happened.

No sooner had she completed her testimony than four former police commissioners issued a statement criticizing her for giving evidence that they said was characterized by vagueness, generalizations, and hearsay. The police, they insisted, had done everything possible to ensure the welfare of detainees. They were clearly confident that their counterattack would succeed in discrediting her and other witnesses.

Next came the widows of the "Pebco Three," members of the Port Elizabeth Black Civics Organization who had disappeared without trace in May 1985 after receiving a message to meet a British consular official at the local airport.

Elizabeth Hashe described how she and her husband had endured years of harassment at the hands of the security police. They had both been detained without trial, and their house had been raided at night, time and again. Since her husband's disappearance, she had searched for him constantly, telling her story to magistrates and judges, but in vain. "I just want the commission to have sympathy with me, to understand what I went through when these things happened," she pleaded, breaking down in tears.

All she wanted now was to be allowed to bury her husband in a dignified manner. She asked, too, for help in obtaining the return of a photograph that police had confiscated after his disappearance. It was the only one she had of him.

The widows of the Pebco Three were followed by the widows of the "Cradock Four," four activists whose bodies had been found badly mutilated near Port Elizabeth in June 1985, several days after they had disappeared. Their deaths had ignited popular revolt throughout the Eastern Cape. One inquest had led nowhere. A second inquest in 1994 held the security forces responsible for the killings but still failed to identify any culprits. Now the widows hoped that Tutu's commission might provide them with answers. "We need an inside person, a witness," said Nyameka Goniwe. "We need the people out there who are still concealing the truth to come forward."

Her husband, Matthew Goniwe, the principal of a secondary school in Cradock, had been one of the most effective political organizers in the Eastern Cape. "He was seen as a dangerous man and a threat to the state," his widow told the commission. "They hated him for raising the level of political awareness of people." For years the family had been persecuted by the security police. "This took the form of early-morning raids and short-term detentions, death threats and tampering with our cars." Their movements had been closely watched; their phone calls had been tapped. And therefore, she said, the police must have known what had happened when her husband and his three colleagues left home by car to attend a political meeting in Port Elizabeth.

For another Cradock widow, Nomonde Calata, the grief of those days was still raw. Recalling the moment when she first heard the news about her missing husband, she threw her head back with a wail of such anguish that it sent a shudder throughout the audience. "I was only twenty at the time, and I couldn't handle this," she recalled. A family friend had subsequently gone to identify her husband's body. "He discovered that the hair was pulled out. His tongue was very long. His fingers were cut off. He had many wounds in his body. When he looked at his trousers he realized that the dogs had bitten him very seriously. He couldn't believe that the dogs already had their share."

Two weeks after Fort Calata's funeral in July 1985, Nomonde gave birth to a daughter. A few days later, the security police turned up to search her house. "Hau, you've got a baby without a father," one of them jeered at her in Afrikaans "Don't you want us to be the father of the baby?"

"I kept quiet. I didn't give them an answer. They waited a few minutes and then left. After a few minutes they came back. They said: 'We want to evict you from this house. You do not have money to pay for the rent. . . . Even in Fort's account there is not a cent left. So we are here to take you out of the house.' . . . I said to them I am not going to get out of the house. They could take a gun and shoot me, but I'm not getting out of the house. . . . I do not know the reason for their cruelty. I just want to know."

The family of Sicelo Mhlawuli, another of the Cradock Four, added further detail about their fate. His widow, Nombuyiselo Mhlawuli, described how, when reading the postmortem documents, she had discovered that her husband's face had been disfigured by acid and that his right hand had been chopped off. She had subsequently heard that the hand had been seen preserved in a bottle at security police headquarters in Port Elizabeth.

Her daughter, Babalwa, now nineteen but only eight years old at the time, took the tale further. She related how a few days after her father's body had been found, security police raided their house and made fun of sympathy cards sent to her mother. One of the policemen had shouted and screamed at her mother and stayed in the house for some six hours. He returned day after day, standing outside the house, howling like a dog and waving his hand loosely in the air.

Nombuyiselo Mhlawuli was asked by one of the commissioners what her reaction would be if the perpetrators came forward and requested amnesty for their crimes, as they were entitled to do. "Even if I say these people should be given amnesty, it won't return my husband," she replied. "But that hand, we still want it. We know we have buried them, but really to have the hand which is said to be in a bottle in Port Elizabeth, we would like to get that hand."

As well as the widows who testified, there were the mothers. Charity Kondile had spent nine years searching for her son, Sizwe, after the police claimed to have released him from detention in 1981. She had traveled to Lesotho hoping that the African National Congress would help find him. But ANC officials there had spurned her, telling her that Sizwe had turned traitor and defected to the police. "When I tried to reassure them that he had been kidnapped, they would not believe me."

Then, in 1990, she had been told of a newspaper story relating how Sizwe had been so badly tortured by the security police that they had decided to take him to a remote spot on the Mozambique border and kill him. "They put his body on a pile of wood with a tire near the Komati River at night, where it took them nine hours to burn his body," she said; and they passed the time drinking beer and enjoying a barbecue while the body burned nearby.

"As a mother, I feel that, no matter whether it was politics, fighting for his land, I don't think that he deserved all that treatment. I feel it was grossly inhuman. I feel if they could have killed him and given us the body or left it in the veldt. I feel that this was tantamount to cannibalism, or even Satanism."

Not all the testimony related to police brutality. Nontuthuzelo Mpehlo described how her husband, Mick, a businessman in Grahamstown, had been victimized for years after being falsely accused of betraying Steve Biko, the black consciousness leader who died in police custody in 1977. "My husband told me that he thought he was going to die but that he would die an innocent man," she said.

"While dressing for church, we heard the noise. The youths were coming down the road. . . . They surrounded the house, and they shouted, 'Let the spy *die*! Let the spy *die*!' They threw stones through the window. When they left, he said to me, 'Don't cry, Nontuthuzelo. A person dies only once, not many times. I know where these things are leading to.' . . . Then someone we knew knocked at the door. 'The comrades are burning your shop, Uncle Mick!'

"'I'll be back for lunch,' he said to me. They told me afterwards, he walked up to the door of his shop. He didn't look back. . . . Someone in the crowd shot him in the back."

There were also white victims who came forward, survivors of armed attacks carried out in the Eastern Cape by members of the Azanian People's Liberation Army. Beth Savage, a librarian, described how a group of friends belonging to a wine-tasting club were enjoying their annual Christmas party at a golf club in King William's Town in 1992 when gunmen burst in, opened fire, and tossed hand grenades in their midst.

"We were seated at one long table. . . . I suddenly became aware of something that sounded like firecrackers. I saw Rhoda Macdonald throw back her arms and die, and Ian [Macdonald] did exactly the same thing. I swung around to look at the door to see what was happening, and I saw a man there with a balaclava on his head—but not over his head—with an AK-47 [an assault rifle], and my immediate reaction was, 'Oh, my goodness, this is a terrorist attack!' After that I blacked out."

In the hospital, she was haunted at dusk each evening by the appearance of a man at her window. Unable to speak, she wrote messages to her family, "Please tell them to take the man away from the window." Eventually, her daughter brought her a photograph of one of the suspects. "It was this face at the window. . . . This was the gentleman at the door with the AK-47. . . . So that actually was a tremendous healing thing for me."

She recounted how much harm had been done. Four of her friends had died in the attack. Her father, whom she described as a staunch opponent of apartheid, had fallen into a deep depression and died; her mother, distraught without him, had died a few months later; her daughter had suffered a nervous breakdown. Her own injuries had been horrific: half of her large intestine had been removed, her heart had been damaged, and she still carried shards of shrapnel in her body.

Yet she was remarkably resilient. "All in all, what I must say is, through the trauma of it all, I honestly feel richer. I think it's been a really enriching experience for me and a growing curve, and I think it's given me the ability to relate to other people who maybe go through trauma." She added: "You know there are people here who have had far worse problems than I ever had."

She was asked whether it was important for her to know the identity of her attacker. "What I would really like," she replied, "is to meet that man that threw that grenade, in an attitude of forgiveness and hope that he could forgive me too for whatever reason."

After four days of hearings, Tutu concluded the commission's first session, encouraged by the fortitude shown by the thirty-three witnesses who had testified. "It is like a weight has been taken off their shoulders," he said. "The country has taken the right course in the process of healing to hear these stories."

Hundreds more witnesses were to tell their stories in the coming months at hearings held in towns and cities across South Africa. But there were few signs of any perpetrators coming forward to take advantage of the amnesty the commission was empowered to offer.

And the need for victims to know what had happened went unful-filled. "I would love to know who killed my father," said nineteen-year-old Babulwa Mhlawuli. "It is hard to forget and forgive if we don't know who to forgive."

Against all odds, however, the commission eventually succeeded in breaking through the barriers of silence. Like the unfolding of a complex detective story, the secret world of the security police was slowly exposed, and many of the killers and torturers were forced out into the open. What was even more unexpected was that once the security police network began to unravel, Tutu's commissioners found it possible to probe higher and higher up the chain of com-mand, reaching the highest levels of government.

2

Reconstructing the Past

In the struggle to end apartheid, South Africa came close to open civil war. The cycles of violence, which first erupted in the mid-1970s, flared up again and again with ever-increasing intensity, drawing in whole communities embittered by decades of white rule. In the mid-1980s, groups of black youths—"comrades," as they were known—set out to make black townships "ungovernable"; with stones, catapults, and petrol bombs, they defied armed police and soldiers in the dusty and decrepit streets. Urged on by the exiled African National Congress to mount "a people's war," comrades enforced consumer boycotts, organized rent strikes, attacked government buildings, set up "people's courts," and hunted down "collaborators"—township councillors, local policemen, and others deemed to support "the system." They were joined by small groups of ANC guerrillas infiltrating across the borders from neighboring states, bringing with them arms supplies to intensify the conflict. Marches, demonstrations, and labor strikes all added to the climate of insurrection. Many comrades saw themselves as the shock troops of revolution and believed that it was within their reach.

South Africa's white rulers responded with brute force. Claiming that the unrest was all part of a "total onslaught" orchestrated by the Soviet Union to enable communists to seize control of the country, President Botha declared successive states of emergency, giving the security forces virtually unlimited powers to deal with the truculent black population. A national security management system he established allowed army and police commanders control not only of security but of a vast range of other government activity. Hoping to decapitate black resistance, the government detained hundreds of community leaders, student activists, church workers, and union officials, holding them for months on end without trial. To counter the influence of radicals in the townships, the government supported right-wing vigilante groups. And to curb ANC infiltration, it launched cross-border raids into neighboring countries and trained and supplied rebel groups to disrupt governments there. The only way to combat "total onslaught," said Botha, was through "total strategy."

Botha was willing to modify the apartheid system, but only insofar as reform did not undermine white control. In the forty-year period that Afrikaner nationalists had held power, they had developed the apartheid system into the most elaborate racial edifice the world had ever seen, intending it to ensure white supremacy for all time. The black community was subjected to a vast array of government controls and segregated from whites wherever possible. Every facet of their life—residence, employment, education, public amenities, and politics—was regulated to keep them in a strictly subordinate role. In the name of apartheid, more than 3 million people were uprooted from their homes to satisfy government planners; millions more were imprisoned for infringing apartheid regulations. Black "homelands" set up ostensibly to allow blacks a measure of self-government remained dependent ultimately on white control.

In their attempts to resist apartheid, black nationalists tried public protest, petitions, passive resistance, boycotts, sabotage, and eventually urban insurrection. But although at each stage the confrontation became more widespread and more violent, South Africa's white rulers still showed no sign of willingness to lessen their hold on power. Botha in particular was confident that the government's security forces could overcome any threat the black nationalists posed. He declared that there would be no surrender to the communists.

His successor, F. W. de Klerk, however, on taking office in 1989, saw no long-term future in pursuing "total strategy" and sought a way out of the confrontation. In 1990, he released Nelson Mandela from twenty-seven years' imprisonment, lifted the thirty-year ban on the African National Congress and the Pan-Africanist Congress, and set out to secure through negotiation a new political dispensation that would leave the whites powerfully entrenched.

Yet the conflict only grew worse. Violent rivalry between Mandela's African National Congress and Chief Buthelezi's Inkatha Party, a Zulu nationalist movement, erupted first in the KwaZulu homeland and Natal, then spread to areas of the Witwatersrand, South Africa's industrial heartland. Security force elements still wedded to the idea of "total strategy" aided and abetted Inkatha, determined to thwart any prospect of the ANC coming to power. Massacres by one side or the other became commonplace. Death squads were known to be at work. Armed groups belonging to the Azanian People's Liberation Army, which was opposed to negotiations, singled out white civilian targets for attack. White right-wing paramilitary organizations embarked on their own vigilante action and threatened to wreck the whole negotiation process. Only by a narrow margin did South Africa succeed in holding its first democratic election in April 1994.

Despite the enormous task of reinventing South Africa as a democracy and of delivering the economic and social change that had been promised to an impatient electorate, President Mandela was determined to deal with its violent past. Unless the crimes of the apartheid era were addressed, he said, they would "live with us like a festering sore." He proposed that human rights violations should be investigated by a truth commission, not for the purpose of exacting retribution but to provide some form of public accounting and to help purge the injustices of the past.

Mandela's proposal was denounced both by de Klerk and by Buthelezi. De Klerk argued that a truth commission would result in a "witch-hunt" that focused upon past government abuses while ignoring ANC crimes. It was likely to "tear out the stitches of wounds that are beginning to heal." Buthelezi made clear that he would have nothing to do with a truth commission.

In the national debate that followed, some argued, as the ANC had once done, in favor of Nuremberg-style trials, claiming that apartheid was "a form of genocide" equivalent to Nazi atrocities during the Second World War, atrocities for which Nazi leaders were subsequently prosecuted. Some demanded reparations from the white community on the grounds that they were the main beneficiaries of the apartheid system.

Others argued that the best way to improve the chances of peace and reconciliation would be to grant a general amnesty to all sides. A large segment of the white community opposed the whole process, maintaining that the only result would be to reopen old wounds and revive old animosities still close to the surface. A common theme in the Afrikaans-language press was: "Atrocities were committed on both sides, so let us just forgive and forget."

There were conflicting views about what the central purpose of a truth commission should be. Some argued that the overriding imperative was the need to achieve justice and to bring to account those guilty of gross human rights violations. Others maintained that truth was at least as important as justice and that knowledge of the truth alone would contribute significantly to the cause of peace and stability; avoiding trials would also reduce the risks of a backlash from the security forces, still largely under the control of whites. Mandela himself once remarked privately that if he were to announce a series of criminal trials, he could well wake up the following morning to find his home ringed by tanks.

There were also differences of opinion about what period should come under review. Some wanted the review to cover the three centuries since white settlers first arrived in the Cape from Europe in 1652. Other suggestions included: the period from 1910, when South Africa was formed as a union between the two Afrikaner republics—Transvaal and the Orange Free State—and the two British colonies—the Cape and Natal; the period from 1948, when the National Party swept to power on a surge of Afrikaner nationalism and launched its apartheid policies; the period from 1960, when the National Party government first imposed a state of emergency and introduced detention without trial; and the period from 1976, when the cycles of violence first erupted.

The debate about a truth commission was pursued at conferences, at workshops, and in parliamentary committees. Much attention was paid to lessons learned from truth commissions that had been set up in countries in Eastern Europe and South America, in particular in Chile and in Argentina, to deal with their difficult pasts. Foreign experts were invited to give their views on how South Africa should proceed. From newspaper articles, South Africans became familiar with the words of wisdom from other lands: "Those who cannot remember the past," warned George Santayana, "are condemned to repeat it."

The Truth and Reconciliation Commission (TRC) that emerged in 1995 was born inevitably of compromise. The remit it was given by parliament was relatively narrow. The commission's focus was limited to the investigation of gross violations of human rights in the thirty-four year period from 1960, starting with the massacre at

Sharpeville. These violations were defined as the killing, abduction, torture, or severe ill-treatment of any person, or any attempt, conspiracy, incitement, instigation, command, or procurement to commit
those acts. Thus the wider injustices of the apartheid system—such
as the forced removal of some 3 million people from their homes,
the imprisonment of millions for pass-law offenses, and the widespread use of detention without trial—would not be addressed. Only
the extremes of apartheid would be examined, not its normality.

To help it develop "a complete picture" of the causes and extent
of gross violations of human rights, the TRC was given powers of
subpoena and of search and seizure. It was supported by its own
investigative unit. It was required to pay as much attention to violations committed by liberation movements as by the security police.
But it was not a judicial body or a court of law. It could not carry out
prosecutions or hand out punishment. Its aim was not so much to
reach a judgment about culpability as to establish a process of disclosure.

The most contentious part of the TRC's remit involved the
amnesty clauses. During the final stages of the negotiations that
ended white rule, de Klerk had insisted that a guarantee of amnesty
be written into the new constitution; Mandela was obliged to concede. Without amnesty, the white establishment might not have
agreed to give up power. Amnesty therefore became the price for
peace. A special "post-amble" inserted into the constitution spoke
of the priority that had to be given to national reconciliation in
overcoming past divisions and strife:

> There is a need for understanding but not for vengeance, a need for
> reparation but not retaliation, a need for ubuntu [humaneness] but
> not for victimization. In order to advance such reconciliation and
> reconstruction, amnesty shall be granted in respect of acts, omis-

sions, and offenses associated with political objectives and committed in the course of the conflicts of the past.

In giving effect to this constitutional requirement, Mandela's government decided to link amnesty to truth-telling. Only if perpetrators agreed to make full disclosure of their crimes would they be granted amnesty. No general amnesty would be given. Each individual would have to apply for amnesty separately. Applicants would have to convince a panel of commissioners that their crimes had been carried out with a political objective. In making their decision, the commissioners would weigh six factors, known as the "Norgaard principles": the motive; the objective; the context; whether the deed was authorized; its "legal and factual nature"; and its proportionality to a political goal. Amnesty would not be granted for acts driven by personal gain or malice, nor would it be granted if the panel was not convinced that an applicant had made a full disclosure. But applicants would not be required to express any remorse. Once amnesty had been granted, perpetrators would no longer be liable to criminal or civil suits. But if they failed to apply for amnesty, they would remain at risk of prosecution. Despite the incentive, TRC officials expected relatively few perpetrators to take advantage of the offer.

The initial focus of the commission's work therefore became the testimony of the victims. Commission officials began taking statements from hundreds of victims who wanted their stories heard, selecting from their number a group of cases deemed appropriate for public hearings. It was recognized that the proportion of victims making contact with the commission would be only a fraction of the total. The number of cases heard in public would be even smaller. But the commission hoped that from all the fragments of evidence it collected, the pattern of human rights abuses in the past would become clearer, and that at least the victims who had been heard would gain some sense of relief as well as a measure of compensation.

The format chosen for the public hearings produced further controversy. In recounting their stories, victims were to be allowed to name perpetrators, provided that the perpetrators had been given sufficient warning, but the victims themselves were not to be subjected to any rigorous cross-examination, as would happen in a court of law. The commission wanted to ensure a friendly environment in which victims could relate their ordeals without fear of interrogation. Their testimony would thus be largely untested by the normal rules of evidence. The risk was that a flawed or a false version of the truth might emerge.

There was serious concern about how much importance would be attached to victims' evidence of events ten or twenty years distant. A leading academic, Tom Lodge, stressed the pitfalls of oral history corrupted, as it often was, by flaws in memory; Lodge warned of the danger that the TRC might degenerate into an "untruth commission."

There was also concern about the license allowed the TRC to name perpetrators who were to be given only limited opportunity to defend themselves. Critics maintained that this collided with a fundamental rule of natural justice—*audi alteram partem*—both parties must be afforded a proper hearing. One of the first challenges the commission faced was from two former security policemen who, on the grounds that they were not offered a fair chance to respond to her allegations, took legal action to prevent a victim's mother from giving evidence against them on the first day of the commission's hearings in April 1996.

The commission encountered a torrent of other criticism. Families of several prominent victims, most notably Steve Biko, were outraged that the amnesty provisions deprived them of their right to seek redress from the courts; these families challenged the validity of the provisions in the Constitutional Court, though without success. Opposition to the amnesty provisions came not just from the black community but from sections of the white community. "The amnesty process breeds a contempt for the rule of law in our society by placing a section of our political class above the law," complained the business magazine *Finance Week*. "If politicians and their followers are not subject to trial and punishment for their crimes, why should the rest of society be?"

ANC officials abhorred the commission's intention to treat ANC violations on an equal basis with government violations, as it was required to do. They argued that because the liberation struggle against apartheid had been a just cause, violations of human rights on their side were of less significance than government violations committed in defense of an unjust order.

The appointment of commissioners aroused further controversy. Candidates were interviewed in public by a selection panel. They were required to be able to make impartial judgments and to possess moral integrity with a known commitment to human rights, reconciliation, and disclosure of the truth. They could not be high-profile members of any political party. Out of 300 nominations, the panel eventually selected a short list of twenty-five names that were submitted to President Mandela.

The seventeen commissioners appointed by Mandela came from diverse backgrounds. Four were from the white English-speaking community; two were Afrikaners; two were from the Indian community; two were from the Colored (mixed-race) community; seven were Africans. By profession, they included four churchmen, six lawyers, two doctors, two psychologists, and a psychiatrist. Several were unknown in public. But all of them possessed liberal or anti-apartheid credentials. This immediately opened the commission to the charge that its membership was biased in favor of the liberation movements. Most commissioners might realistically have been described as "pro-ANC"; perhaps two might have had some sympathy for the National Party; none were supporters of Inkatha. Buthelezi's Inkatha Party declared that the "truth commission, through its party political appointments, is beginning to resemble the make-up of Stalin's show trials, where accuser, judge, and jury are one and the same."

As chairman, Archbishop Tutu tried to ride out each storm with grace and goodwill. His credentials were impeccable. His defiant stand against apartheid had earned him the Nobel Peace Prize in 1984. Yet he had also made clear his opposition to violent means to overthrow the system of apartheid, and he had often endeavored to damp down the fires of black anger. On one occasion, he had intervened physically, trying to prevent a crowd from killing a suspected police informer. He was a close friend of Nelson Mandela; indeed, he had invited Mandela to stay at his home in Cape Town on his release from prison in 1990. Yet he had not shrunk from criticizing the new government for greed and corruption. As much as he had been during the apartheid era, Tutu remained a voice of conscience for the new South Africa.

A diminutive figure with expressive eyes and animated hands, Tutu exuded Christian bonhomie, laughing and crying with equal facility. At the age of sixty-four, he was on the verge of retirement when he was invited to head the commission. It was a position he neither sought nor wanted but felt duty-bound to accept. Like other prospective commissioners, he had been interviewed by the selection panel.

"What should one call you?" asked a panel member. "Wouldn't people find you intimidating? . . . Here I am, and I don't know whether I should say 'Your Highness' or 'Father' or 'Bishop.'" Tutu replied, laughing: "You can call me anything as long as you don't call me 'Your Graciousness.' No, I don't think I intimidate people, I hope they think I'm fun."

With his customary ebullience, Tutu brought to the commission not only Christian terminology but Christian habits. His deputy, Alex Boraine, a white Methodist minister, had similar inclinations. When introducing the commissioners to press photographers at his official residence at Cape Town, Tutu bowed his head and began to pray, ". . . that we may have the strength to listen to the whispers of the abandoned, the pleas of those afraid, the anguish of those without hope." As part of their preparation, he took the commissioners for a retreat under the guidance of his personal spiritual adviser, Father Francis Cull; during the retreat the commissioners were not permitted to talk, even during mealtimes. The day before the first public hearings began in East London in April 1996, he led a church service in Mdantsane township at which he offered to forgive "the sins of those burdened by sins."

Not all this was appreciated. A white anti-apartheid activist, Marius Schoon, whose wife and six-year-old daughter had been blown apart by a parcel bomb sent by security police to their home in exile in Angola in 1984, wrote to a Sunday newspaper complaining that Tutu had no right to impose his beliefs on others: "As a religious leader, the Archbishop is completely entitled to make this type of appeal to his faithful. However, as chairperson of an important government commission, it is important that the Christian ethic is not viewed as the law of the land. Not all of us are Christians."

Schoon said he was aware of "good political reasons" for the establishment of the TRC. "These reasons do not include the imposition of Christian views on all of us. There is no feeling of forgiveness in my heart. There is no constitutional duty placed on me to forgive."

Thus the TRC began its journey into the past, bearing the hopes of many but the scorn and derision of others. The Afrikaner community, believing that it would become the main target of opprobrium, was overwhelmingly hostile. Buthelezi's Zulu nationalists dismissed it as worthless. De Klerk's National Party was skeptical. Whatever progress it made, the TRC suffered from those handicaps from the start.

From East London, the commissioners moved to Cape Town, Johannesburg, and Durban, then dispersed to other towns across South Africa, traversing a landscape marked by suffering and pain. "The depth of the depravity was breathtaking," recalled Tutu. Yet for all the stories they heard from victims, they gathered little new evidence about the perpetrators. The old security network was effective in covering its tracks and maintaining silence. A few cracks in the facade had appeared, however, and they were suddenly to widen.

3

Vlakplaas

DURING THE 1980s, anti-apartheid activists blamed many murders on the security forces; but there was little evidence to support their claims, and the government curtly dismissed all such allegations. It was not until 1989 that a sudden breakthrough occurred.

On 19 October 1989, a few hours before he was due to be hung for the murder of a white farmer, a thirty-two-year-old black security policeman, Almond Nofomela, hoping to gain a stay of execution, swore an affidavit that he had been a member of a police death squad. He had kept silent hitherto, he said, because senior officers had assured him that they would step in to save his life. But three days before he was due to be hanged, a security policeman visiting him in the condemned cells in Pretoria prison told him he would have to "take the pain."

Nofomela claimed that he had been involved in some nine assassinations. In eight cases he was unable to recall their names. But one name he did remember was Griffiths Mxenge.

Griffiths Mxenge was a popular Durban lawyer who worked tirelessly on behalf of victims of the apartheid system caught daily in the web of pass laws, curfew laws, liquor laws, residence laws, and employment laws that made criminals of ordinary people. A former Robben Island prisoner who had served two years there for "furthering the aims" of the banned ANC, he was also renowned for his work defending anti-apartheid activists.

On 20 November 1981, Mxenge's badly mutilated body was found outside a football stadium near Durban. His watch, wallet, jacket, and car had been stolen, suggesting a robbery. But, as an inquest noted, he had been stabbed more than thirty times and sustained a dozen other wounds. His widow, Victoria, remarked, "My husband died in great pain. His throat was slashed, his stomach ripped open, and his ears almost cut off. The rest of his body was covered with stab wounds. I don't believe this is the work of ordinary thugs. It was done by someone who was opposed to what he stood for."

The security police were the main suspects. But the head of the security police, General Johan Coetzee, pointed a finger at the ANC, claiming that there was dissatisfaction within the ANC with the manner in which Mxenge had handled funds from overseas. At the inquest, after noting how little the police had investigated, the magistrate recorded that Mxenge's death had been caused by persons unknown.

At his funeral, a massive crowd of mourners heard Desmond Tutu, then a bishop, speak of how costly liberation from apartheid would be and of how, nonetheless, freedom would come in the end. As the coffin was lowered into the ground, a black security policeman was found trying to tape-record the proceedings covertly; a frenzied group of mourners seized upon him, screaming "Kill! Kill the *impimpi* [spy]!" Tutu and another priest struggled in vain to protect him. "Have you come here to bury Griffiths or kill one another?" shouted Tutu, his white robes spattered with blood, as the battered policeman lay dying behind the speakers' platform.

Victoria vowed to continue his work. "If by killing my husband they thought the work he was doing would come to an end, they have made a mistake. I'll continue even if it means I must also die. A rough life is part and parcel of me now." A newly qualified lawyer, she took up his crusade in the courts and in anti-apartheid organizations like the United Democratic Front (UDF), an internal ally of the banned African National Congress.

On 1 August 1985, Victoria Mxenge was shot by four men who ambushed her as she arrived at her home at Umlazi near Durban. Her murder caused widespread outrage reaching as far as London and Washington. A State Department spokesman denounced the killing and called on the South African government to find and arrest the perpetrators.

The murder also led to rising tension between supporters of the UDF and its rival Inkatha, the Zulu nationalist movement. At a memorial service held in a cinema in Umlazi, mourners were attacked by a group of assailants, whom they identified as Inkatha supporters, carrying assegais and knobkerries. Seventeen people were killed.

In his affidavit in October 1989, Almond Nofomela described how in 1981 two senior white officers, Brigadier Willem Schoon and Captain Dirk Coetzee, had ordered him and three black colleagues from the police death squad based outside Pretoria to travel to Durban to eliminate Griffiths Mxenge. "I was told . . . that Mxenge was to be eliminated for his activities within the African National Congress," he stated. At the main police station in Durban beforehand, Coetzee, in command of the operation, had instructed Nofomela to use only knives in the killing and to make it appear as a robbery. After monitoring Mxenge's movements for a few days, Nofomela and his colleagues had waylaid Mxenge as he was driving home from his office at night, forced him into a car, taken him to a football stadium, and assaulted and stabbed him to death. Then, after stripping his body of items of value and taking his car, they had reported back to Coetzee. They had subsequently been paid a special cash bonus for a job well done. Coetzee later mentioned that

Victoria Mxenge might also need to be killed, but Nofomela heard nothing more of the plan.

The Nofomela affidavit was the first hard evidence about the existence of government death squads. But the credibility of Nofomela's allegations was diminished by his own admission that he was seeking to escape the death penalty.

A few weeks later, however, Dirk Coetzee broke ranks. His police career had ended ignominiously in 1986, after a series of internal disputes had culminated in his discharge; he had left bitter and disgruntled, an outcast from the service he had once revered. Nofomela's affidavit made him willing to talk. With the help of an investigative reporter from the radical Afrikaans newspaper *Vrye Weekblad*, he fled South Africa and placed himself in the hands of the African National Congress.

Coetzee's disclosures, published in *Vrye Weekblad* on 17 November 1989, caused pandemonium in the security establishment. He admitted that he had commanded a police counterinsurgency unit based at Vlakplaas, a secluded farm near Pretoria; the unit had been involved in assassination, bombing, arson, and kidnapping. He had initially set up Vlakplaas in 1980 as a base for handling antigovernment guerrillas who had defected—"askaris," as they were called—and who were to be used to hunt down their former colleagues. But it had swiftly become a death squad. Coetzee admitted his involvement in the murder of Griffiths Mxenge. He also disclosed that he had been called on to help dispose of Sizwe Kondile; he described how security policeman had enjoyed a "braai" (a barbecue) while Kondile's body burned beside them. By the time he was transferred from Vlakplaas in December 1981, he had chalked up involvement in six murders and seventeen other serious crimes. "I was prepared to kill as many people as I was instructed to kill. I absolutely felt like a hero. I mean, you were there to please your bosses."

The impact of these disclosures was all the greater since at the time there was growing public alarm at the possibility that death squads might be in action. Six months before, in May 1989, a white university lecturer, David Webster, who had worked assiduously on behalf of political detainees and their families, was shot dead outside his house in Johannesburg by a gunman from a passing car. Webster's death had all the hallmarks of a professional assassination. In September, on the eve of elections in Namibia, a neighboring territory that South Africa controlled, Anton Lubowski, a prominent white supporter of Namibian independence, was shot dead in front of his home in the capital, Windhoek, in what was clearly another professional assassination.

The security establishment was quick to deny any involvement. When Coetzee's disclosures were published, a massive campaign was launched to discredit him. He was dismissed as a crank, mentally unstable, bent only on revenge for his discharge in 1986. The police admitted the existence of Vlakplaas but insisted it was used only for "rehabilitating" former terrorists. As for death squads, they were no more than a figment of his imagination.

Investigations into Lubowski's murder, however, soon led to a notorious assassin named Donald Acheson, a former Rhodesian soldier who was known in the trade as "The Cleaner." From Acheson the trail led first to his "handler," Ferdi Barnard, a convicted murderer and drug dealer recently released on parole, and then to Barnard's employer, a secret defense force unit called the "Civil Cooperation Bureau," or CCB. The CCB also appeared to be linked to Webster's murder.

As public alarm mounted, President de Klerk hoped initially that an internal inquiry would be sufficient to quell the matter. Only recently installed in office, he had little experience of the security establishment. During the Botha era of "total strategy," when defense and security officials were given a free hand to act as they saw fit both in South Africa and abroad, de Klerk had been preoccupied with domestic issues like education. Along with a large section of the National Party, he had come to dislike the way in which the security establishment had tended to usurp the role of parliament and the National Party itself. Soon after taking office, de Klerk had dispensed with the elaborate system of national security management that Botha had constructed as part of his total strategy. Nevertheless, de Klerk remained heavily dependent on the security establishment to maintain control while he embarked on reform, and he feared antagonizing it.

The internal inquiry duly reported to de Klerk in November 1989 that there was no evidence to substantiate the allegations made by Coetzee and Nofomela. But public opinion was far from satisfied. In January 1990, de Klerk was obliged to concede a judicial commission of inquiry under Judge Louis Harms to investigate "murders and deeds of violence allegedly committed with political motives," and he promised to "cut to the bone" to reach the truth about the death squad issue.

The Harms commission was largely a farce. De Klerk restricted its terms of reference to South African territory alone, thwarting all attempts to investigate assassinations in neighboring countries; the Lubowski case and others like it were thus off-limits. Security force operatives showed their contempt for the proceedings by appearing in clownlike disguises and using pseudonyms. One after another they denied all knowledge of criminal activity. The commander of Vlakplaas, Major Eugene de Kock, who was later revealed as one of South Africa's most prolific killers, added his own denial: "I was never involved in any assassination outside the borders of South Africa. My duty was restricted to collecting information on the activities of terrorists. The accusations of Almond Nofomela and

Dirk Coetzee are untrue. There was never a death squad at Vlak-plaas."

The only help Harms received was from Tim McNally, an attorney general who had previously headed the internal inquiry dismissing Coetzee's claims as worthless, and from a team of senior police officers, one of whom, Colonel Hermanus du Plessis, had been implicated by Coetzee in death-squad activity.

Harms interviewed Coetzee in exile in London and Nofomela in Pretoria but decided to discount their evidence. Coetzee, he said, "showed strong psychopathic tendencies"; his evidence was unreliable; and he clearly had a grudge against the police. Nofomela was probably just trying to save his life. Neither was telling the truth. Major de Kock, on the other hand, he found to be an "impressive witness."

In tackling the CCB, Harms hit the same wall of lies and deception. The minister of defense, General Magnus Malan, a central figure in "total strategy" operations for more than ten years, claimed that only recently, in November 1989, had he been informed of the CCB's existence and that he knew little about it. The CCB's commander, Joe Verster, a former special forces officer, appeared before the commission wearing a wig and a long, false gray beard down to his chest. At every turn, Harms was blocked. Files went missing; documents disappeared. Requests for information, complained Harms, "were treated with contempt."

What Harms managed to establish was that the CCB had been formed officially in 1988 from an amalgam of special force units to carry out a wide range of dirty tricks, including assassinations. It employed some 300 members and operatives, drawn mainly from the ranks of the military and the security police but also including gangsters like Ferdi Barnard and freelance killers like Acheson. To distance itself from the defense force, it operated ostensibly under a civilian cover; its commander, Joe Verster, was termed "managing director." But the chain of command still ran through military headquarters, and its official budget was part of the defense budget. It operated in eight regions, including every neighboring country and Europe. It had been active in what was known as Region Six—South Africa—since 1988, employing members recruited from a notorious Johannesburg police unit, the Brixton Murder and Robbery Squad.

After seventy days of hearings, Harms had little more to show. Only one witness, "Slang" van Zyl, a former Brixton detective, decided to break ranks, explaining that since de Klerk had released Mandela and lifted the ban on the ANC in February 1990, he no longer saw the need for units like the CCB. He had joined the CCB, he told Harms, believing that clandestine warfare was needed to deal with the enemy. During his instruction course, he had been told that CCB's primary task was to cause "maximum disruption to the enemy," which could involve "anything from the breaking of a window to the killing of a person." Members were guaranteed immunity: "The managing director told us that we would be indemnified against prosecution for acts of violence that we committed during the execution of authorized projects."

Van Zyl gave various examples of his activities. These included a murder plot, duly approved by Joe Verster, to steal heart pills from a radical Cape Town lawyer, Dullah Omar, and substitute them with poison pills; the plot subsequently failed. He was also ordered by Verster to hang up a monkey fetus at Archbishop Tutu's residence in Cape Town. "I just received an instruction from the managing director who told me that the fetus of an ape would be made available to me and that he would accompany me to Cape Town to hang the ape there. . . . It was a very sensitive case and there was no discussion about the reason for placing the fetus. We live in a military environment where you receive a command which you have to obey." This project he duly carried out, hanging the fetus in a bottle on a tree.

Van Zyl was also given the task of monitoring the movements of Lubowski before his death. But Harms refused to pursue any investigation into the Lubowski killing. Van Zyl confirmed that Webster's death had all the hallmarks of a CCB assassination. Harms agreed but came no closer to identifying the culprits. Only in one other murder case—the assassination of a popular Pretoria doctor, Fabian Ribeiro, and his wife at their home in Mamelodi township in 1986—did Harms establish a link to the CCB; but the matter was taken no further. In the case of Griffiths Mxenge, Harms decided that there was no clear answer about who had committed the murder. He saw no reason to trust the evidence of Coetzee or Nofomela.

Harms made no attempt to establish who had political responsibility for the CCB and declined to ask General Malan, the defense minister, to give evidence. Harms's conclusion was that the CCB had its own political agenda that did not correspond with "the expressed agenda of the political authority." Its actions, he said, had "contaminated the whole security arm of the state."

The government was generally pleased with the outcome of the Harms commission. The police minister, Adriaan Vlok, declared jubilantly that the police had been vindicated. "Death squads never existed in the South African police," he declared. "The police don't kill people, they arrest them." General Malan dismissed the fuss over the CCB as "the unauthorized activity of five or six people" whose actions had unfortunately blemished the image of the armed forces. De Klerk ordered the CCB to disband and tried to put the whole controversy behind him: "The events dealt with in the report took place in an era of serious conflict, now belonging to the past.

We should act with a view to our future and take conciliatory steps which are necessary to again create a peaceful South Africa."

What lay ahead, however, was violence on a scale that South Africa had never before experienced. In KwaZulu and Natal, the endemic conflict between Buthelezi's Inkatha movement and the pro-ANC United Democratic Front, which by 1990 had left more than 3,000 dead, erupted with ever-increasing ferocity after the ANC was unbanned and spread like a contagion to black townships on the Witwatersrand. In the year between July 1990 and June 1991, some thirty-six major massacres occurred, perpetrated by one side or the other.

The government blamed the violence on "black-on-black" rivalry. But the suspicion soon grew that something more sinister was happening. In September 1990, twenty-six people died and more than one hundred were injured when a six-man gang ran through a black Johannesburg commuter train shooting passengers at random; a second gang, lying in wait on a station platform, attacked survivors trying to escape from the train. The attack had all the hallmarks of the kind of terrorist activity carried out for years in Mozambique by rebels trained and supported by South African military intelligence.

In the light of the evidence that surfaced during the Harms commission, it seemed all the more plausible that a conspiracy of right-wing elements in the military and the police was at work aiming to wreck the negotiation process. Mandela raised the question of "a third force" with de Klerk, at first in private and then in public. But all that de Klerk was prepared to admit was that "a few rogue individuals" might be involved.

For several months, Mandela gave de Klerk the benefit of the doubt. But as the violence continued, reaching the proportions of a small-scale civil war in Natal, he began to suspect that de Klerk was pursuing a "double agenda"—talking to the ANC in negotiation while supporting the violent activities of its opponents. He refused to believe that de Klerk did not have the power to curb the violence. In Mandela's view, there were only two possible explanations: either the security forces were out of control or de Klerk was conniving with them. "He might not be aware of every attack. But generally speaking, the fact that the police and security services are involved, he would know very well," said Mandela.

Evidence about security force involvement in the conflict mounted steadily. Press investigations revealed that 200 Inkatha hitmen had been trained secretly by South African military intelligence in the Caprivi Strip, before being deployed in Natal and on the Witwatersrand. Buthelezi confirmed the training but said the men had been attached to KwaZulu officials to act as bodyguards. In July 1991, the government was forced to admit that it had secretly channeled funds to Inkatha, lending weight to Mandela's claims about a double agenda.

To keep the negotiations process alive, de Klerk agreed to establish a judicial commission, headed by Judge Richard Goldstone, for the purpose of investigating public violence and intimidation. Goldstone's first interim report, in May 1992, concluded that the primary cause of the violence was not security force activity, as Mandela maintained, but the political battle between supporters of the ANC and Inkatha. There was no credible evidence, he said, of a "third force."

Then in November 1992, Goldstone's investigators uncovered a secret operation that had been set up in 1991 by the Department of Military Intelligence (DMI) to run a dirty-tricks campaign against the ANC, using a covert unit based in Pretoria. The unit, part of a DMI section known as the Directorate of Covert Collection, had employed Ferdi Barnard as a "chief agent" in 1991 to establish a network of "prostitutes, homosexuals, shebeen [speakeasy] owners, and drug dealers" to incriminate ANC officials in criminal activity.

A subsequent investigation carried out by the defense force chief of staff, General Pierre Steyn, uncovered evidence of military intelligence involvement in train massacres, assassinations, gunrunning, smuggling, and other criminal activity. Unable to dismiss the problem any more as "a few rogue individuals," de Klerk ordered a purge of military intelligence staff. Several special force units, like the notorious Koevoet, a police counterinsurgency unit previously stationed in Namibia, were disbanded. Military personnel, de Klerk admitted, had been involved in "illegal and unauthorized activities and malpractices."

Goldstone continued with his investigations but made little notable progress until January 1994, three months before South Africa's election, when he was approached by Captain Chappies Klopper, a disgruntled former member of Vlakplaas. Klopper had left Vlakplaas with an abiding hatred of his former commanding officer and with a desire for revenge; twice Colonel Eugene de Kock had assaulted him. Klopper implicated de Kock in a host of crimes, including murder, fraud, and gunrunning.

De Kock had retired from the police in 1993, after serving for seven years as commander of Vlakplaas, where he had gained the nickname of "Prime Evil." Vlakplaas, too, had been closed down. In what was a clear attempt to buy their silence, de Klerk's cabinet authorized payment of R1 million to de Kock and R17.5 million to some eighty other Vlakplaas policemen. But Klopper's disclosures now broke through the silence.

As well as implicating de Kock, Klopper named a number of senior officers and former colleagues, including Willie Nortje, de Kock's closest confidant. Nortje had served with de Kock for twelve years, first in Koevoet and then at Vlakplaas. When called in for questioning by Goldstone, Nortje quickly took advantage of a witness protection program. In his testimony, he implicated de Kock in some 100 crimes.

In March 1994, Goldstone announced that he had acquired "convincing evidence of criminal activity" involving high-ranking police officers in Pretoria, the KwaZulu police, and Inkatha. This activity included, he said, assassinations, train massacres, hostel violence, gunrunning, and the subversion of justice. Factories in the Transvaal had been used by a police covert unit to manufacture homemade guns that, along with large quantities of other weapons, had been smuggled to Inkatha and used in attacks in Natal and on the Witwatersrand. Goldstone emphasized that only a small group within the police force was involved, but he added, "The whole illegal, criminal, and oppressive system is still in place, and its architects are in control of the South African police." Among the officials whom Goldstone named were the head of police counterintelligence and the police second-in-command. Goldstone recommended that the police commissioner himself should be removed from office forthwith.

By sheer chance, Goldstone had found a tip of the iceberg.

4

Prime Evil

On taking office in May 1994, Mandela's government was determined to pursue the leads that Goldstone's investigators had uncovered and to bring perpetrators to justice. A special team of prosecutors led by Jan d'Oliveira, an attorney general, was assigned to the task. While plans for a truth commission were still being discussed, d'Oliveira's team set to work, armed with the power to offer witnesses indemnity in exchange for court testimony and a witness protection program.

D'Oliveira's first target was Colonel de Kock, whose reputation was fearsome. Within the security establishment, he was known as an officer who would undertake whatever dirty business was necessary. He was no renegade; he was not one of the "rogue individuals" whom de Klerk liked to blame for "third force" activities; rather, he was a highly decorated commander, valued by police generals for his expertise in counterinsurgency and the ultimate product of the "total strategy" system. When politicians like Magnus Malan and Adriaan Vlok spoke repeatedly of the need to "eliminate" and "annihilate" enemies of the state wherever they appeared, they relied on officers like de Kock to make sure it happened. For his efforts, de Kock was twice awarded the Police Star for Outstanding Service and the Silver Cross for Bravery. In the security police, he was regarded as part of an elite.

De Kock had spent most of his life in combat roles. As a young policeman, he had sought a posting to neighboring Rhodesia, where South African paramilitary units were helping to prop up Ian Smith's white minority regime against guerrilla incursions. He returned to Rhodesia for nine tours of duty. His next posting was to South West Africa (Namibia), where South Africa was engaged in a brutal war against nationalist guerrillas fighting for independence. De Kock became a founding member of Koevoet, a counterinsurgency unit that used "turned" guerrillas to hunt down their former colleagues; prisoners were routinely tortured and executed. In 1983, as internal resistance against apartheid in South Africa was mounting, he was transferred to Vlakplaas, the counterinsurgency unit stationed on a farm twenty miles outside Pretoria; he became its commander in 1985. "I walked from one war to the next," he said at his trial. "There was a difference in tactics, but the enemy remained the same. The war never stopped."

There was never any doubt about who the enemy was. As the government stressed persistently, it was Soviet communism together with its front organizations like the African National Congress, all bent on taking control of southern Africa through "total onslaught." De Kock explained:

> The government impressed on the security forces that the ultimate objective of the Soviet Union was to overthrow the government and to replace it with a Marxist-oriented system, and that the communists would do anything to achieve this goal. We were told that the communists were responsible for instigating social and labor unrest, civil disobedience, attacks by terrorists on the country's infrastructure, and the intimidation of black leaders and members of the security forces. . . . We were told the enemy was "everywhere"—in universities, in trade unions and cultural organizations. They all harbored enemies of the state who were waging psychological and economic warfare against us.

As commander of Vlakplaas, de Kock transformed it into a major operational base. During Dirk Coetzee's period in control in 1980–1981, it had remained a small unit, consisting of less than twenty askaris in four groups. Given access to huge secret funds, de Kock added new offices, new living quarters, garages, an arsenal, a club house, a shooting range, a soccer stadium, and a "braai" area next to the Hennops River. Police generals enjoyed visiting Vlakplaas for parties; one of them kept his own personal bottle of Chivas Regal whisky on the farm. Adriaan Vlok was a regular guest. It became such a popular venue for police functions that a chef was employed there. A lot of drinking went on. By 1990, the number of askaris based at Vlakplaas had reached about seventy.

As commander, de Kock was universally feared, both by his white colleagues and by black security policemen and askaris. His ferocious temper made him a dangerous man, liable to explode into violence. He expected orders to be carried out without question. He never smiled, and his eyes remained shielded by thick spectacles.

A revealing exchange took place during his trial when a state prosecutor, Anton Ackermann, asked him: "How would your enemies describe you?"

DE KOCK: Cold-blooded.

ACKERMANN: Other words you want to use?

DE KOCK; Determined and persevering.

ACKERMANN: How do your enemies see you?

DE KOCK: As merciless.

ACKERMANN: What else?

DE KOCK: I haven't met that many, because most are dead.

ACKERMANN: Mr. de Kock, have you ever tried to establish how many lives you've taken?

DE KOCK: No. One doesn't do it. It's a terrible thing to think about.

In the ten years he served at Vlakplaas, from 1983 to 1993, de Kock was involved in at least seventy killings. Some were accounted for during cross-border raids into Swaziland, Botswana, and Lesotho, others in South Africa. Yet tests he underwent showed no sign of a psychopathic personality, as most people assumed there would be. Like many other security policemen, de Kock explained himself as simply a loyal defender of the white state. "I'm a relentless hunter who stays on the track until the problem is solved," he said in a police questionnaire in 1993. "I act without mercy against the country's enemies and criminals."

At his trial, Ackermann asked de Kock why he had lied at the Harms commission of inquiry.

DE KOCK: It was in the interests of the police. It was in the interest of the government. We had to protect the police and army so that the revolutionary forces couldn't flood into the country and cause the same bloodbaths as in Angola, Mozambique, and the former Congo.

ACKERMANN: So you committed perjury for *Volk en Vaderland*.

DE KOCK: Yes, that is correct.

De Kock's trial at the Transvaal Supreme Court in Pretoria began in February 1995 and ended in October 1996. For eighteen months, he watched tight-lipped and expressionless as some of his closest colleagues, who had killed and tortured with him, gave evidence to save themselves from prosecution. Only a fraction of his record was examined, but what it revealed was a depth of depravity that South Africans had never witnessed. In his opening address, Ackermann endeavored to portray de Kock as no more than a common criminal using the cover of state security to perpetrate his crimes. But at the end of the trial, a different picture emerged.

One of de Kock's victims was Japie Maponya, a young security guard who was abducted and taken to Vlakplaas in 1985 because he was suspected of knowing the whereabouts of his brother, a trained ANC guerrilla recently returned to South Africa. Japie was interrogated at first by askaris who hit and kicked him repeatedly, demanding to know where his brother was. Then de Kock and Willie Nortje arrived.

"De Kock asked me if I had some tear gas with me," testified Nortje. "He grabbed Japie behind his head, forced his mouth open, and sprayed the tear gas into his mouth. Japie said he knew nothing about his brother. We then knew that he was not going to speak."

They agreed he would have to be killed. The following night, Japie was taken to a plantation in Swaziland. While de Kock started to clear an area for the grave, using a spade, Nortje was supposed to shoot him dead with a machine pistol. "I couldn't get myself to do it and hit him behind the head with the Uzi. I felt sorry for him. I wanted him to be unconscious before I shot him. . . . Japie tried to get up, and that was when de Kock hit him with the spade."

Another victim was an askari named Phemelo Nthehelang, who was accused of selling his service pistol in a shebeen for drinking money. He claimed he had lost it, but de Kock told him he was lying. "De Kock was very aggressive," testified Sergeant Douw Willemse. "I know him well, and when he gets like that, few people can stop him. I was scared and knew that something was going to happen, and so I walked out."

De Kock hit Nthehelang over the head with a snooker cue, breaking it. Other white policemen joined in the assault. One of them, "Brood" Van Heerden, decided he would "tube" him, a favorite method of torture that involved smothering a victim with the inner tube of a tire. "At that time it was general practice for good policemen," Van Heerden told the court. "If I had to 'tube' a man to get information, I would do it." When Van Heerden's hands became tired, another policeman stepped in to finish him off. Nthehelang's body was dumped on a farm in Western Transvaal.

Another askari who was murdered was Brian Ngqulunga, a member of the death squad that had killed the lawyer Griffiths Mxenge in 1981. Implicated in Mxenge's killing by Almond Nofomela eight years later, Ngqulunga had appeared before the Harms commission in 1990. Like other Vlakplaas operatives, he had been thoroughly coached beforehand and calmly denied any involvement. But subsequently he had become nervous and agitated. Worried that he might break ranks, de Kock ordered a group of Vlakplaas assassins to abduct and execute him.

De Kock was also involved in a plot to kill the former Vlakplaas commander, Dirk Coetzee, who had defected to the ANC. A Vlakplaas explosives expert, Steve Bosch, was told to construct a parcel bomb to send to Coetzee at a postal address in Lusaka, where he was staying. Bosch decided to use a Walkman cassette player to conceal the device, bought a pig's head for a trial run, and went down to the river with earphones to test it. Willie Nortje witnessed the event. "The pig's head was put down, the earphones were put on, and it was detonated. It blew a hole right through the pig's head."

The parcel bomb was sent to Coetzee in Lusaka in May 1990, but because he could not afford to pay a customs charge he did not collect it. Eight months later, the parcel found its way to a Johannesburg lawyer, Bheki Mlangeni, who acted for Coetzee and whose name appeared as the sender. Opening it in his Soweto home, Mlangeni found the Walkman inside. When he put the earphones on to listen to the cassette, his head was blown apart.

In 1991, with de Klerk's reform process underway, de Kock managed to keep Vlakplaas in business by agreeing to concentrate on fighting organized crime and on tracing illegal weapons. Officially Vlakplaas became a unit within the Crime Intelligence Service. But de Kock and his colleagues spent most of their time devising schemes to pilfer police funds and fraternizing with gangsters like Ferdi Barnard.

One incident, however, did stand out. In 1992, de Kock led a hit squad that ambushed a gang of four men in a minibus on their way to rob a security firm in Nelspruit in Eastern Transvaal. The ambush group included Willie Nortje, Chappies Klopper, and ten others. The would-be robbers had been set up by a Vlakplaas informant who suggested the target and supplied them with the minibus. The Vlakplaas aim was to "show results" in order to prove their worth and to claim cash bonuses for weapons supposedly retrieved from the robbers.

All four men died in a hail of bullets and grenade explosions. But their leader, Tiso Leballo, was not among them; he was waiting for them at a nearby petrol station. De Kock dispatched a team to deal with him. Leballo was caught, locked in the boot of a car for twelve hours, taken to an open cast mine, interrogated, assaulted, and then shot dead.

To dispose of the body, the Vlakplaas team decided to use explosives, a method they favored. They put the body in a sitting position and packed it with "sausages of explosives." After the explosion, they drank through the night and returned in the morning to collect the bits and pieces. "For the next three hours, we walked around looking for pieces of human flesh to make certain that we had destroyed all evidence," said Rolf Gevers, a police captain who, like other witnesses, testified in return for indemnity from prosecution. "The biggest piece we got was the size of a fingernail—in all only about half a kilogram of flesh and bone. We held this in our hands. We put the pieces of flesh in the hole and blew them up. We searched again for pieces of flesh and blew them up again."

De Kock also meddled in the Inkatha conflict, supplying tons of weapons to Inkatha groups operating on the Witwatersrand and in Natal. A large part of the Vlakplaas armory was transferred to Inkatha. One consignment of grenades, mortars, rocket launchers, and mines took a convoy of six ten-ton trucks to move it. As well as providing Vlakplaas weapons, de Kock helped organize the manufacture of homemade weapons, using police funds. Inkatha officials were registered as informants and paid monthly salaries.

In August 1996, de Kock was found guilty of six murders, conspiracy to murder, attempted murder, culpable homicide, abduction, assault, possession of illegal arms, and sixty-six charges of fraud. Determined to gain revenge for what he saw as his "betrayal" by the security establishment and the politicians in power, he finally broke his silence, naming police generals and government ministers, implicating them in murders and criminal activity and revealing a host of dirty-tricks operations. His orders, he said, had come from police generals. They in turn had received their instructions from the highest levels of government. He was guilty of many crimes, he said, but so were they. The evils of the old regime could not all be blamed on one lone colonel.

His testimony, in mitigation of sentence, lasted for twelve days. He described how, in 1987, he had been called to security police headquarters where a senior officer, Brigadier Willem Schoon, had instructed him to destroy Cosatu House in Johannesburg, the headquarters of an anti-apartheid trade union organization. "I was speechless, because we were now talking about pure terrorism. I asked him who gave the orders. He told me it came from the highest authority. I asked if this included the President [P. W. Botha], and he said yes." De Kock and his team carried out a reconnaissance for two weeks, then placed two massive bombs in the basement; the bombs caused severe structural damage.

The following year, he claimed, he was asked to help blow up Khotso House in Johannesburg, the headquarters of the South African Council of Churches, which security police believed was used by the ANC as "a sort of internal headquarters." The explosion at Khotso House in August 1988 wrecked the building and shook the whole of central Johannesburg. At a celebration party at Vlakplaas, the guest of honor was Adriaan Vlok, the minister of law and order. "The minister thanked us for our services and said that we would fight till the bitter end. We would never give over to the ANC. He said we would fight them for a thousand years."

Vlok later named Shirley Gunn, an ANC activist, as a suspect in the bombing, claiming she was a trained terrorist but knowing full well that she was entirely innocent. She was detained in 1990 for two months, along with her baby son, but never charged.

Two months after the Khotso House episode, de Kock was asked to set fire to Khanya House in Pretoria, the headquarters of the South African Bishops' Conference. "After the fire started raging, we were watching the building when we realized, for the first time, that there were people in it. We saw clergymen being helped down ladders by the fire department. It was a huge shock."

As well as implicating Botha, de Kock turned his venom on de Klerk. De Klerk, he said, knew full well that death squads were at work during his presidency. He himself had ordered an attack on a house in the Transkei in 1993; de Kock and his men had carried it out, killing five youths.

De Kock accused de Klerk of using police and army covert units when it suited him, then discarding them when it was opportune.

F. W. de Klerk abdicated when he unbanned the ANC. He wasn't in control of the country any more. De Klerk is one of the biggest traitors in the history of this country. De Klerk was like a petrified puppy who lay on his back and wet himself. He just gave over. He handed a section of his security forces over to the mercy of the ANC. There were only two factions that kept the National Party in power all those years: the police and the defense force. The people who helped him stay in power, the people who helped him to start this peace process, were the people he threw to the wolves.

De Kock went on to implicate police generals in the arms traffic to Inkatha, in the Dirk Coetzee bomb plot, and in the murders of Japie Maponya and Brian Ngqulunga. He painted a picture of sleaze and corruption, which he said pervaded the security police, giving examples of how senior officers used secret funds for their own private benefit. And he provided details of his role in the bombing of the London headquarters of the ANC in 1981, for which he had been awarded the Police Star for Outstanding Service.

In a rare moment of emotion, de Kock remarked: "I can't tell you how dirty I feel. I shouldn't have joined the South African police. We achieved nothing. We just left hatred behind us. There are children who never knew their parents, and I will have to carry this burden for ever. . . . I sympathize with my victims as if they were my own children. This is all I can say."

In October 1996, at the age of forty-seven, de Kock was given two life sentences plus 212 years of imprisonment. His next move was to apply to the Truth and Reconciliation Commission for amnesty.

5

Chains of Command

A s d'Oliveira's team of prosecutors probed ever deeper into security police activities, the old security police network began to crumble. Rather than risk prosecution, a group of five white security policemen from the Northern Transvaal Security Branch decided in October 1996 to jump for the safety of the Truth and Reconciliation Commission and to apply for amnesty for a series of murders, in the hope that eventually they would go free. Their initial murder tally was forty, but they later raised this to more than sixty. It was the TRC's first breakthrough after six months of work.

Before beginning their testimony at an amnesty committee hearing, they read out an eloquent joint statement asking for compassion and understanding. Not once did they use the word "murder." Their actions, they said, had all been carried out for political reasons, namely, "to uphold the National Party government and apartheid, to fight communism and to resist liberation."

> We are not criminals. We have never committed any criminal deed outside the spheres of conflicts of the past. . . . We believed that we acted bona fide in the interests of our country and our people. We will show that we, at all times, believed that we were acting in the course and scope of our duties and within the scope of our authority. . . .
>
> We will endeavor to enlighten the world to the environment and

background against which we acted, the beliefs we held which were impressed upon us from our birth, the indoctrination to which we were subjected, and the political motives with which we acted.

We were brought up to believe in apartheid. We were made to believe that apartheid was sanctioned by God through the church. We were made to believe that our participation in the security forces was justified to uphold apartheid. We were made to believe that black people were inferior and that the needs, emotions and aspirations of black people differ from ours. We were made to believe that we were superior and that these differences justified apartheid. We have come to realize that these beliefs were wrong. . . .

We, as proud Afrikaners, are part of this country and shall be part of this country in the future. We are prepared to forgive those who have sinned against us in the past. We have forgiven the concentration camps of the Boer War, where innocent women and children had died. We are prepared to forgive those who have waged war during the struggle, also on innocent women and children. We similarly ask forgiveness for those who lost their lives and those who were injured, and we share the grief of those family members of victims who have suffered during the era of conflict. We have sincere regret that people have suffered on both sides, and we wish to express the sincere hope that the time for truth and reconciliation in South Africa has now arrived. . . .

We call upon our superiors and the previous government not to deny responsibility but to stand by the people and to admit responsibility for what was done by us in our endeavors to keep them in power. We all supported the National Party until 1994. What we had done was always in the interests of the National Party and its objectives. We believed in the policies of the National Party and believed that we had to carry out our duties in support of our party.

We state emphatically that we have been deserted by the National Party and that we have, so to speak, been thrown away in the gutter. . . . We call upon the previous government and our superiors to explain certain orders given to us . . . and to admit to authorizing actions outside the normal processes of the law. . . . We ask you: Do not desert us further; do not turn your backs on us; help us.

The names of the five policemen had originally been given to d'Oliveira's investigators by an African assassin, Joe Mamasela, who had agreed to collaborate in exchange for indemnity from prosecution. Mamasela himself had killed as many as forty people during his career in police death squads. A former student activist who had taken part in the Soweto uprising in 1976, he had joined the ANC in exile in Botswana but had been captured in 1979 after returning to Johannesburg to organize students cells. After agreeing to become a police informer, he returned to Botswana to spy on the ANC, but his cover was blown in 1981. Escaping back to South Africa, he was sent to Dirk Coetzee's new outfit at Vlakplaas. Coetzee remarked of him: "He was ruthless and had the killer instinct. He was a born killer."

Mamasela became a member of the four-man group that Coetzee used to kill the Natal lawyer Griffiths Mxenge in 1981. Implicated in the killing by his fellow assassin, Nofomela, Mamasela was paid large sums by the security police to keep quiet and lie to the Harms commission.

Mamasela left Vlakplaas in 1985 shortly before de Kock took command and transferred to the Northern Transvaal Security Branch, a new unit led by Brigadier Jack Cronje. One of the first tasks Mamasela was given by Cronje was to infiltrate activist groups on the East Rand and supply them with booby-trapped grenades.

Posing as an ANC guerrilla from Lusaka, he made contact with student activists in three townships, gave them a quick demonstration with real grenades, then returned the following night with booby-trapped grenades fitted with zero ignition and designed to explode in the hands of the thrower pulling the pin. The operation was given the code name "Zero Zero." Eight students died, blown to pieces; seven were seriously injured.

The death of the students provoked fury in the townships. At a funeral for four of them, a young mother, Maki Skosana, wrongly identified as a police informer connected to their murder, was chased, beaten, and stoned by a mob of mourners. While television cameras filmed the scene, a tire was placed around her neck, filled with petrol, and set alight. Her death marked one of the first examples of the "necklace" method of killing that soon became a trademark of young "comrades" operating in the townships.

The security police were well pleased with the outcome of Operation Zero Zero. Mamasela was rewarded with a cash bonus and a promotion to the rank of sergeant. The death of Maki Skosana, meanwhile, shocked all who saw it on television and enabled the government to point to the mindless brutality of black activists in the townships.

In 1986, Mamasela was sent on a similar mission. Posing once again as an ANC guerrilla, he lured a group of ten township youths from Mamelodi, near Pretoria, into setting off with him to Botswana for military training, taking them in a minibus toward the border. Two of the group were only fifteen years old. Along the way, he gave them enough beer to make them all drunk. Near the border post of Nietverdiend, their journey ended. Four armed men with balaclavas stopped the vehicle, pushed it down an embankment, filled it with explosives, and blew it up. Newspapers subsequently reported that a group of "trained terrorists" infiltrating from Botswana had been killed in a vehicle accident. The following year, Mamasela lured nine more youths from Mamelodi to their deaths in KwaNdebele in a similar scheme.

At his amnesty hearing, Brigadier Cronje was asked what the objective of such operations was and who gave the orders for them.

CRONJE: The purpose of the operation was to eliminate the prospective activists before they could leave the country, so that it could serve to frighten other prospective activists from joining MK [Umkhonto we Sizwe, the ANC's armed wing]. A further purpose was to eliminate prospective MK soldiers who at a later stage could return as well-trained terrorists and commit acts of terror.

QUESTION: Was there any other way in which you could have dealt with these prospective soldiers?

CRONJE: No. We did not see any other way of dealing with them.

QUESTION: No attempt was made to get hold of these youngsters, to talk them out of it, to educate them differently, no attempt was made to treat them in that fashion?

CRONJE: Mamasela had instructions to talk to them, and it turned out that they were extremely convinced of their intentions.

QUESTION: You made no attempt to prosecute them, did you?

CRONJE: At that time I had no testimony which I could use in a case against them.

QUESTION: Arresting them and sending them to prison for a number of years, you would achieve that would you not? Many people were prosecuted, many people were sent to prison, but you chose not to take that route, is that not so?

CRONJE: I did so because I had insufficient testimony for a court case.

QUESTION: You made no attempt to get any, did you?

CRONJE: Not at that time, no.

QUESTION: Brigadier, there was no urgency to execute this operation. There was no great urgency to eliminate the young activists, was there?

CRONJE: They wanted urgently to leave the country, and therefore I had no choice.

QUESTION: But you could have made attempts to verify the information that you received from Mamasela—that they wanted to train. Why didn't you do that?

CRONJE: The fact that they were on their way with Mamasela convinced me that it was with the intent of receiving training.

QUESTION: These men died on Mamasela's word, with no check from you, is that what you are now telling us? You accepted what Mamasela told you?

CRONJE: Yes, I did.

QUESTION: The action you took in the circumstances was totally excessive. It was disproportionate in relation to what they had done prior to their elimination.

CRONJE: I disagree. Were they to return as well-trained terrorists, then they could have struck anywhere in the republic and I wouldn't have known how to prevent them from doing so.

QUESTION: Your prospect of them returning was nil, so that is hardly an issue for debate.

CRONJE: This was preventative. We had to eliminate them to prevent that they would come back as trained terrorists.

QUESTION: But you could have prevented them going, couldn't you?

CRONJE: Maybe once, but they would have tried again to go.

QUESTION: Because they might have tried again to go. Is that the reason you are now advancing, Brigadier?

CRONJE: If these persons' purpose was to go for training, I would never again have been able to prevent them going had they so intended.

Cronje described the situation in South Africa in the mid-1980s as tantamount to war. There were car bombs, sabotage incidents, land mine explosions, necklace murders, petrol bombings, riots, and group murders, all carried out in the name of liberation. The security police were in the front line. "It was war. . . . Full-scale guerrilla tactics were used against the liberation movements. . . . It didn't matter what was done or how we did it, as long as the flood-tide of destabilization, unrest, and violence was stopped."

Cronje testified that in 1986 he had been called in by Brigadier Johan Viktor, the deputy head of the police counterinsurgency division.

He said that Pretoria was burning and that South Africa was burning. He said that all necessary steps should be taken to normalize the situation and bring it under control. He further said that if a policeman's house was attacked, immediate steps had to be taken against the person who was responsible for that act. Such a person's house would then have to be burned down as well.

His orders were to the effect that when we retaliated we should just go a step further than the enemy each time. His instructions amounted to the security police taking active steps in the struggle against terrorists and activists. What his orders in reality amounted to was that the same methods had to be used and that there was in reality an active guerrilla war to be waged against the ANC, SACP [Communist Party], and PAC activists. . . . From that stage onwards use was made of guerrilla warfare tactics, and a full-scale guerrilla war was waged against the liberation organizations.

Later in 1986, he received a phone call from Brigadier Willem Schoon, head of the security police antiterrorist division, telling him that the commissioner of police, General Johan Coetzee, had issued orders that henceforth the security police had to work in conjunction with Special Forces combat groups.

The instruction to work with special services was a direct instruction to become engaged in military warfare. . . . This was no longer normal policing functions or normal policing tasks which I was authorized to exercise. My responsibilities became far broader. . . . All instructions, therefore, which I gave my subordinates . . . must be seen as instructions to act in a situation and circumstances of war.

Cronje's death squads had license to murder and bomb activist targets virtually at will. Night after night they would go out to fire-bomb activists' houses. Mamasela estimated that they had attacked some 350 homes in the Pretoria area. "We could do as we wished," said Paul van Vuuren. "When we had to kill somebody, we would say, 'We are going to steal him tonight.' He was as good as dead."

Cronje testified about the death of an activist in 1987 whose name he did not know. After being detained and interrogated, the unknown activist was taken in a minibus—a kombi—to identify houses in Mamelodi where MK guerrillas were thought to be staying.

CRONJE: He did not point out houses in Mamelodi and also did not point out terrorists. We then drove along a gravel road to Bophuthatswana, where the man was further questioned. Prinsloo and du Plessis sat at the back of the kombi and interrogated this man, and during questioning he was assaulted. He was inter alia beaten and throttled, and during interrogation he died. He was then blown up in a deserted area with a limpet mine.

ADVOCATE: Brigadier, was the intention during this interrogation to eventually eliminate him?

CRONJE: No, that was not the intention, because we wanted more information out of him. . . . The activist's death was an accident; it was not our intention to eliminate him, and I never gave such an instruction. A limpet mine was available in the vehicle. My members always used to carry these around with them. . . .

JUDGE WILSON: I have been engaged in trials both as counsel and as a judge for many years where the police have given evidence about interrogations, where the accused has given evidence about interrogations, and it was not considered necessary to take a man off into the bush and strangle him to interrogate him. Why didn't you question him in the normal way? You had powers to detain him?

CRONJE: It was at night. We didn't want to do it in a built-up area. We wanted to do it outside somewhere where it was quieter. You're correct, we did have powers to question him further, but that was the practice. They beat him during interrogation.

JUDGE MALL: By interrogation, you really mean torturing him, don't you?

CRONJE: Yes, he was assaulted.

JUDGE MALL: It was not merely an interrogation where questions are put and answers elicited? He was tortured physically?

CRONJE: Yes, he was.

JUDGE WILSON: And as a result of that torture he died?

CRONJE: Correct.

JUDGE NGOEPE: Brigadier, it must have been clear at some stage that the deceased was severely beaten with obvious injuries?

CRONJE: Yes, I saw that, and I didn't stop it.

JUDGE NGOEPE: You say that the intention was not to kill him?

CRONJE: Correct.

JUDGE NGOEPE: What did you intend to do with such a severely beaten person with obvious injuries?

CRONJE: At this stage, I can't say. If it was so serious that we couldn't detain him any further, then the possibility would have been that we would have eliminated him.

JUDGE NGOEPE: Well, that is what is troubling me. It seems to me that the person was so severely injured that you had no option but simply to eliminate him, and therefore in that sense you cannot say that there was no intention to kill him.

CRONJE: Let me put it this way. The injuries which he sustained as a result of the beating weren't that serious. But he died because they strangled him. That was not the aim.

ADVOCATE: You didn't take part in the torture yourself?

CRONJE: No I didn't, not myself.

JUDGE NGOEPE: Were you not in charge of the operation?

CRONJE: Yes, I was.

JUDGE NGOEPE: Now if you were in charge of the operation and, as you have testified, it was an accident that this man was eliminated, why didn't you stop the throttling of him?

CRONJE: Well, I could have stopped it, but I did not expect that they would throttle him so long that he would die.

JUDGE NGOEPE: Brigadier, really. Did you expect the man to survive being throttled by two men, and after this man has been tortured and assaulted?

CRONJE: I did not expect that they would throttle him that long, so long that he would die.

JUDGE NGOEPE: Well, as the officer in charge, why didn't you watch and when you could see what was going on tell them to stop? You were responsible. You gave the orders.

CRONJE: Yes, I was responsible. But I did not watch all the time. I was looking in front of me.

Cronje insisted that the State Security Council, consisting of top politicians and senior government officials, knew full well about the existence of death squads. They received monthly reports from the "Sanhedrin," the regional desk heads of the security police, who met daily to assess the security situation, review incidents, and discuss action plans.

A secret unit known as "Trevits"—an acronym for *Teen Rewolu-*

sionêre Inligting Taakspan, or "Counterrevolutionary Intelligence Task Team"—held monthly meetings to evaluate intelligence reports and identify targets. Its members included representatives from the security police, military intelligence, Special Forces, and the national intelligence agency.

> Records were kept at every region of who the activists were and who the troublemakers were. A list of priorities was also maintained. In some cases, it was necessary to eliminate the targets by killing them. That was the only way in which we were able to act effectively against activists in the war situation.
>
> Detention in terms of the emergency regulations was not enough, because it was only of limited duration. To prosecute a person through the normal court structure was too much trouble and sometimes totally impossible. There was no other choice but to resort to acts of war and to eliminate activists.
>
> Reports about the death of activists were sent to head office and there was never any objection, repudiation, or orders that the eliminations should stop.

As the violence spread, security police commanders resorted to issuing general orders allowing subordinates to take initiatives as they saw fit, said Cronje.

> Subordinates were told to take whatever steps were necessary to deal with the situation. . . . The orders were couched in general terms and meant that permission did not have to be sought for a specific operation. . . . Authority was delegated down the line, and officers were increasingly confronted with general orders in terms of which they could act within broader parameters than would have been the case under normal circumstances.

Cronje said he accepted full responsibility for the actions of his own subordinates and asked senior officers and politicians to do the same. As an example of orders from the top, he cited the Zero Zero incident. The instruction to supply booby-trapped grenades to ANC activists on the East Rand, he said, had come from General Johan van der Merwe, a former head of the security police and subsequently the national police commissioner.

> This instruction was given to me in Springs [on the East Rand] by General van der Merwe, and during this instruction he specifically indicated to me that this came directly from Minister Le Grange [the minister of law and order] and that it had indeed been authorized by President P. W. Botha.

Suddenly, the TRC found itself reaching the highest levels of government. General van der Merwe appeared dramatically before the TRC's amnesty hearing to testify in support of Brigadier Cronje and his four fellow applicants. He confirmed that he had given the order for the Zero Zero operation, after receiving an instruction from the minister of law and order, Louis Le Grange. "He was not likely to have taken the decision without the knowledge of the president," said van der Merwe.

The operation was launched, he said, after he had received reports that a group of ANC activists on the East Rand were preparing to launch a campaign to drive black policemen out of the townships. The police could not act against them because informers would not testify.

> It was abundantly clear that other preventative measures would have to be taken so as to protect the lives of the policemen concerned, who by now were very frightened and totally demoralized.

Information to hand indicated very clearly that the group of activists concerned were only awaiting the delivery of a consignment of hand grenades from an arms cache before launching their attacks against the homes of the policemen. . . .

I decided that the only way the black members could be protected against such attacks was to ensure that the activists were provided with hand grenades which had been suitably modified.

Van der Merwe made a recommendation to the then police commissioner, General Johan Coetzee, who passed it to Le Grange who approved it.

General van der Merwe also took the opportunity to admit to his role in the 1988 bombing of Khotso House, the headquarters of the South African Council of Churches. He received an instruction to render Khotso House unusable, he said, from Adriaan Vlok, the minister of law and order.

According to Mr. Vlok this instruction had come from President P. W. Botha personally. It was common knowledge within security circles at the time that the building concerned served as a sort of internal headquarters of the ANC, where resistance campaigns, unrest, and violence were planned and where financial and other assistance was provided to MK members who had infiltrated into the country. According to information, explosives were also stored in the basement of the building.

Despite being in possession of a great deal of information regarding certain unlawful activities taking place within Khotso House, the police were powerless in putting a stop to it, as no informer or agent was prepared to give evidence in court regarding such activity.

Vlok himself now came forward to apply for amnesty. He said

that Botha had ordered the destruction of the building because it had become "a house of evil." According to Vlok, Botha took him to one side after a meeting of the State Security Council at the president's official residence in Cape Town in July 1988 and told him: "I have done everything possible to persuade them [the South African Council of Churches] to come to their senses, but nothing helps. We cannot act against the people. You must render that building unusable."

Vlok said that at a subsequent meeting of the State Security Council Botha congratulated him and the police on the success of the operation.

6

Room 619

THE FLOODGATES OF THE PAST now opened. In January 1997, a group of notorious security policemen from regional headquarters in Port Elizabeth applied for amnesty for a string of murders in the Eastern Cape. For years their names had struck terror in the townships as they cruised about acting with impunity. Now their only hope of avoiding prosecution was to testify before the Truth and Reconciliation Commission.

Their most famous victim was Steve Biko, a dynamic young leader from the Eastern Cape whose short life had a profound impact on black politics and thinking and whose lonely death was to stand as a permanent monument to police brutality. A former medical student, he was the inspiration behind the black consciousness movement of the 1970s, arousing a new mood of defiance among the black population, which culminated in the Soweto revolt of 1976.

The security police harassed him endlessly. Over a three-year period he was arrested and detained twenty-nine times. But despite a series of banning orders restricting him to the King William's Town district, he continued to travel, to write, and to campaign.

Returning from a secret meeting in Cape Town on 18 August 1977, he was arrested at a roadblock outside Grahamstown. For the next twenty days, he was held in solitary confinement, kept naked, given no proper washing facilities, and allowed no exercise. He was then taken from his cell at Walmer police station to security police headquarters in the Sanlam Building in Port Elizabeth for interrogation, still naked and now held in leg irons and handcuffs. During interrogation, he suffered severe head injuries. According to police evidence at the inquest, the injuries occurred when Biko's head hit a wall in the course of "a scuffle" that started after he had become violent.

During the next four days, Biko's condition deteriorated steadily. A doctor was called but said he found no apparent injury. Biko was moved to a prison hospital, but doctors there said there was no evidence of brain damage. A prison guard found him during the night lying in a bathtub of water, fully clothed. By morning he was foaming at the mouth. The doctors reexamined him in the afternoon and concluded he should be sent to the hospital for treatment.

Though Biko was nearly comatose, the security police decided he should be taken to a prison hospital in Pretoria some 700 miles away. He was put naked into the back of a police van, covered with a prison blanket, and given nothing more than a bottle of water for the eleven-hour journey. He died on September 12, a few hours after arriving in Pretoria, lying on a mat on a stone floor. He was thirty years old.

Two days later the minister of police, Jimmy Kruger, announced that Biko had died after a hunger strike. Kruger provoked laughter at a National Party conference when referring to Biko's death: "I am not glad and I am not sorry about Mr. Biko. It leaves me cold. [Dit laat my koud.] I can say nothing to you. . . . Any person who dies . . . . I shall also be sorry if I die."

A postmortem performed the next day by a private neuropathologist showed the cause of death to be extensive brain damage. Biko's injuries included a major blow to his left forehead; his body had been beaten; and he had suffered kidney failure.

At the inquest in November 1977, the security police version was that Biko, with "a wild expression in his eyes," had suddenly attacked them; it had taken five members of the interrogation team to subdue him. The magistrate subsequently ruled that "on the evidence available, the death cannot be attributed to any act or omission amounting to a criminal offense on the part of any person."

Twenty years later that version was to be tested at a TRC amnesty hearing at a hall in the New Brighton district of Port Elizabeth. Five members of the interrogation team were present: Major Harold Snyman, Captain Daantjie Siebert, Warrant Officer Johan Beneke, Warrant Officer Rubin Marx, and Detective Sergeant Gideon Nieuwoudt. Their commanding officer, Colonel Piet Goosen, who had ordered Biko's detention and his transfer to Pretoria and who had subsequently risen to the rank of deputy police commissioner, had since died.

Snyman was the first to testify. Once feared for his ruthless reputation, he now appeared an old and broken man, sixty-nine years old, suffering from stomach cancer. He kept his eyes cast down, avoiding the gaze of Biko's widow, Ntsiki, who was in the audience. Speaking in a nervous, high-pitched voice, he stuck closely to the version he had told the inquest, but there were some significant differences.

His instructions from Goosen, he said, had been to question Biko "intensively" and to deprive him of sleep to break down his resistance. Biko was brought at 9 A.M. to Room 619 at security police headquarters, a small file room that became infamous among detainees.

> We wanted to prove his involvement in the instigation of violence and rioting . . . in order to charge him so that he could be neutralized as a leader. Biko was handcuffed when he arrived. I ordered the handcuffs removed.
>
> Captain Siebert initially started questioning Biko, but it was clear that he was not going to cooperate with us. His attitude was ill-tem-

pered, confrontational, and aggressive. He refused to answer questions. He tried to sit down on a chair. Siebert told him to stand up while we were talking to him.

He tried again to sit on the chair. Siebert shouted at him to stand up. He did not react. Siebert grabbed him by his chest and pulled him off the chair. Biko aimed a blow at Siebert, but missed. He pushed the chair in the direction of Siebert. Beneke then shoulder-charged him. He staggered backwards towards the wall. Marx and Nieuwoudt joined in. They were trying to corner him so they could handcuff him. There was a full-scale fight, blows were traded left and right. . . . All of them collapsed to the ground against the wall. One fell on top of Biko.

Biko was lying with his head against the wall. He appeared confused, like a person who had been knocked out in a boxing match. . . . His speech was impaired; he slurred his words. His lip was injured.

Despite his injuries, Biko was chained hand and foot to a metal grille, with his arms stretched out as if on a crucifix. He remained in this position for most of the day while his interrogators waited for him to recover so that they could continue their questioning. Although he had visible head injuries and his speech was incoherent, he did not receive any medical attention. During the evening, when night staff took over, the handcuffs holding him against the grille were unlocked, but the leg iron was kept on. He was given some mats to sleep on.

Only the next day, on 7 September, twenty-four hours after the assault, was a district surgeon, Dr. Ivor Lang, called to examine him, but he could find no apparent injury. Biko was kept at security police headquarters for the rest of the day before being taken to a prison hospital.

Snyman admitted that he and his colleagues had lied at the inquest by covering up the fact that the police had waited twenty-four hours after the "scuffle" before requesting medical assistance. After Biko's death, he said, Colonel Goosen had summoned every member of the interrogation team to tell them what line to follow. "He told us Mr. Biko's death was an embarrassment to his branch and the government." The incident would create a negative picture of South Africa abroad. It needed to be managed "to protect the interests of the Security Branch and the South African government." Snyman therefore officially recorded the incident as occurring on 7 September when in fact it had happened on 6 September.

Snyman was cross-examined by George Bizos, an advocate acting on behalf of the Biko family.

BIZOS: On your version, the security policemen did nothing wrong. They acted in self-defense?

SNYMAN: That is correct.

BIZOS: And you did nothing wrong?

SNYMAN: We had to restrain him.

BIZOS: Now, he died as a result of violence to his person. You didn't apply any violence to his person at any time?

SNYMAN: That is correct.

BIZOS: Nor did any of your colleagues in your presence?

SNYMAN: We have said that during the scuffle, he bumped his head against the wall. . . .

BIZOS: If your story is true, that was his own fault and not the fault of anyone else?

SNYMAN: In order to restrain him, we had to follow that course of action, and in the process thereof he fell with his head against the wall.

As the relentless grilling continued, Snyman complained he was tired.

BIZOS: Why did you use the handcuffs to spread out the arms of Mr. Biko? . . .

SNYMAN: The intention was to reduce his resistance.

BIZOS: But you told us that he had been confused and hardly in a position to speak, and you had the benefit of the handcuffs in order to put an end to his resistance. Why would you have to put his arms out in a comparatively uncomfortable position?

SNYMAN: This was done after he had been lying on the ground for a while, and as it appeared that he was improving, we shackled him again and put on the foot shackles.

BIZOS: Why did you put his arms up in a manner which would have given an injured man some additional discomfort to that of his injuries?

SNYMAN: At that stage we did not bear knowledge of the nature of his injuries.

BIZOS: What did you think had caused his slurred speech and his inability to behave in the normal aggressive way that he had behaved before? Did you not think that it was an injury?

SNYMAN: It might well have been the knock against the wall.

BIZOS: No, listen to the question please. Why was it necessary to break the resistance of an injured man? If you've got a pair of hand-cuffs—and that one handcuff on the grille would have been suffi-cient, with his arm in a comfortable position—why was it necessary to put his arms out in an uncomfortable position?

SNYMAN: It was in order to break him down. We did this when it appeared as if he had improved. . . .

BIZOS: You also used leg irons. . . . Why was it necessary to use both hands to be handcuffed on the grille and the leg irons, with the chain passed through one of the bars, was it? So that he didn't have free movement of his legs? Have I got the picture correctly?

SNYMAN: We were not aware of whether he would be able to come up with his tricks again, and that is why we chained him like that.

BIZOS: Why was the chain put on the other side of the one bar, other than to restrict even the movement that leg irons allow?

SNYMAN: It is possible that we acted in an inhumane manner.

BIZOS: Well, that's one of the franker answers that you've given the committee. Can we summarize that the putting up of his arms and using the leg irons in the manner in which you did was a form of torture?

SNYMAN: That is correct. That might have been the case.

The testimony of the other policemen revealed other details. Captain Siebert, who subsequently rose to the rank of brigadier, admitted that he had lost his temper. Biko, he said, had been unco-operative from the start of the interrogation. He refused to answer any questions and became "angry and upset" when confronted with information gained from other detainees.

He again sat down. I lost my temper and pulled him up by his chest. He stood up and shoved the chair in my direction, as if he wanted to say "take the chair if you want it."

I bent down to stop the chair from hitting my legs and saw a movement above my head. It appeared to me that Biko was trying to slap me. I deflected his blow with a push. The push did not make much impression because he was bigger and heavier than me. The next moment Beneke came in from the side and charged with his shoulder into Biko's body.

A "full-scale fight" developed, said Siebert. Nieuwoudt joined in, striking Biko with a piece of hosepipe. "Subsequently, all three of us grabbed Biko and moved with him in the direction of the corner of the office and ran with him into the wall." "That's not an accident," Bizos remarked. "That's using him as a battering ram."

The five policemen applied for amnesty for culpable homicide. Bizos, on behalf of the Biko family, opposed the amnesty. The applicants, he said, had not made a full disclosure of what had happened. "Statements made at the inquest have merely been modified to try to explain away concrete evidence which did not fit in with the false evidence given at the inquest." Nor did they have a political motive when they fatally injured Biko. "Torturing helpless detainees for the purposes of extracting information to the point that they end up dead is not a political objective."

T HE SAME SECURITY POLICE UNIT in Port Elizabeth was responsible for a number of other infamous murders. These included the killing of the young activist Sizwe Kondile, whose mother had pleaded at the TRC's opening session in April 1996 for help in finding out what had happened to her son.

Kondile was a significant prize for the security police. A close aide to Chris Hani, the ANC guerrilla leader based in Lesotho, he had been arrested in the Orange Free State in June 1981, after driving across the border from Lesotho into South Africa in Hani's car. Handed over to the Port Elizabeth security police, he was held in a police station in the coastal town of Jeffrey's Bay.

In August, according to the original security police version, Kondile was taken back to the Orange Free State and released. Captain Hermanus du Plessis sent a message to security police headquarters in Pretoria on 10 August, informing them that the interrogation of Kondile had been completed and that there was no case against him but that he was willing to become a police informer. Kondile's mother, Charity, searching for her son, was told repeatedly that the police knew nothing of what had since happened to him; the police suggested that he had returned to Lesotho.

But Dirk Coetzee, the former Vlakplaas commander who applied for amnesty for his own role in Kondile's death, told a different story. Visiting Jeffrey's Bay police station in September 1981 while on assignment from Vlakplaas, Coetzee caught sight of Kondile handcuffed to a bed in a back room and guarded by a black policeman. His colleague, Colonel Nic van Rensburg, later explained who he was. He said that Kondile had sustained head injuries during interrogation. He had dived through a window with his hands handcuffed behind his back and landed on his head. "He told me a doctor had said Kondile had blood on the brain and if they wanted to avoid a Steve Biko case, they would have to do something." Coetzee offered his services.

Several weeks later, Coetzee was contacted by the Port Elizabeth security police; he arranged to meet them at a farm near Komatipoort on the Mozambique border. Coetzee arrived there with a group bringing wood and tires. The Port Elizabeth men brought Kondile. He was given a cold drink spiked with a drug, shot dead, and then cremated.

In his testimony, Coetzee seemed to relish giving details.

> We were all drinking. We gave Kondile his spiked drink. After twenty minutes he sat down uneasily; . . . then he fell over backwards. Then Nic van Rensburg said: "Well chaps, let's get on with the job." Two of the younger constables with the jeep dragged some dense bushveld and tires and made a fire. . . .
>
> The burning of a body on an open fire takes seven hours. Whilst that happened we were drinking and braaing next to the fire. I tell this not to hurt the family, but to show you the callousness with which we did things in those days.
>
> The fleshier parts of the body take longer. . . . That's why we frequently had to turn the buttocks and thighs of Kondile. . . . By the morning we raked through the ashes to see that no piece of bone or teeth was left. Then we all went our own ways.

Three senior officers—van Rensburg, du Plessis, and their commanding officer, Colonel Gerrit Erasmus—eventually admitted to the murder but denied that Kondile had been killed because he had suffered brain damage during interrogation. The reason for his death, they claimed, was that after agreeing to become a police informer, Kondile had been given the name of a security police agent; the name, if it had fallen into the ANC's hands, would have caused severe damage. No longer trusting Kondile, they had decided to kill him. Erasmus admitted making the final decision.

At the end of his testimony, Dirk Coetzee turned toward Charity Kondile to ask for her forgiveness, saying he hoped to meet her one day to "look her in the eye." Mrs. Kondile's lawyer, Imram Moosa, gave a swift response: "You have said you would like to meet Mrs. Kondile and look her in the eye. It is an honor she feels you do not deserve. And if you were really remorseful, you wouldn't apply for amnesty, but in fact stand trial for what you did."

A long, uncomfortable silence filled the hall. The amnesty panel, the legal representatives, the audience, all seemed distraught. Coetzee turned away slowly, his hands clutched together.

In a newspaper interview afterwards, Mrs. Kondile said: "It is easy for Mandela and Tutu to forgive. . . . They lead vindicated lives. In my life nothing, not a single thing, has changed since my son was burnt by barbarians . . . nothing. Therefore, I cannot forgive."

T HE WIDOWS OF THE Pebco Three—the three activists from the Port Elizabeth Black Civics Organization who had disappeared without trace in May 1985—also learned what had happened to their husbands.

The same group of security policemen responsible for so many murders—van Rensburg, du Plessis, Nieuwoudt, and Snyman—were once more involved. The trail leading to their doorstep started when the former Vlakplaas askari, Joe Mamasela, admitted to Jan d'Oliveira's team of investigators that he had participated in the killing. He had been among a group of Vlakplaas operatives sent to Port Elizabeth to assist with the abduction.

In October 1996, Colonel Roelof Venter, seeking amnesty along with Brigadier Cronje for his role in a number of murders, admitted to the TRC that he had led the group to Port Elizabeth. He had been involved in the abduction of the Pebco Three, he said, but not their killing. "To this day, I do not know how they were killed or what happened to their bodies." But he named several Port Elizabeth security policemen who he knew had participated in the operation.

The key figure in the operation was du Plessis, then a major. At an amnesty committee hearing in November 1997 he described how, in 1985, Pebco had established street and area committees in townships, which enabled it effectively to take control of the city. Whenever police arrested political activists, Pebco launched bus and consumer boycotts to force their release. "Port Elizabeth was ungovernable," said du Plessis. "If there was a war going on, then they won it." He discussed the problem with Colonel Snyman, then regional head of the security police.

Snyman testified that he was under constant pressure from the government to quell the unrest. Politicians like President Botha, Defense Minister Magnus Malan, and Police Minister Louis Le Grange attended meetings of the local Joint Management Center and stressed the need for drastic steps to restore control. "Fire must be fought with fire" was their message.

At a government conference in Cradock in February 1985, Snyman explained the difficulties he was facing to Louis Le Grange during a tea break.

SNYMAN: We discussed the fact that the normal, legal methods of policing were no longer effective, and the minister said to me very clearly, "Colonel, you have to make a plan with these activists in the Eastern Cape."

ADVOCATE: How did you interpret that? How did you understand that?

SNYMAN: My understanding was that these people had to be eliminated.

In April, du Plessis approached Snyman with a plan to "eliminate" the three Pebco leaders. It was the only way that the police would regain the initiative, said du Plessis.

> The information at my disposal was that they were the most radical. I believed that if we eliminated them we would harm Pebco irreparably. It would take them a long time to reorganize and regroup. . . .
>
> Snyman did not give a direct instruction, but he did say he realized there were no other options and I had to proceed and do the best I could in the interest of the country. I interpreted this as an instruction to go ahead and eliminate them.

On 8 May 1985, the Pebco Three—Sipho Hashe, Champion Galela, and Quqawuli Godolozi—were lured to Port Elizabeth airport by a police agent posing as a British embassy official; they were abducted by Colonel Venter and his Vlakplaas team and taken to the disused police station at Post Chalmers, where they were interrogated. According to members of the Vlakplaas group, including Mamasela, they were brutally tortured, one by one. According to Nieuwoudt, they were given spiked coffee and executed. Their bodies were burned on a pile of wood, and the ashes were collected in plastic bags and emptied into the Fish River.

"It was war. It was unfortunate that it happened," said du Plessis. "It's entirely possible that our plans were grossly ineffective."

THE PUZZLE OVER who killed Matthew Goniwe, Fort Calata, and the two other members of the Cradock Four, whose bodies were found badly mutilated near Port Elizabeth in June 1985, was also solved. The first inquest had found, like so many other verdicts on political assassinations, that their deaths had been caused by persons unknown. Then in 1992, a Johannesburg newspaper, *New Nation*, published details of a military signal that had been sent by the Eastern Cape military commander, Brigadier Joffel van der Westhuizen, to the secretariat of the State Security Council in Pretoria; the signal implicated the army in the killing.

Van der Westhuizen was a former combat officer who had set up an irregular unit known as the Hammer to carry out specialist operations against dissidents in the townships in the Eastern Cape. On 7 June 1985, three weeks before the Cradock Four were murdered, he discussed the Goniwe problem on the phone with General Hans Janse van Rensburg, a senior official seconded to the State Security Council; van der Westhuizen then sent a summary of the conversation, headed "Extremely Secret," to van Rensburg by military signal. In the summary, van der Westhuizen proposed that Goniwe and Calata should be "permanently removed from society as a matter of urgency." He warned: "Widespread reaction can be expected, locally as well as nationally, because of the importance of these persons."

In the light of the evidence published in the *New Nation*, a second inquest was held, opening in 1993 and concluding eighteen months later. Van der Westhuizen testified about the key role that Goniwe played in black opposition to the government: "Through him, town councils resigned; boycotts took place; stayaways [strikes] were instigated." The Eastern Cape, van der Westhuizen said, was "getting out of control." Van der Westhuizen denied, however, that his signal was tantamount to a death warrant; it had meant only that Goniwe should be detained indefinitely. To eliminate him would have been "unproductive" because it would have made a martyr of him.

A Supreme Court judge, Neville Zietsman, ruled in 1994 that

members of the security forces had indeed murdered the Cradock Four, but he was unable to identify any individuals. He said he could find no direct link between van der Westhuizen's military signal and the murders.

What the inquest precipitated, however, was a sharp dispute between the military and the security police. Embarrassed by its connection with the murders, the military pointed the finger at the security police. Odd items of evidence also suggested security police involvement: A false car number plate left at the murder scene was linked to security police headquarters. In his conclusion, Judge Zietsman found that a "case of suspicion" had been made not only against officers like van der Westhuizen but also against "certain members of the police force," including Colonel Harold Snyman. But that was as far as the matter was taken.

Then other evidence surfaced, relating to events in 1989, when three black policemen and a police informer were killed in a car bomb near Motherwell, outside Port Elizabeth. The car bomb was blamed on the ANC, and the ANC, handily enough, claimed responsibility. But a different explanation eventually emerged.

In 1994, Colonel Gideon Nieuwoudt, the commanding officer of the three dead policemen, was put on trial for their murder. The motive for the killing, according to the prosecution, was that Nieuwoudt had feared that they might divulge information to the ANC about the Goniwe murders and other security police activities. Nieuwoudt denied the charge.

The evidence against Nieuwoudt was far from conclusive. But during the course of his trial, Colonel de Kock, the former Vlakplaas commander who was himself still on trial for murder, made a dramatic intervention. De Kock had been infuriated by the remarks of several police generals who, in the course of his own trial, had dissociated themselves from his activities and claimed that he had been acting on his own authority. Among the generals was Nic van Rensburg, formerly head of the Port Elizabeth security police who had subsequently been promoted to security police headquarters in Pretoria. "It was complete treason," said de Kock. "It was another case of [the generals] running away. It was time for them to answer for their deeds." De Kock consequently decided to testify in the trial against Nieuwoudt and reveal the role that General van Rensburg had played in the plan to kill the four policemen.

De Kock's version was that in December 1989 he was summoned to van Rensburg's house in Pretoria for a meeting with Nieuwoudt. Nieuwoudt said he had a problem with a group of black security policemen who were engaged in fraud. "The drift of the discussion was that these people should be killed," said de Kock. When de Kock subsequently expressed doubts to van Rensburg about killing policemen involved in nothing more than fraud, van Rensburg confided that the real reason was that the policemen were about to defect with information about the Goniwe case and other similar cases. "We realized it was an extremely high-profile matter and could be extremely damaging to the security police if it were to leak out," said de Kock. Accordingly, he organized a car bomb device and sent two Vlakplaas officers to Port Elizabeth with it to assist Nieuwoudt.

With security policemen busily implicating each other, the remaining dominoes soon fell. Largely on the basis of de Kock's testimony, Nieuwoudt was convicted of murder and sentenced to twenty years' imprisonment. Seven security policemen now came forward to apply for amnesty in connection with the Goniwe killings, including van Rensburg, Snyman, and du Plessis.

The key figure in the operation was Captain Johan van Zyl, a former Koevoet officer with recent combat experience who had been posted to the Eastern Cape only a few months beforehand. In his testimony to the TRC in 1998, he said Goniwe was known as the most effective activist in the Eastern Cape. "We had to chop off the head of the destabilizing forces in the area," he said. The plan was approved by van Rensburg and ultimately by Snyman.

On 27 June 1985 Goniwe, Calata, and their two friends were abducted near the Olifantshoek Pass as they were returning to Cradock from a meeting in Port Elizabeth. They were handcuffed and taken in two cars to an area near St. George's beach in Port Elizabeth. There they were killed. Their bodies were mutilated, to make it look as though they were the victims of a vigilante attack, and then burnt. Their murder, far from quelling black opposition, set the Eastern Cape on fire. On the day after Goniwe's funeral in July 1985, President Botha was forced to declare a state of emergency.

One of the assassins, Lieutenant Eric Taylor, testified that he was convinced that the death squad would never be uncovered. When it was, he approached Nomonde Calata, Fort Calata's widow, whose appearance at the TRC's first hearing in 1996 had been so memorable; Taylor sought a fifteen-minute meeting so he could ask for her forgiveness.

"You have teased our grief for nearly twelve years," she told him when they met, "and you think you can reconcile in fifteen minutes?"

ONE OTHER MURDER CASE involving the Port Elizabeth security police gained particular public attention for the way it showed how far the Port Elizabeth security police went in persecuting their victims.

The story of Siphiwo Mtimkulu, a twenty-two-year-old student leader, was first told to the TRC in Port Elizabeth in June 1996 by his mother, Joyce. She described how he had been repeatedly harassed and detained. "Every time he was detained, he came out stronger than before. . . . Nothing could separate him from the struggle." One policeman, Gideon Nieuwoudt, had pursued him relentlessly, once even appearing at the Mtimkulu's house in New Brighton disguised as a Methodist priest and carrying a Bible.

During a protest march in May 1981, Mtimkulu was arrested and then held in Algoa Park police station for five months. By the time of his release, he had become a shadow of his former self, said his mother. He had lost his usual spirit; he complained of stomach pains; he had cold feet; his limbs were swollen.

> He said: "The Boers have finished me. I am totally finished. There is nothing that you can do about me." I asked him, why don't you stop this involvement with the struggle? He replied, he cannot do that. . . . The time for him to stop has passed. He stated he would rather die than stop what he was doing.

He told how he had been severely beaten, given electric shocks, and made to stand for hours on end. He gave her a diary that she had kept hidden for years. "Although he is dead, he can still talk. And he's talking now," she said, reading passages from the diary at the TRC hearing.

> I still had on my underpants. Nieuwoudt left the office with the towel. He returned. The towel was wet and dripping with water. He tied it over my nose and mouth. Breathing was difficult. I lost consciousness and fell. The towel was removed. It was done until I lost consciousness several times. Each time I fell on my back. At times he would hit me. The others would kick me.

The day after his release, his parents found him crawling on the floor, unable to walk. He was taken to a hospital in Cape Town, where doctors diagnosed that he had been poisoned with thallium, a tasteless, colorless, and odorless poison unavailable in South Africa except to the government. "Siphiwo was unrecognizable," said Joyce. His hair started to fall out. Holding up a fistful of hair, she told the commissioners: "This is Siphiwo's hair."

After three months of hospital treatment, he began to recover, but he was confined to a wheelchair. He brought two civil suits against the police: one for torture, the other for poisoning. An official inquiry into Mtimkulu's claims of torture was due to start in May 1982. On 14 April 1982, Mtimkulu went to Livingstone hospital in Port Elizabeth, accompanied by a friend, Topsy Madaka. Then he disappeared.

For years Joyce Mtimkulu searched for him. The police suggested he had crossed the border into Lesotho. Nieuwoudt came by her house to ask where he was.

Now, as she appeared before the TRC, she said she wanted answers to her questions. "Where did they leave the bones of my child? Where did they take him from Port Elizabeth? . . . What did they do to him?"

A year later the questions were answered. In September 1997, Erasmus, van Rensburg, du Plessis, and Nieuwoudt appeared before a TRC amnesty committee to account for their role in Mtimkulu's abduction and murder. All had prospered greatly during their service in the security police. Erasmus and van Rensburg had been promoted to the rank of general, du Plessis and Nieuwoudt to the rank of colonel.

General Erasmus admitted giving the order to kill Mtimkulu and his fellow activist Topsy Madaka, but he denied he had done so because of Mtimkulu's impending suit against the police. He described Mtimkulu as a "troublesome activist" who needed to be dealt with. He could have been arrested under the Internal Security Act, but this would have led to widespread unrest and riots. Moreover, headquarters in Pretoria would probably not have sanctioned detention of such a sick person.

Erasmus held several discussions with van Rensburg about the problem.

ERASMUS: Our final conclusion was that there was no other way—detention or any other thing—other than to eliminate these people.

ADVOCATE: When you are talking about elimination, you mean to kill them?

ERASMUS: That is correct.

ADVOCATE: Now, how did you feel about that personally—about this decision?

ERASMUS: This decision was a very, very difficult one. It's not something which you decide to do lightly. Gerrit Erasmus is not a murderer—the way he was brought up—and in all these years I still remember it. I tried to get this decision right out of my system, but it constantly came back to me. . . .

ADVOCATE: And what purpose did you try to achieve with that?

ERASMUS: What I tried to achieve was to break this power basis which was developing around these people.

The committee chairman, Judge Andrew Wilson, was incredulous of this explanation. He pointed out that after five months in detention, Mtimkulu was in such poor health that he had to spend several months in the hospital.

JUDGE WILSON: And when he was released, he was in a wheelchair?

ERASMUS: That is correct.

JUDGE WILSON: And up to the time of his death, he was still hobbling around with a stick, he couldn't walk properly?

ERASMUS: That is correct.

JUDGE WILSON: Is this the man—the man you considered so potentially dangerous as an activist that he should be killed—this invalid?

ERASMUS: That is correct.

Erasmus said that there was not sufficient evidence to gain a conviction against Mtimkulu and Madaka in the courts.

ADVOCATE SANDI: You did not seek the opinion of the attorney general to see whether one could secure any conviction?

ERASMUS: No I did not.

ADVOCATE SANDI: If I understand you clearly, that is to say that you were a judge as well as an executioner in your own case?

ERASMUS: You can call me that.

Although he did not consult headquarters about this particular case, he said the government was well aware of such operations. "I'm still under the impression that the politicians had to know. They were aware of what was going on." That included President Botha.

What we did, we did exclusively to safeguard the government of the day in power and to keep in place norms and structures that were important to us as white South Africans. That created gray areas as

far as policemen's work was concerned, more specifically security
policemen's work.

In his testimony, General van Rensburg described Mtimkulu and
Madaka as "two large cogs in the revolutionary struggle ... By
eliminating them we thought we would possibly be able to succeed
in stabilizing the area and preventing the revolutionary onslaught
from continuing locally."

The two young activists were abducted outside a Port Elizabeth
hotel on 14 April 1982 by du Plessis and Nieuwoudt and taken to a
disused police station at Post Chalmers near Cradock, which the
security police used for interrogation. Van Rensburg killed
Mtimkulu by shooting him behind the ear. Nieuwoudt shot Madaka
dead. Their bodies were placed on piles of firewood, doused with
diesel, set alight, and burned for six hours. The following morning,
Nieuwoudt and du Plessis raked up the remaining fragments of
bone, put them in plastic bags, and threw them into the Fish River.

At a ceremony on the banks of the Fish River in 1997, the families of Siphiwo Mtimkulu and Topsy Madaka cast flowers on to the
water and said prayers in remembrance of the two young men.

> In the midst of big things, in the midst of strong winds, the father of
> my king, Jesus Christ, you looked after us. Today, at the start of 1997,
> our God, who is extremely good, said we must come and stand over
> this river.
>
> We heard, after these long years when we were in the dark, that
> the bones, the remains, of our husbands and children got thrown
> here in plastic bags by the Boers, the people who were ruling at the
> time. But they got caught out, because you said a human being's
> bones can't just disappear.

7

Operation Marion

The GREATEST AREA of human rights violations the TRC was called upon to investigate was the conflict in KwaZulu-Natal. Starting in the mid-1980s, the conflict had grown into a Zulu civil war, pitting Chief Buthelezi's conservative Inkatha movement against radical pro-ANC groups; at one stage the war threatened to wreck the 1994 election. More than 20,000 people had died there in a decade of warfare; countless more had been injured.

In an attempt to ensure that the conflict did not erupt anew, Mandela gave Buthelezi a cabinet post in the 1994 coalition government, but there was considerable friction between the two men over several issues. In particular, Buthelezi was adamantly opposed to Mandela's plans for a truth commission and refused to cooperate.

Explaining his position in April 1996, as the TRC's first public hearings got underway, Buthelezi said that his Inkatha Freedom Party (IFP) had "as much interest as any party in reaching the truth of South Africa's recent history." Over a ten-year period, he said, some 430 IFP leaders and 12,000 IFP members had been murdered. The IFP had been the victim of a so-called "people's war" conducted by the ANC and its internal surrogate, the United Democratic Front (UDF).

"It is important that history records the pogrom against elected black leaders and councillors in KwaZulu-Natal and the campaign of assassinations against traditional structures in this and other provinces," Buthelezi said. However, he insisted that Tutu's TRC was not the appropriate organization to undertake the work. It was biased in favor of the ANC. Tutu himself had once been a patron of the UDF. "Our concern is not the truth emerging," declared Buthelezi, "but whether the whole truth will emerge."

In September 1996, after discussions with Tutu, Buthelezi agreed to make a submission to the TRC, but he spent his time placing all blame for the violence on the ANC. He denied any personal role in the strife, though he admitted that, despite the IFP's "constant vigil" to keep violence out of IFP politics, "IFP members and supporters have been drawn into violence."

> I say I am sorry to South Africa for this because, although I have not orchestrated one single act of violence against one single victim of political violence that has cost us many lives, as the leader of the Inkatha Freedom Party I know that the buck stops right in front of me.

Having proffered this apology, Buthelezi went on to deliver a 700-page report containing a litany of accusations against the ANC.

The TRC's investigations into the complexities of the KwaZulu-Natal conflict were thus conducted in hazardous circumstances. The picture the commission developed was inevitably fragmented and flawed, but what was most striking about it was that it displayed the extent to which Buthelezi and the apartheid government had combined their forces in an attempt to defeat the ANC.

AS CHIEF MINISTER SINCE 1976, Buthelezi had run the rural KwaZulu homeland as a one-party state, controlling its parliament, its civil service, and its police. His party, Inkatha, was a well-organized political movement drawing support from the Zulu establishment, from legislative assembly members, councillors, indunas, businessmen, and government employees. As a member of the Zulu royal family, he could also rely on the support of a powerful network of traditional chiefs—"amakhosi"—whom he in turn rewarded with power and privilege. In many respects he resembled a tribal potentate: intolerant of criticism, brooking no opposition, given to making interminable speeches, and constantly reminiscing about the past exploits of the Zulu people.

His role in the apartheid system was a complex one: He developed the art of opposing Pretoria's homelands policy while also playing a prominent part in it. Initially, he managed to remain on good terms with the exiled leaders of the ANC. Opinion polls during the 1970s showed that he was regarded by many Africans as South Africa's most important black politician.

In the early 1980s, however, his relationship with the ANC turned sour. To the fury of radical activists, he vociferously opposed the armed struggle and economic sanctions and praised the free-enterprise system. From Lusaka, the ANC denounced him as "a counter-revolutionary," "a puppet," and "a snake poisoning the people of South Africa"; the ANC urged its supporters inside South Africa, who had recently formed the United Democratic Front (UDF), to hit Inkatha "on the head."

Buthelezi responded in kind. "We must prepare ourselves not only to defend property and life, but to go beyond that and prepare ourselves to hit back with devastating force at those who destroy property and kill us," he told the KwaZulu legislative assembly in 1984. The following year, according to a secret State Security Council document obtained by the TRC, the Inkatha central committee resolved that "the whole of KwaZulu and Natal must be turned into a so-called 'no-go area' for the UDF, regardless of the consequence."

In the mid-1980s, the UDF began to make increasing inroads into Inkatha territory, organizing strikes and consumer boycotts. Its supporters came from the ranks of urban blacks in Natal, from community groups, the landless, the unemployed, and the youth, all struggling for survival in crowded shack settlements and townships and all resentful of the power and patronage enjoyed by the Zulu establishment. The numbers of this constituency were forever swelling.

Buthelezi soon turned to Pretoria for help. After hearing of a plot to assassinate him, he arranged a meeting in November 1985 with the director of military intelligence, General Tienie Groenewald, to ask for military protection; he wanted, among other things, a KwaZulu defense force, a KwaZulu state security council, and a Zulu battalion in the defense force. The matter was taken up quickly at an extraordinary meeting of the State Security Council attended by Magnus Malan and Louis Le Grange. In further discussions with General Groenewald, Buthelezi asked the defense force to give him a "contra-mobilization capability," an intelligence capability, and an offensive capability that could be used to prevent the UDF from disrupting Inkatha meetings and terrorizing Inkatha supporters.

Defense chiefs subsequently agreed that a paramilitary unit was needed to "neutralize" the UDF; they stressed, however, that the unit should not be traceable to the defense force but should appear to originate from KwaZulu. Buthelezi was asked to select 200 candidates for special training. The plan was given the code name "Operation Marion."

Two hundred and six recruits were flown in conditions of utmost secrecy from Durban to Camp Hippo, a guerrilla warfare school on the Caprivi Strip; the school was used by the defense force's Directorate of Special Tasks (DST) to train antigovernment rebel groups operating in Mozambique and Angola. The recruits were divided into four separate units, each specializing in different aspects of paramilitary work. The largest unit of 114 men was trained in contra-mobilization tactics; two other units concentrated on intelligence and VIP protection. There was also an "offensive" unit of thirty-three men. The recruits were given training in weapons and explosives, ambush and abduction techniques, house penetration and killing. They were taught how to conceal evidence, evade arrest, and lie to the police. They were also schooled in anticommunist propaganda. The enemy, they were told, was the ANC and its paymasters in Moscow. Their task was to hunt down ANC and UDF members and kill them.

The training at Camp Hippo lasted from April to September 1986. The recruits were paid in cash brought by military intelligence officers. They were also visited by Zakhele Khumalo, Buthelezi's personal assistant who served as Inkatha's liaison man on Operation Marion. On their return to KwaZulu, the recruits were called to meet Buthelezi, who congratulated them on their training.

From 1987, the Natal Midlands descended into ever-increasing bouts of violence. The conflict was essentially territorial. Inkatha leaders, known as "warlords," formed armed groups—"impis"—to drive out their opponents. The police were frequently accused of collusion in Inkatha attacks, of standing by while the impis went to work, and of failing to deal with the activities of warlords and known killers. Attackers, heavily armed, were sometimes transported in buses in broad daylight. Records obtained by the TRC showed that in 1987 some 700 UDF activists were detained by police, but not a single IFP activist.

UDF groups retaliated with similar ferocity. The main organizer in this Zulu civil war was the Natal Midlands boss, Harry Gwala, a modern-day Stalinist and former political prisoner who harbored an abiding hatred of Buthelezi and all that he stood for and who believed military victory over him was possible. Gwala publicly declared that Inkatha warlords should be killed. Hit squads operating in his area, some of them belonging to the ANC's armed wing, MK, were responsible for murdering scores of middle-ranking Inkatha officials.

The government was open about where it stood. At a police ceremony in the provincial capital, Pietermaritzburg, in February 1988, Adriaan Vlok, the police minister, declared: "The police intend to face the future with moderates and fight against radical groups. . . . Radicals, who are trying to destroy South Africa, will not be tolerated. We will fight them. We have put our foot in that direction, and we will eventually win the Pietermaritzburg area."

Police reinforcements were deployed in areas where UDF groups appeared to be getting the upper hand. As well as using regular policemen, the government recruited several thousand special constables—"kitskonstabels"—mainly from the ranks of Inkatha, gave them limited training, and sent them back to their communities armed with pump-action shotguns.

Amid the daily toll of death and destruction, there were appalling massacres. Both sides were culpable. In many cases, the perpetrators were never identified. In later years, however, two massacres in particular became infamous, not because they were any more brutal than others but because of why they happened.

The first massacre occurred in January 1987 when gunmen opened fire on a group of villagers holding a prayer meeting at a house belonging to a local pastor in the rural settlement of Kwa-Makutha, near Amanzimtoti. Thirteen people, mostly women and children, were killed. Local residents blamed Inkatha and the security forces, but for eight years the case remained unsolved.

The second massacre occurred in December 1988 when gunmen burst into a house in Trust Feed, a small village in the district of

New Hanover in the Natal Midlands, and killed eleven villagers attending a candlelit funeral wake. Once again, Inkatha and the security forces were blamed, but all attempts at investigation came to nothing, even though a number of policemen were implicated. Like most incidents in Natal's war, it was soon forgotten.

Three years later, however, Frank Dutton, a police captain attached to a special investigation unit, stumbled across evidence that a number of suspected murderers were being hidden within the ranks of the KwaZulu police at a camp called Mkuze, which was run by military intelligence. Among these suspects were two special constables implicated in the Trust Feed massacre. A police brigadier had previously submitted affidavits stating that the two men had deserted the police force.

In August 1992, the two special constables were taken before a magistrate, and they admitted taking part in the Trust Feed massacre. Their former commanding officer, Brian Mitchell, was arrested later that day. Shortly afterward, four other policemen implicated in the massacre were arrested. All seven policemen were subsequently indicted to stand trial on eleven counts of murder and eight counts of attempted murder.

Both at his trial and at a TRC amnesty committee hearing in 1996, Brian Mitchell described how he regarded himself as "a soldier engaged in a civil war." As the new station commander at New Hanover and as head of the local Joint Management Center, his task had been to turn the tide of war against the UDF. "It was my duty to see to it that the UDF/ANC were countered effectively within my area. This included favoring the IFP and groups not perceived to be state enemies."

Mitchell admitted that when he was posted to New Hanover in January 1988, Trust Feed had been a peaceful community. But he considered the local Inkatha leadership to be weak and vulnerable, losing ground to the UDF, and he set about trying to bolster it. His instructions were that "not an inch of Natal was to go to the UDF/ANC—irrespective of the costs." The police objective, he said, was to confine revolutionary violence to the black communities, to wage war by proxy, so that white men could drink beer and watch rugby on Saturday afternoons untroubled by the townships burning.

In collusion with the local IFP leader, Jerome Gabela, Mitchell established a landowners' association to oppose the residents' association, an elected organization recognized by regional planners but regarded by the police to be dominated by the UDF. Within months, Trust Feed descended into turmoil as Inkatha members tried to force out UDF supporters.

At a meeting in November attended by Lieutenant Mitchell, Inkatha officials, and Captain Terblanche, the head of the local riot police, it was agreed that a night of attacks would be launched on remaining UDF supporters. A detachment of special constables in civilian clothes would be sent to Trust Feed, ostensibly to guard Gabela's house. A curfew would be imposed, enabling the police to detain UDF supporters while their houses were set on fire. The day before the attack was due, the riot police would sweep the area removing what weapons they could find. "This would render UDF/ANC supporters more vulnerable to the attack, which would take place with the assistance of the special constables and in conjunction with the Inkatha Youth Brigade," Mitchell told the TRC.

During the attack on 3 December, Mitchell ordered four special constables, armed with pump-action shotguns, to attack a house in which they believed UDF activists were gathered. In the darkness, they chose the wrong house. The policemen opened fire through the back windows and front entrance of the house. Then two of them went inside and moved from room to room to finish off the occupants. Eleven innocent mourners were killed, most of them IFP supporters. It was, said Mitchell, "a stupid mistake."

In the aftermath, police investigators covered up evidence linking Mitchell to the attack. After being questioned about his role in the killings, he was told "not to worry," he said. "I accepted the incident would be covered up." The residents' association was blamed for the killing, and its members fled, allowing Inkatha to take over the township. The special constables were given positions in the KwaZulu police. Mitchell himself was promoted to captain and transferred to another town in Natal.

In 1992, Mitchell was convicted of murder and sentenced to death. His sentence was commuted two years later to thirty years' imprisonment. He was one of the few police officers ever to face prosecution for involvement in political violence.

I NVESTIGATIONS INTO THE KwaMakutha massacre, which took place almost two years before the Trust Feed massacre, eventually led far higher up the chain of command.

In 1993, after a prolonged period of violence in the Esikhawini area near Richard's Bay, police uncovered the existence of a hit squad within the KwaZulu police; the squad was responsible for scores of murders. One of its members was Daluxolo Luthuli, a relative of the former ANC leader Albert Luthuli.

Daluxolo Luthuli had led a checkered career. As a young man, he had joined the ANC's armed wing, MK, received military training in the Soviet Union, and participated in a guerrilla offensive in Rhodesia. Arrested in 1967, he was sentenced to ten years' imprisonment on Robben Island. On his release he returned to his family home in Georgedale and joined Inkatha. After the UDF was formed in 1983, he became increasingly resentful of its activities.

Militant youth affiliated to the UDF were very active in black areas. They were forcing people to support them in their efforts to make the country ungovernable. People's courts were held, and the sentences that were meted out by youngsters were often inhumane and barbaric. People were sentenced to hundreds of lashes, forced to parade naked through townships, and death by necklace was a common sentence.

Inkatha and its supporters were labeled collaborators of the white government. It was common for Inkatha leaders and supporters to be attacked and murdered.

In 1986, Luthuli was asked by Buthelezi's personal assistant, Zakhele Khumalo, and other Inkatha officials to join Operation Marion.

> I was told that because the ANC had declared war on Inkatha and its supporters, Inkatha had decided to form an armed wing to fight the ANC. I was told that if an armed wing was not formed, Inkatha, its leaders and supporters, would be destroyed by the ANC.
>
> Khumalo asked me to act as the political commissar to this group. I immediately agreed. The fact that Khumalo was involved in this project convinced me that Dr. Buthelezi approved the formation of the armed wing.

Within a week, Luthuli was flown to Camp Hippo on the Caprivi Strip to help supervise the 206 recruits sent there by Inkatha. On his return he was given command of two Caprivi groups, including contra-mobilization. Over the next seven years, he was involved in so much hit-squad activity, he said, that it was impossible for him to remember it all.

Pursuing the links between the Caprivi group and hit-squad

activity, police investigators led by Colonel Frank Dutton focused upon the KwaMakutha massacre and eventually found two army officers—Major Johan Opperman and Sergeant André Cloete—willing to testify as state witnesses about what had happened.

Opperman, the deputy commander at Camp Hippo, had been assigned to work with the Caprivi group on their return to Natal. His version was that some weeks later he was approached by Khumalo, who told him that they were restless and wanted to "practice their training." Opperman asked Colonel John More, a staff officer at the Directorate of Special Tasks, for permission to launch an operation; permission was granted.

Opperman then asked Daluxolo Luthuli to select four people "whose death would have a positive impact on Inkatha." Four members of the "intelligence-gathering" group were instructed to compile a dossier each. Opperman checked to see that none of the intended targets was a police or military informer and then traveled to Pretoria to obtain final approval from the DST.

The first target they chose was Victor Ntuli, a UDF activist who lived in KwaMakutha at the house of his father, the Reverend Willie Ntuli. AK–47 assault rifles were supplied to the hit squad from a military base in Natal. The weapons were to be collected after the operation and destroyed.

Opperman and Khumalo met Luthuli and eleven members of the hit squad at a deserted spot in Ulundi to brief them on the mission. One of the gunmen was given a piece of paper on which was written "Chapter 1, Verse 1," with instructions to leave it at the scene, for effect.

Victor Ntuli was not at home when the gunmen struck. Instead the house was full of visitors resting after attending a late-night prayer meeting. Thirteen people were killed, including the Reverend Ntuli and three of his children.

During 1995, a series of arrests were made in connection with the KwaMakutha massacre, including Brigadier More, Zakhele Khumalo, and six former KwaZulu policemen. Then in November 1995, General Magnus Malan—the former defense minister—and ten retired senior officers, including two former chiefs of the defense force, were indicted on charges of murder and conspiracy to murder. The prosecution's aim was to prove that all those involved in setting up Operation Marion were directly responsible for the massacre at KwaMakutha.

There was, however, one notable omission: Chief Buthelezi, currently serving as minister of home affairs in Mandela's coalition government. When the judge, Jan Hugo, asked why Buthelezi had not been listed as a coconspirator, the KwaZulu-Natal attorney general, Tim McNally, replied that Buthelezi was known to be "a man of non-violence, a man who favored the peaceful option."

The trial lasted for seven months. The judge's verdict was that there was no doubt that the KwaMakutha massacre had been planned by two members of the army's Directorate of Special Tasks—Opperman and Cloete—and carried out by a group of Caprivi-trained Inkatha gunmen paid by the South African Defense Force. But, he said, there was no evidence that Malan and his defense chiefs had set up Operation Marion with the aim of establishing hit squads, nor was there any proof that the military had authorized the KwaMakutha massacre. The judge also found that it could not be proved beyond reasonable doubt that the six former KwaZulu policemen on trial were the actual perpetrators. All twenty accused were consequently discharged. The Ntuli family was dismayed by the result. Mbusi Ntuli, who lost his father and three sisters, remarked: "They were murdered, yet it seemed no one killed them."

When Archbishop Tutu suggested that Buthelezi should visit

KwaMakutha to apologize to the relatives of the thirteen victims, Buthelezi retorted that he had already apologized on two separate occasions. "If that is not good enough, then no theatrics of the kind that is now being suggested will improve in any way the apologies that I have already made before the whole world."

In 1998, Daluxolo Luthuli and six other members of the Esikhawini hit squad—all Caprivi graduates—applied for amnesty in connection with fifty-six incidents in northern KwaZulu-Natal in which more than 100 people had been killed. They recounted how they had fired indiscriminately into crowds at bus stops, at roadsides, and at political rallies, without knowing how many people they had killed or injured. Individuals were targeted as they walked home or sat in their homes. The expression the hit squad used when a victim had been identified was: "He must take the first bus."

All their actions, they said, had been carried out under orders from senior IFP officials and with the support of high-ranking KwaZulu police officers. Luthuli testified that he had no doubt that Buthelezi knew of hit-squad operations; he said that Zakhele Khumalo, Buthelezi's personal assistant, had given him direct orders. Public statements by Buthelezi urging Zulus to fight against their enemies were taken as a call to attack ANC supporters.

Another member of the hit squad, Romeo Mbambo, serving a life sentence for two murders, spoke of the bitterness he felt toward the IFP, which had abandoned him after using him and others to do its dirty work. "The youth should not fall into the trap of being manipulated and exploited by people of authority in the community."

At their hearing before the TRC in Richard's Bay, the former members of the Esikhawini hit squad came forward to ask for forgiveness from the audience, which included many of their victims. Each man was applauded.

B RIAN MITCHELL, SERVING A thirty-year sentence for his role in the Trust Feed massacre, also applied for amnesty. In his judgment in December 1996, Andrew Wilson, the same judge who had sentenced Mitchell to death for murder, accepted that his activities had been "part of the counterrevolutionary onslaught against the ANC and UDF activists" and that "he had acted within the course and scope of his duties as an officer in the South African police force." Wilson was also satisfied that Mitchell had made a full disclosure of the facts. Accordingly, he was granted amnesty.

There was outrage that Mitchell was allowed to walk free, particularly among the residents at Trust Feed who had opposed amnesty. Mitchell made an emotional plea for forgiveness and pledged himself to work for the reconstruction of the local community, but his attempts at reconciliation were rebuffed. Residents denounced the amnesty process for favoring perpetrators rather than victims.

Mitchell was the first security force member to be granted amnesty for apartheid crimes. "Amnesty," warned Archbishop Tutu at the time, "is going to cause people a lot of heartbreak."

8

In Police Custody

FOR A PERIOD OF thirty years, the government's standard method of dealing with political dissidents and troublemakers was to imprison them without trial. Between 1960 and 1990, some 80,000 people were detained without trial, among them 10,000 women and 15,000 children and youths under the age of eighteen. Initially, detainees were treated little differently from ordinary prisoners, an experience that was grim enough. But from 1963, when the security police were given virtually unlimited powers to crush armed rebellions started by the ANC's military wing—Umkhonto we Sizwe (MK)—and the Pan-Africanist Congress, torture became commonplace.

Under the General Law Amendment Act of 1963, detainees could be held in solitary confinement, without access to lawyers and family, until they had replied "satisfactorily" to all questions put by police interrogators. The initial period for which they could be held was 90 days; this was later extended to 180 days. But the police were entitled to renew the order again and again—"until this side of eternity," in the words of the justice minister, John Vorster. And the courts were expressly prohibited from interfering.

Scores of men and women vanished into jails, to be subjected to solitary confinement and prolonged interrogation. They were allowed no reading material except the Bible, no writing material, no visitors; and their interrogators taunted them constantly with the threat of holding them without trial indefinitely. When ordinary interrogation methods failed, the security police readily resorted to physical assaults and torture.

A favorite method was "statue" torture. Detainees were forced to stand in a small chalk square for periods ranging from six hours to sixty hours. If they tried to sit down, they were jerked to their feet again; and if they fainted or lost consciousness, they were revived and forced to stand again. A white communist activist, Ivan Schermbrucker, described in a note smuggled out of prison how he was made to stand until exhaustion brought him to the ground after twenty-eight hours: "I fell twice, had cold water thrown over me, and was pulled to my feet. . . . I nearly committed bloody suicide by jumping out of the window. This is torture. . . . They threatened to keep me standing for four days and nights and even longer."

An MK member, Laloo Chiba, described to the TRC his interrogation in Johannesburg in 1964:

> There were about five or six people who were actually present in the room. They started assaulting me, punched me, kicked me, and in the process my face was badly bruised. My left eardrum had been punctured. They wanted to know who my contact in MK was. . . . I pleaded ignorance. . . . The assault must have lasted half an hour or so. It is very, very difficult for me to assess the passage of time in these circumstances. But what was to follow was far more serious.

Chiba was covered with a wet burlap sack, then subjected to electric shock treatment: "Every time I resisted answering the questions, they turned the dynamo, and of course, violent electric shocks started passing through my body. . . . After the electric torture was over, I was unable to walk. I collapsed. They then carried me out."

A fellow detainee, Reggie Vandeyar, described Chiba's condition on his return to the cells:

His face was swollen severely. His eyes appeared to be coming out of their sockets. He was walking with great difficulty and was supported by a policeman. His legs were rigid. His knees could not bend. His hands were almost like he had severe arthritis. He looked like a Frankenstein monster.

Another MK member, Abdulhay Jassat, told the TRC how he had first been given electric shocks, then dangled by his ankles outside a third-floor window in a Johannesburg building:

> Two policemen. . . dragged me to the window, and then they said I can now jump. . . . I refused. . . . They grabbed me by my shoulders and lifted me physically up and pushed me out of the window, . . . and they were holding me by my ankles, . . . each policeman holding one ankle. All I could see was the concrete floor at the bottom. We were three floors up, and all of a sudden one would let go of one foot—as he's about to catch my foot, the one he had released, the other chap let's go—and they played like that. . . . And you know, you thought: God, this is the end.

It was not long before the casualty list mounted—activists were said to have hung themselves, or thrown themselves out of high windows, or slipped fatally in showers on bars of soap. The first was Looksmart Ngudle, an MK commander, reported to have committed suicide by hanging himself in September 1963. A fellow prisoner told the TRC how he had last seen him in a badly beaten condition.

The following year, Suliman Salojee was said to have committed suicide by jumping from the seventh floor of the security police headquarters in Johannesburg. His widow told the TRC that the bloodstained clothes she had collected from the police suggested he had been tortured.

Each year, more victims were added to the list. Mapetla Mohapi, whose widow testified at the first TRC hearing in 1996, was the twenty-fifth detainee to die in prison. Steve Biko, the following year, was the forty-seventh. A white trade unionist, Dr. Neil Aggett, became the fifty-third in 1982. During three months in detention, Aggett received no medical attention, despite injuries he had sustained during interrogation. Shortly before his body was found hanging in his cell, he told a police sergeant that he had been interrogated continuously for sixty-two hours, during which time he had been given electric shocks. At his inquest, a human rights lawyer described his death as "induced suicide." The magistrate found that nobody could be held responsible for his death. By 1990, the number of detainees dying in police cells had reached seventy-three.

Throughout the 1980s, as the government sought to crush black resistance through mass detention, torture was used routinely. Colonel Roelof Venter, head of the security police interrogation division, told the TRC that the usual method of interrogation was "to use violence, to humiliate people, to assault, to intimidate as a means of gaining information from them." He admitted: "Any effective method was acceptable in the context of war and the total onslaught." Some detainees would speak after an hour, others after a few days. If the victim held out, the questioning and assaults would go on and on, day and night, for as long as it took.

Independent investigations at the time showed the use of torture to be widespread. "There can be little doubt that the security police regard their ability to torture detainees with total impunity as the cornerstone of the detention system," concluded a report by the Detainees' Parents Support Committee in 1983. "Sometimes torture is used on detainees before they have even been asked their first question in order to soften them up. Other times, torture is used late in the interrogation process when the detainee is being stubborn and difficult."

A study on torture published in 1985 by the Department of Psychology at the University of Cape Town showed that 145 of 175 people in its sample—83 percent—had suffered some form of torture. Beating was the most common; other methods included electric shocks; suffocation; hair-burning; genital abuse; and forced postures—requiring detainees to sit in an imaginary chair for hours on end. The "helicopter" technique, which involved suspending detainees from a pole while handcuffed at the ankles and wrists, was employed frequently.

At one TRC hearing after another, victims came forward to describe their experience; some of the victims appeared quite dispassionate; others struggled to control their emotions. Haroon Aziz, an underground ANC cell leader in Natal, recounted how he had been subjected to the "invisible chair" method:

> They used to make me sit on what they used to call an invisible chair. An invisible chair is [where] you pretend to sit on a chair, but there's no chair there, and you hold your hands out and you flick your fingers. They interrogate you, and you have to answer the questions. This invisible chair position was quite close to the wall, but I wasn't allowed to lean against the wall. In front of me one of the special branch policemen used to hold a knife at my navel so as to prevent me from falling easily to the ground. And if they were not satisfied with the answers I gave, from time to time they would hit me on my penis, and sometimes squeeze it. It was very difficult to fall down because of the knife in front, but eventually, when I fell, I was kicked, and this kicking used to go on, and I used to scream and shout, and they used to laugh at me like mad hyenas.

Greta Apelgren, arrested in connection with a car bomb attack outside a bar on the Durban beachfront, spoke of her ordeal of being held in solitary confinement in a small cell for seven months:

> I don't even want to describe psychologically what I had to do to survive down there. I will write it one day, but I could never tell you. It did teach me something, and that is that no human being can live alone for more than I think a month. . . . The basement . . . was . . . at the bottom with high walls. I felt as the months went by that I was going deeper and deeper into the ground. . . . I became so psychologically damaged that I used to feel that all these cells are like coffins and there were all dead people in there, because they were not there, no one was there. It was as if I was alive and all these people were dead.

Sexual torture was inflicted both on men and women. Ntombizanele Zingoxondo testified: "They unbuttoned my shirt and pulled my breast out of my bra. They emptied one drawer, and my breast was squeezed in the drawer. They did this several times on each breast until white sticky stuff burst out of the nipples of my breast."

Patrick Mzathi, a fourteen-year-old youth, was subjected to the male version of the drawer method: "They put my penis and my testicles into a drawer. It was the first time I experienced a pain of my private parts. I went unconscious."

Women, in particular, found difficulty in talking about the humiliation they had endured. Testifying to the TRC, Thandi Shezi, an ANC youth league member, explained that she had never told her mother the truth about what had happened to her in detention.

At first, her feet and hands were chained and she was severely beaten. Four policemen then placed a plastic sack over her head, poured cold water and acid on her, and sent electric shocks through her until her tongue was swollen and she was close to suffocation. Realizing she would not reveal any information that way, they took her to another room and threw her to the floor. "And one of them said, 'We must just humiliate her and show her that this ANC can't do anything for her.' . . . Then the whole four of them started raping me whilst they were insulting me and using vulgar words and said I must tell them the truth."

Referring to her reluctance to talk about the incident, Shezi said: "I was ashamed. I thought I'd done something to deserve to be treated like this."

As well as the victims who testified, a number of perpetrators came forward. A former member of the Durban Riot Unit, Frank Bennetts described how he practiced electric shock torture:

I did make use of a shocking device. . . . They were available from anyone at Telkom [the national telephone company]. I can go fetch you one now. . . . It was an old crank telephone, . . . and you'd take two wires—well, the best one was just two keys, I presume, was the best way to do it. Just a normal key with a hole in the top. Tie a key on to each wire. The guy's got a hood over his head. Dangle them so that they touch the palms of his hands. When the first shock goes through, his hands close and he can't open them again. While you keep turning the handle, he can't let go of it.

Bennetts also gave a graphic description of the "helicopter" technique:

They would handcuff his feet together round the ankles and handcuff his hands behind his back and then place him on his stomach with his feet in the air and put a broom stick or quite a strong plank of wood between his ankles and then through his legs coming out the top here and pick him up and hang him between two desks like that. The result was similar to crucifixion. It pulled all your muscles. It closed up your chest. You couldn't breathe. Leave the guy there long enough, he's going to talk.

Jeffrey Benzien's specialty was the wet bag. He liked to boast that no one could resist his technique. Usually it took less than thirty minutes for detainees to start talking. Few held out any longer. His reputation among Western Cape dissidents was so fearsome that in some cases it was sufficient for him just to walk into the room to produce results. By his own admission, he was Cape Town's most successful torturer. His former commanding officer, Lieutenant Rudolf Liebenberg, head of the Terrorist Tracing Unit based at Culemborg in Cape Town, described him as "the best exponent of unconventional methods of extracting information from suspects." According to his victims, he was a man totally oblivious to screams of agony.

At his amnesty hearing in Cape Town in 1997, Benzien, a former warrant officer still employed by the police in its air wing, was remarkably forthcoming about the tricks of his previous trade. But even more remarkable were the exchanges he had with former victims who were allowed to question him. Ostensibly, it was the turn of the victims to interrogate, but the outcome was not so straightforward.

The first to question him was Tony Yengeni, a former MK commander and at the time of the hearing a member of parliament; Benzien had tortured him with his wet bag technique.

YENGENI: Now, I was blindfolded and then the bag was used on me. The point, the question that I want to ask you is, I have never seen this bag being used myself on any other person. Even when it was used on me, I never saw it. And I think it would be in the interest of the public and the commission for you to demonstrate the use of this bag.

BENZIEN: It was a cloth bag that would be submerged in water to get it completely wet. And then the way I applied it was, I get the person to lie down on the ground on his stomach, normally on a mat or something similar, with that person's hands handcuffed behind his back.

Then I would take up a position in the small of the person's back, put my feet through between his arms to maintain my balance, and then pull the bag over the person's head and twist it closed around the neck in that way, cutting off the air supply to the person.

A volunteer came forward so that Benzien could give the commissioners a practical demonstration. As they stood up, watching intently and asking questions, Benzien squatted on the back of the volunteer lying face down on the floor and pulled a bag over his head.

YENGENI: At what point do you release the bag to give the person who is tortured more air? Is there something, are you counting time, or is there something that you feel and then you release the bag? What happens, what makes you to release the bag?

CHAIRMAN: I imagine that when you are in that position, you are asking questions?

BENZIEN: That is correct.

CHAIRMAN: And you are expecting answers?

BENZIEN: That is correct.

CHAIRMAN: And whether you release it and when you release it, would depend upon whether you are getting answers from this person.

BENZIEN: Answers, and also I would release it—the intention was never to kill somebody, but the possibility, the real possibility was always there. I did realize that.

YENGENI: But was there any physical condition that would make you to release the bag on the part of the person who is tortured?

BENZIEN: On occasions people have, I presume, and I say presume, lost consciousness. They would go slack and every time that was done, I would release the bag.

CHAIRMAN: What happens to the person while he is being choked? Can you describe [that]? . . .

BENZIEN: There would be movement. There would be head movement, distress. All the time there would be questions being asked: Do you want to speak? And as soon as an indication was given that this person wanted to speak, the air would be allowed back to this person to say what he wanted to say.

YENGENI: Would the person groan, moan, cry, scream? What would the person do?

BENZIEN: Yes, the person would moan, cry, although muffled, yes, it does happen.

YENGENI: And you did this to each and every one of us?

BENZIEN: To the majority of you, yes. . . .

YENGENI: How did I react and respond to you at the bag?

BENZIEN: Individually, I cannot say how you reacted. I know that after the method was applied, you did take us to the house of Jennifer Schreiner, where we took out a lot of limpet mines, hand grenades, and firearms. In other words, your reaction, as far as I understand it correctly, was, you told us where your weaponry was. . . .

YENGENI: What kind of man uses a method like this one of the wet bag, to people, to other human beings, repeatedly and listening to those moans and cries and groans and taking each of those people very near to their deaths? What kind of man are you? What kind of man is that, that can do that kind of, what kind of human being is that, Mr. Benzien?

I want to understand really why, what happened? I am not talking about now the politics or your family; I am talking about the man behind the wet bag? When you do those things, what happens to you as a human being? What goes through your head, your mind? You know, what [has] that torture activity done to you as a human being?

BENZIEN: Mr. Yengeni, not only you have asked me that question. I—I, Jeff Benzien—have asked myself that question to such an extent that I voluntarily—and it is not easy for me to say this in a full court with a lot of people who do not know me—approached psychiatrists to have myself evaluated, to find out what type of person am I. . . .

I had the fortune or misfortune of growing up in a white environment in Cape Town. I did not—either through my own stupidity or ignorance, as long as I was one of the whites, the privileged whites who had an education, who had a house—I couldn't see it being taken away. If you ask me what type of person is it that can do that, I ask myself the same question.

Though at times apologetic and once even moved to tears, Benzien was not averse to inflicting further humiliation on his victims by reminding them of how they had broken under interrogation, betraying their colleagues, and by refusing to remember details of their ordeal that they were anxious to confirm.

Ashley Forbes, another former MK commander, probed for answers persistently, trying to get Benzien to admit to acts that had driven him to the brink of suicide.

FORBES: When I was arrested, do you remember saying to me that you are able to treat me like an animal or like a human being and that how you treated me depended on whether I cooperated or not?

BENZIEN: I can't remember it correctly, Sir, but I will concede I may have said it.

FORBES: Do you remember that when the wet bag method was used, that I was undressed, that my pants were pulled towards my ankles, and that thereafter the wet bag was pulled over my head and suffocated?

BENZIEN: I cannot remember it specifically, but I am willing to concede.

FORBES: I understand maybe there are many aspects, details that you can't remember, but most of these things, they stand out vividly in my mind, so most of these things are things that I can remember. Can I then also just ask if you remember that while I was laying on the ground, that somebody inserted a metal rod into my anus and shocked me?

BENZIEN: No, Sir. As heinous as it may sound, I used an electric generator on one person. It was on Peter Jacobs, not on you.

FORBES: This is something that I do remember.

BENZIEN: I am sitting in the position, Sir, where I cannot remember that, but if I can remember I am not trying to squirm away from my responsibility.

   You, I can remember especially, because I think that the two of us after weeks of your confinement really became quite close. I may be mistaken, but I think we became relatively, I wouldn't say good friends, but on a very good rapport.

FORBES: Can I then also ask if you remember why the date is significant, is that always on the 16th it would be the day that the assaults would happen? That although the first time this type of assault took place was the day of my arrest, after that, whenever it came to the 16th, it would either be the threat or actual assault on me. That it didn't perhaps take place once, but it took place at least three times? . . .

BENZIEN: Sir, in the spirit of reconciliation—and I have been trying to be as honest with this court as I can—I deny. And Mr. Forbes, if I am denying this, then one of us two [is] lying. Because after your initial arrest and your initial interrogation, I concede, on the Saturday I assaulted you. I then assaulted you, I think it was on the Monday evening—that was after we went for the steak, am I correct?

   After that, I took you on investigation to the Eastern Cape. Whereas to refresh your memory—and I am not saying it flippantly—you said it was the most Kentucky Fried Chicken you have ever eaten. Either after that or prior to that, we attempted to go to the Western Transvaal, where you were going to do some pointing out.

   Can you remember the time that you saw snow for the first time? Can you remember what happened in the snow? The husband and the wife and the two children who were taking photos of you playing in the snow along the N1 [a main road]? Your trip to Colesberg, where you braaied with me that night and with the rest of the unit?

Therefore, Mr. Forbes, in the spirit of honesty and reconciliation, I am sure you are making a mistake about the 16th of every month was the day that I would assault you.

FORBES: Mr. Benzien, maybe I will take you through the next time that I was assaulted, and I will just see if there are aspects of that torture that you may remember. For example, on the second occasion do you remember that I was wrapped in the carpet?

BENZIEN: That was the Monday, the Monday night.

FORBES: Do you remember, for example, that my clothes were removed and that the wet bag method was again used on me?

BENZIEN: I would concede it could have happened.

FORBES: Do you remember after that, putting me onto a chair and then saying to me that you are going to break my eardrum and then hitting me against my ear?

BENZIEN: No, Sir. Not saying I am going to break your eardrum. I gave you a smack that evening on your ear, and days later you told me that you think your eardrum was broken. You were examined by a district surgeon in Queenstown, if I am not mistaken, but you had also been sitting at the open window in the vehicle.

FORBES: Do you remember saying that you are going to give me a blue eye and then hitting me against my eye?

BENZIEN: No Sir . . .

FORBES: Do you remember saying that you are going to break my nose and then putting both your thumbs into my nostrils and pulling it until the blood came out of my nose?

BENZIEN: I know you had a nose bleed. I thought it was as a result of the smack I gave you.

FORBES: Do you remember choking me and then knocking my head against the wall until I lost consciousness?

BENZIEN: No Sir, I am not aware of Mr. Forbes losing consciousness at all.

ADV. DE JAGER: What about the knocking of the head against the wall?

BENZIEN: Sir, I doubt if I hit his head against the wall, because all this could have led to marks.

FORBES: I would just like to say that these are all occurrences that I can clearly remember. But then to continue, could I ask Mr. Benzien, apart from I think the impression that you are giving this commission that we went on these joy trips in the snow and for braais and so forth, can I put it to you that it was always after an assault of this nature that we would be taken on these trips, and that the intention of these trips was to ensure that the injuries would heal and that I would actually not get into contact with the district surgeon?

BENZIEN: No, Sir, I deny. . . .

FORBES: Mr. Benzien, after about three months in interrogation, I tried to commit suicide, just before the 16th, I think it was, of July. As from my perspective I would have seen that particular act, it is something that I have never thought of before, even after—something that I wouldn't ever think of doing. But under those conditions, after three months in your hands and just prior to the 16th, I had tried to commit suicide.

Could you perhaps from your perspective try and explain or try to help the commission to understand why I would have come to that point to have tried to commit suicide?

CHAIRMAN: Were you aware of the fact that he tried to commit suicide?

BENZIEN: I was so informed, Mr. Chairman. What actually led to that, I cannot say, except that I concede the method of detention was a draconian law instituted by the then Nationalist government.

In the case of Peter Jacobs, another MK insurgent, Benzien admitted that his interrogation had been "robust and very long," far longer than the usual thirty minutes.

BENZIEN: The normal interview with you carried on for quite a while and you were giving evasive answers. . . . It was obvious that you were playing for time, and then I resorted to using the wet bag method on you.

During the sessions with the wet bag, we were not getting the desired results. Time was going on, and I think I applied electric shocks to you by means of a hand generator.

JACOBS: In which parts of my body?

BENZIEN: I am not exactly clear on this, but if you told me I could refresh my memory.

JACOBS: [To the commission] It is only when one provides him with information, then he says if that is so, I would concede. . . .

JUDGE NGOEPE: Let's sum up what you were trying to put to the witness. I think Mr. Jacobs is saying to you that you were able to remember the details, the questions that you asked me, for example that you stayed under the bush and so forth, but when it comes to exactly where on my body did you apply electric shocks, suddenly you don't remember. That is what he is saying. And he is asking you, how do you explain that?

BENZIEN: Sir, if I said to Mr. Jacobs I put the electrodes in his nose, I may be wrong. If I said I attached it to his genitals, I may be wrong. If I put a probe into his rectum, I may be wrong. That is why the specific methods—I could have used any one of those three.

ADV. DE JAGER: Did you, during your service, use all three methods?

BENZIEN: In the case of Mr. Jacobs, yes, Sir. . . .

JACOBS: Let's just go to the shock treatment. Why was that necessary given what you were saying about the bag and all of that. I mean, [why] would that make a difference?

BENZIEN: I was using any means at my disposal to get you to tell us where your friend or compatriot was hiding.

JACOBS: Anything to get me to talk—is that what you are saying—anything?

BENZIEN: Anything short of killing you, yes.

JACOBS: So, you would undress me, tie my blue belt around my feet, throw me on the ground, put the handcuffs with the cloth over my arm to prevent marks. You do that [give electric shocks] quite a few times. But at some point, I think it is about the fourth time, when I thought I am dying, you woke me up and you said, "Peter, I will take you to the verge of death as many times as I want to. But you are going to talk and if it means that you will die, that is okay." Do you remember that?

Benzien: I concede I may have said that, Sir.

Jacobs: I want you to tell me, because this is important for me. The truth commission can amnesty, but this is important for me. Did you say that?

Benzien: Yes, I did say that.

There were scores of ANC insurgents caught by the security forces who never survived torture or were summarily executed and then buried in secret graves on police farms or blown to pieces by explosives. The TRC exhumed some fifty bodies but knew of the grave sites of several hundred more. The security forces rarely bothered to take captured insurgents prisoner, and the insurgents themselves, according to the ANC, expected no quarter if they were captured. In several cases heard by the TRC, the security police testified to the courage of the insurgents.

Paul van Vuuren, of the Northern Transvaal Security Branch, described the death of Harold Sefola, a trained insurgent captured in 1987 and taken with two comrades to a deserted mining property near Messina. Sefola, said van Vuuren, was "different," a strong personality who believed deeply in the cause.

He was given a series of electric shocks. "He admitted his involvement in bombings and limpet mine explosions and that he had been responsible for the planning of all these incidents," said van Vuuren. "He admitted to being a trained terrorist."

After watching his two comrades being electrocuted to death, Sefola asked van Vuuren if he could say something before he died. Van Vuuren agreed and untied him. He stood up and sang the African anthem, "Nkosi Sikelel' iAfrika."

"He said we can kill him, but the ANC would rule one day. He said that apartheid could not survive and that democracy would be the end of the Boers. . . . I have tremendous respect for Harold Sefola because of the way in which he behaved during the process of us killing him."

Another tale of courage was told about Phila Ndwandwe, a twenty-three-year-old MK commander and mother of a ten-month old child; Ndwandwe was based in Swaziland and disappeared in 1988 after arranging a rendezvous at a hotel in the capital, Mbabane. Her father, Nason Ndwandwe, had since spent nearly ten years hoping to hear news of her.

She was a bright girl, he said, a final-year dental student at the University of Durban–Westville, a Sunday school teacher, and a fearless activist. "I asked her to concentrate on her studies, but she was committed to the struggle."

In 1997, a TRC exhumation team went to a secret site on a farm at Elandskop in the Natal Midlands, where a group of security policemen had indicated Phila Ndwandwe was buried. She had been kidnapped in 1988, after being lured to the rendezvous by police agents, taken to the farm at Elandskop, and interrogated to see if she would become an informer. For a period of ten days she was held naked in a small concrete chamber. To cover herself, she fashioned a pair of panties from a blue plastic bag.

When grave diggers dug up her shallow grave, the blue plastic bag was still wrapped around her bones. "She was brave, this one. Hell, she was brave," remarked a security policeman, standing nearby. "She simply would not talk."

AMONG ALL THE DISAPPEARANCES and deaths that occurred in the 1980s, one case stood out for the way in which it eventually exposed the involvement of the country's highest-ranking police officers in criminal activity.

Stanza Bopape was a popular community leader from Mamelodi, a black township near Pretoria; he was arrested in Hillbrow in Johannesburg on 9 June 1988 and taken for interrogation to the John Vorster police station. The security police suspected he was a member of a MK insurgent group responsible for several bomb attacks in the Pretoria area.

Bopape's lawyers made repeated inquiries about his whereabouts. But it was not until 13 July that the head of the security police, General Johan van der Merwe, told them that he had "willfully escaped." The escape had taken place, said van der Merwe, while Bopape was being taken by car to Vereeniging, in southern Transvaal. "A flat tire en route necessitated that the police vehicle stop, and whilst the spare tire was being fitted, your client made good his escape." Though Bopape was handcuffed and manacled, he had apparently managed to find keys in a jacket left on a seat beside him and set himself free.

The police kept to this version of events for nine years, but Bopape's family never believed it. At a TRC human rights violation hearing in 1996, his mother, Francina, told the commissioners: "I don't believe Stanza released himself and disappeared. I'm asking the police where they buried him. They know where my son is. They must give me my son. Even if it's his bones, I'll bury him."

When the TRC subsequently began investigating Bopape's disappearance, a group of security policemen applied for amnesty. Among them was General van der Merwe, who had served as police commissioner for five years.

What emerged was that Bopape had been tortured to death. On

12 June, three days after his arrest, he had been taken to the tenth floor for interrogation but proved "stubborn and uncooperative." The officer in charge of the interrogation, Colonel Adriaan van Niekerk, told the TRC: "Some activists never gave any information, despite the force we used. Bopape was not willing to give us any information." So they decided "to give him a bit of a fright." An electric shock device was brought in by Sergeant Johan du Preez. Van Niekerk testified:

> We decided to tie Mr. Bopape to a chair. His shirt was removed; his hands were tied to the supports of the chair, and his feet to the legs.
> . . . Sergeant du Preez had the shock device in his hand. . . . There were two cords running from the device, and at the tip of it, these cords, there were two pieces of cloth which were wrapped around the tips of the cords.
>
> This device was turned three or four times by Sergeant du Preez, and whilst he was turning it, Mr. Engelbrecht [a police constable] pushed these cords against his body. . . . It didn't take very long, maybe two to four minutes. The device was turned, then it was stopped, then someone asked him if he wanted to say something; and if there was no reaction to that, then the machine was turned again, and this must have happened about three times.
>
> By the third time, Mr. Bopape's head fell forward, and I realized there was something wrong. We immediately untied him, placed him on the floor, and Sergeant du Preez gave him mouth-to-mouth resuscitation. It seemed that he was dead already.

Colonel van Niekerk contacted the Johannesburg security police chief, General Gerrit Erasmus, who discussed the matter with General van der Merwe, then head of the security police. "General Erasmus told me that Bopape's death was an unexpected incident, and that only light electric shocks were applied to him during inter-rogation," said van der Merwe. "I did not investigate the matter fur-ther, as I did not see what I could have achieved by that. Bopape was dead."

Fearing that news of Bopape's death would spark off mass demonstrations and riots, van der Merwe agreed that a fake escape should be staged. The body would meanwhile be handed over to security policemen in Eastern Transvaal. Plans were made to dis-pose of it in the Komati River, where it would be eaten by croco-diles or washed over the border into Mozambique. "I thought it an excellent plan," van der Merwe told the TRC amnesty hearing. It would not have been wise to have buried the body in a shallow grave because fresh soil could have aroused the curiosity of a passerby, he said. "The simplest plan is usually the best."

For year after year, van der Merwe kept up the pretense that Bopape had escaped. "In conversations and in letters I wrote, I pre-sented the mock escape as a fact." He denied suggestions that Bo-pape's body had been destroyed because it showed signs of severe torture. "That is far-fetched," he said. "No member of the security branch would make himself guilty of such an act."

Van der Merwe remained unrepentant about what had hap-pened. "In 1988, the security police was the only line of defense against total anarchy in the country."

9

Foreign Ventures

THE STRUGGLE OVER APARTHEID was waged far beyond South Africa's borders. For fifteen years, South Africa was embroiled in a series of conflicts in neighboring states, trying to establish military buffer zones that would prevent the ANC from establishing rear bases there and infiltrating trained insurgents into the country. During the 1980s, the South African defense force supported rebel groups fighting against governments in Angola, Mozambique, Zimbabwe, and Zambia. Covert raids were made regularly on targets in Botswana, Lesotho, and Swaziland. Assassination squads were at work throughout the region. Tens of thousands died in these regional wars, far more than inside South Africa itself.

The theater of war, as the South African government saw it, stretched even further. On a wall in the government's operations room in Pretoria in the 1980s there was a huge map covered with a series of labels and lines linking activists in local townships to larger antigovernment organizations in South Africa, and from there to the ANC headquarters in Lusaka and the offices of the KGB in Moscow.

The government kept in play a variety of military, police, and intelligence units to conduct this warfare and to "keep the pot boiling" in neighboring states. But as the threat of insurrection grew during the 1980s, the security establishment decided that a new organization was needed, a secret covert force able to operate around the world, a civilian outfit, ostensibly with no provable links to the government but in fact under the direct command of the defense force. The name it eventually acquired was the Civil Cooperation Bureau, or CCB.

In its attempts to investigate the activities of the CCB, the TRC encountered difficulties similar to those met by the Harms commission in 1990. General Malan, the former defense minister, admitted that he had approved the formation of the CCB in 1986. "The role envisaged for the CCB was the infiltration and penetration of the enemy, the gathering of information, and the disruption of the enemy," he said. But otherwise he was unhelpful.

QUESTION: What did you have in mind by the disruption of the enemy?

MALAN: Well Sir, there are various things. You can throw sugar in his petrol. . . .

QUESTION: What was it exactly, what did you do?

MALAN: Well, as I say, it depends on the situation, Sir. . . . You would disrupt them if you threw sugar in their petrol and they can't move. You can infiltrate them and you can give them wrong information. . . . So disruption depends on the situation.

He was asked to be specific.

MALAN: You can never specify all situations. That's impossible. But you can say, this is the guideline, disrupt them. And you disrupt them. It's as simple as that.

A more informative answer was given in a submission by General Joep Joubert, a former commanding officer of Special Forces, with overall responsibility for the CCB.

In the mid- to late-1980s, one of the major goals of national security policy and strategy was to bring the revolutionary organization and mobilization by the liberation movements, particularly the ANC, to a halt. . . .

By this time it was clear that the ANC was not going to be stopped by normal conventional methods and that revolutionary methods would have to be used.

Among other things, these methods meant "that ANC leaders and people who substantially contributed to the struggle would be eliminated; that ANC facilities and support services would be destroyed; and that activists, sympathizers, fighters, and people who supported them would also be eliminated."

"At the highest level, people were talking about the neutralizing or the elimination of people," Joubert told the TRC. "Individuals who were eliminated were identified as people who played a material part in the struggle or could play such a part and were thus a serious threat to the state. I regarded it as my duty to counter this threat. I considered the country to be in a state of full-scale war. I never questioned the validity of the war."

The CCB's "managing director," Joe Verster, described his task as setting up a "first line of defense" outside the country. The aim, he said, was to develop "a covert force to counter the covert operations of the ANC." According to the CCB's head of intelligence, Christoffel Nel, the ultimate goal was to create a global subterranean network of companies that would be both legitimate businesses as well as fronts for operational intelligence. The companies would be headed by businessmen who were well integrated into their communities but who remained skilled covert operatives able to run successful firms and to collect intelligence and act on it when instructed.

Before it was officially disbanded in the 1990s, the CCB under-took some 200 projects, about half of them "offensive," most of them abroad. It was involved in assassination, attempted assassination, sabotage, bombing, disinformation, and a range of dirty tricks. Its victims included Dulcie September, the ANC's representative in France, who was killed by a professional gunman in Paris in 1988, and Anton Lubowski, the Namibian nationalist shot dead outside his home in Windhoek in 1989 during a CCB campaign to destabilize Namibia's first election and prevent a Swapo victory. Like other specialist units set up by the security establishment, it was allocated huge sums of money and employed a large network of agents, but it had no effect on turning the tide of war.

T HE FOREIGN INTELLIGENCE SECTION of the security police was also involved in assassination and bombing abroad. One of its favorite techniques was the letter bomb. Because of South Africa's pivotal position in the region's postal system, a large proportion of mail for southern African states passed through sorting offices near Johannesburg's international airport. During the 1970s and 1980s, a staff of some 400 policemen, mostly retired officers, was employed to intercept mail, sending select pieces to police headquarters to be scrutinized and, in some cases, "doctored" before being put back into the system.

The first victims of cross-border letter bombs were killed in Botswana and in Zambia in 1974. In subsequent years, two cases in particular came to symbolize the indiscriminate brutality of the trade: a letter bomb that killed Ruth First, the wife of Joe Slovo, MK's chief of staff, in Mozambique in 1982; and, two years later, a letter bomb that killed the wife and six-year-old daughter of Marius

Schoon, an ANC activist living in Lubango, Angola. In both cases, it was widely assumed that the letter bombs were the work of the South African security police, but there was no possibility of proof. Then in 1995, a former security policeman, Craig Williamson, decided to break ranks.

Williamson had already achieved a certain notoriety. An obese figure with a liking for publicity, he had signed up as a police spy while he was a law student in Johannesburg, feeding the security police with information about his friends and colleagues. A consummate organizer, he rose rapidly in the student world to become acting president of the National Union of Students. On one occasion, he led a delegation to the police minister to protest the detention of fellow members of his own executive. Claiming that the police were after him, he "fled" to Europe in 1976, slipped easily into anti-apartheid circles, joined the ANC, and was appointed deputy director of the Geneva-based International University Exchange Fund, a funding agency that supported the anti-apartheid cause. When his cover was blown in 1980, Williamson returned to South Africa to be hailed as a national hero—a "super spy"—relishing the attention he was given by the press. He was promoted to the rank of major and assigned a post as deputy head of the foreign intelligence section. He resigned in 1985, ostensibly to go into business but in fact to work for military intelligence in a front company called Longreach.

Like many others in the security establishment, he regarded himself as a hero in the war against communism and became increasingly angered by the ease with which politicians from the apartheid era began to disown their links to the murky world of murder and mayhem they had once sponsored so eagerly. When a former foreign minister, Pik Botha, dismissed Williamson as "a clown you have to be careful of," Williamson retaliated with a letter

to a Johannesburg newspaper in January 1995, giving vent to all the
loathing he now felt:

> I hope that those politicians, who are in such an incompetent, self-
> serving, pension-protecting and cowardly way betraying the mem-
> bers and political heads of the security forces which kept the NP
> [National Party] in power for so long, do not think that we have for-
> gotten who gave us the orders to do what was done during the con-
> flicts of the past.
>
> Those who sat on the State Security Council, those who chaired
> the National Security Management System structures, those who
> signed the orders, those who often begged us to restore order in their
> ideological apartheid creations must now know that we remember
> them, though they seem too frightened to remember us. I suppose
> they also believe that it was the NP's political brilliance which kept
> them in power for 46 years and not security force action.
>
> We remember, too, those who were paid to serve on state-funded
> gravy train projects—on women, youth, the church, black political
> groupings and others, especially those who are currently serving NP
> members of parliament.
>
> In the absence of a general amnesty, the truth commission is the
> only alternative we have. We must trust the interim constitution, the
> president and the ANC when they say that amnesty will follow full
> disclosure and that reconciliation is their objective. I believe them.
> They have proven themselves to be honourable, which is more than I
> can say for the National Party, about which hangs a stench of
> betrayal, decay and fear.

Williamson followed this letter with newspaper interviews in
which he admitted that his section of the security police had assem-
bled the letter bombs that killed Ruth First and Jeanette and Katryn

Schoon. He also disclosed that he had participated in the bomb attack on the ANC's London offices in 1982, which had been carried out, he said, with the full approval of government ministers. "I and other serving men suspect there is a strategy afoot to see individuals pilloried for so-called human rights abuses rather than the system that gave the orders. There is a cynical move underway by some people to save their skins."

Three years later, in September 1998, Williamson appeared before a TRC hearing in Pretoria among a group of eight security policemen seeking amnesty for their role in the bombings. The occasion was all the more poignant because present in the audience were Ruth First's three daughters and Marius Schoon, together with his son who had survived the blast; all opposed the amnesty application.

Ruth First was an internationally respected academic and writer working at Maputo University as director of the Center for African Studies. Though a member of the Communist Party, long married to Joe Slovo, and an ardent anti-apartheid campaigner, she had played no role in the armed struggle or MK activities. Her daughter, Gillian Slovo, claimed that her mother became a target because the security police were frustrated by their failure to kill her husband. The bomb exploded in her university office.

Williamson's explanation was that South Africa at the time was under siege from the "ANC–Communist Party" alliance. Bomb attacks carried out by the security police were aimed at psychologically destabilizing and disrupting the alliance "by causing confusion and fear in their ranks, especially through killing or injuring high-ranking officials."

Williamson said that on the instructions of his commanding officer, Brigadier Piet Goosen, who had since died, he had organized the letter bomb that had killed Ruth First. A letter on its way to

Maputo from a United Nations agency in Lesotho had been intercepted in Johannesburg, sent to police headquarters in Pretoria, and fitted with an explosive device.

The person to whom the letter was addressed was a matter of dispute. Williamson's version was that it was addressed to Joe Slovo. Ruth First, he claimed, was the unintended victim. But Gillian Slovo insisted that her mother would never have opened a letter addressed to her father. The letter had been addressed to her in the first place. The issue was important in establishing whether Williamson had targeted an innocent person.

Under cross-examination by advocate George Bizos, Williamson said that it made no difference anyway. Both the Slovos were important targets because of the positions they held.

BIZOS: So you didn't care whether the right victim was killed, or his wife, or his child?

WILLIAMSON: I have to concede that whether it was the victim or his wife, it made absolutely no difference to me. It would have been better if Joe Slovo was killed, but if it was Joe Slovo or Ruth First . . . made no difference.

Sitting behind Bizos, Gillian Slovo bowed her head and wept.

In her testimony, Gillian Slovo said she had mixed feelings about the work of the TRC. By attending the hearings and listening to the truth, she had hoped to be able to put her mother's death in the past. "I thought that coming here would give me—and my two sisters—some sense of closure," she said. "But I have been shaken up in that belief. I do not think we have been told the truth. I cannot believe that my mother, not even in their terms, was a legitimate target."

THE HEARING OF Williamson's application for amnesty for the murder of Marius Schoon's wife and daughter—Jeanette and Katryn—was even more highly charged, for Williamson and Jeanette Curtis had been fellow students at the University of the Witwatersrand, and Williamson had subsequently befriended the Schoon family, on one occasion staying with them at their home in Botswana after they had gone into exile. Despite offering Williamson hospitality, the Schoons had long suspected that he was working for the security police and warned ANC colleagues against him. Williamson thus had a personal motive for taking action against them.

Marius Schoon described to the TRC how he had found the bodies of his wife and daughter blown to pieces in their flat in the Angolan town of Lubango, where he taught English at the university. "Every pane of glass in the flat had been blown out. One wall was covered in blood—that had been Jenny. On the floor, there was a little pile of flesh and blood—that had been Katryn." Somehow, his two-year-old son, Fritz, had survived.

Williamson was as indifferent about the fate of Jeanette Schoon as he had been about that of Ruth First. Once again, he claimed he had been instructed to organize the bomb by Brigadier Goosen. A parcel for Marius Schoon had been intercepted on its way from Botswana to Angola. It made no difference to him whether Jeanette Schoon or Marius Schoon had been the victim. Either would have been justified in the fight against communism. But the death of six-year-old Katryn had shocked him. "When I heard what the results of the attack had been, that a child had been killed, it was like being hit by a bucket of cold water. I was not aware there were children in Lubango. There is nothing in my life I regret more."

Marius Schoon dismissed Williamson's show of emotion as "crocodile tears"—a carefully rehearsed ploy to strengthen his plea for amnesty. "I remain to be convinced personally that we have heard the truth of what occurred. Reconciliation without truth is very, very difficult."

T HE EVIDENCE HEARD by the TRC about the bombing of the ANC's London offices in 1982 showed that the order had come from high in the chain of command. The team that carried out the attack had been led by Brigadier Piet Goosen, head of the foreign section of the security police. It had included Craig Williamson, Major Eugene de Kock, and five other policemen. But the planning for it had been authorized by General Johan Coetzee, the head of the security police who subsequently became the police commissioner.

In his testimony, General Coetzee said that the order had come to him personally from the police minister, Louis Le Grange, and he added: "I doubt that he would have decided this on his own. He wouldn't have placed his own political career in jeopardy to do that." The clear implication was that President Botha had approved the bombing.

"We were informed that the [South African] government had decided to demonstrate to the British government that there were serious risks involved in continuing to allow the ANC to operate from the United Kingdom," Coetzee testified. He said that the government had been prepared to risk the diplomatic repercussions of planting the bomb to demonstrate that the ANC was vulnerable. The attack, he said, was in part retaliation for an ANC rocket assault on a military base outside Pretoria the previous year, in which two British citizens had participated. The British government had subsequently failed to respond to diplomatic overtures to refuse hospitality to the ANC.

The bombing was regarded by the government as a great success. Later that year, members of the team were reassembled in Le Grange's office and awarded the Police Star for Outstanding Service.

S HORTLY AFTER Craig Williamson admitted in 1995 that he had organized the bomb that killed Ruth First, Gillian Slovo, attempting to understand more of the circumstances of her mother's death, sought an interview with Williamson.

Asked by Slovo whether his work weighed on his conscience, Williamson replied: "You can wish or regret or whatever, as much as you like, but you can't change what happened. What's done is done, and if you try and analyze why and how, and what the strategy behind it was . . . it becomes very difficult to believe it could have been done, but it was."

Williamson tried to explain the anger and emotion that had driven him and his security police colleagues.

> You're involved in a war which has huge dimensions. I mean, we're fighting a superpower that wants to destroy us, wants to destroy our country, and is being assisted by our own people who are helping this superpower monster to destroy us. . . .
>
> It's just virtually impossible to tell you how. . . . I want to use the word "hate"; I don't think it was hate, but how totally and utterly determined we were to win the war and eliminate and destroy the enemy. . . . It was an obsession.

10

Race Poison

Just how far South Africa's white rulers contemplated going to retain their grip on the country became apparent during the TRC's investigations into Pretoria's most secret endeavor: its chemical and biological warfare program.

The program had been started in the early 1980s, ostensibly for defensive purposes. Its mastermind was an Afrikaner medical scientist, Dr. Wouter Basson, who had joined the defense force in 1975 and who had subsequently been given command of a special operations medical unit, the Seventh Medical Battalion. Basson recruited a team of scientists, doctors, veterinarians, and toxicologists, many of them academics from Pretoria's universities and research institutes, intending to develop not only expertise on producing chemical and biological weapons but methods of reducing the birth rate of the black population.

Basson toured the world gathering information from scientists in Britain, the United States, Canada, Germany, and Japan about their biological warfare programs, explaining that South African forces operating in Angola in the 1970s had found themselves "absolutely defenseless" against Cuban troops using Soviet-made chemical weapons there. According to Basson, Western scientists were only too willing to exchange information. "I had good access to senior government officials at that time," Basson told the TRC.

Basson's program was officially approved in 1983 by the defense minister, Magnus Malan, and given the code name "Project Coast."

Two "front" companies were established to handle its business: Roodeplaat Research Laboratories (RRL), based near Pretoria; and Delta G. Scientific, based in Midrand. Scientists from both establishments were summoned before the TRC to give an account of their work.

A key figure recruited to the program was Dr. Daniel Goosen, a former director of animal research at the University of Pretoria's medical faculty; he was appointed managing director of RRL in 1983. Goosen and his colleagues embarked on a series of experiments on chimpanzees, baboons, and dogs, looking for a vaccine that would curb the fertility of the black population.

> I was told the growing black population and, of course, "communism" were the overwhelming threats to white South Africa. The anti-fertility project was approved by the SADF [South African Defense Force] at the highest levels. . . .
>
> Lieutenant-General Nico Nieuwoudt, then surgeon general, not only ordered the project but said it was our most important task. Nieuwoudt said there were "too many blacks." His successor, General Niel Knobel, also knew about it.
>
> We believed at the time this was legitimate. If we developed an anti-fertility vaccine, we would have curbed the birth rate, there would be less starving kids. . . .
>
> It wouldn't have been like a contraceptive pill that had to be 100 percent effective. If we had done that and there were suddenly no babies coming out of Soweto . . . well, we couldn't do that, so we wanted a vaccine 70 to 80 percent effective.

As well as working on an anti-fertility vaccine, Goosen investigated the possibility of developing a poison that would be effective against "pigmented people only"—a race poison. After extensive studies, he concluded that it was technically feasible: "We decided it would be good if the government had this weapon. It could be used as a negotiation backup. A thing like this could have been used to maintain peace. It was a case of being the strongest."

The race poison was never developed, but RRL scientists produced vast quantities of other poisons and of potentially lethal bacteria—including cholera, anthrax, and salmonella—capable of wiping out millions of people. The deadly bacteria were freeze-dried and kept in cold storage, whence they were dispensed on demand to police and military operatives. "I had no problem working on this case for *Volk en Vaderland*," Goosen told the TRC. "We were in a climate of war. The politicians talked all the time about total onslaught."

He recalled that he had once asked Basson about his motivation, and Basson had replied: "I have a daughter. We know that one day the blacks will take over this country. But when my daughter asks me, 'Daddy, what did you do to prevent this?' my conscience will be clear."

Another scientist, Dr. Schalk van Rensburg, an internationally renowned veterinarian who joined RRL as director of laboratory services, recalled how Basson was obsessed with developing poisons that would kill but make the cause of death appear to have been natural. "That was the chief aim of the Roodeplaat Research Laboratory," he said.

In this work, Basson enjoyed close collaboration with General Lothar Neethling, a German-born scientist who headed the police forensic laboratories. Neethling had arrived in South Africa in 1948 at the age of thirteen among a group of Nazi war orphans adopted by Afrikaner nationalist families and had assimilated himself rapidly into the Afrikaner community. After working as a research chemist, he joined the police in 1971 and established its forensic department, gaining an international reputation. Like Basson, he was obsessed by the search for undetectable poisons.

In addition to producing lethal poisons, Basson's team experimented with poison gases, investigating the use that could be made of chemical warfare agents, insecticides, and virulent forms of tear gas. They tried out new gases, using drugs like methaqualone (mandrax), LSD, and ecstasy—"incapacitating agents" aimed at controlling black unrest. General Neethling admitted to entrusting to Basson for destruction vast quantities of drugs that had been seized during police raids. It was all "for the good of society," Neethling told the TRC: "The idea was that the substance would be released into the air, which would cause a change of mood so that people who wanted to throw stones would suddenly not feel like doing it any more." He claimed that Louis Le Grange (the police minister), Nico Nieuwoudt (the surgeon general), and Johann Coetzee (the former police commander) all knew of and approved the project.

Huge sums of government money were spent on obtaining materials from abroad and on paying the necessary bribes. Basson's men chartered jets to fly around the world on purchasing trips, staying in the world's best hotels. Over the years, about R100 million was spent on RRL, according to Goosen. Having set vague guidelines, defense chiefs were content to allow Basson to do as he pleased.

In his testimony to the TRC, General Niel Knobel, the surgeon general from 1988 and the person who was technically responsible for the program, insisted that the mandate it was given was clearly defensive. "At no time were classical chemical or biological weapons developed. But incapacitating agents and irritant agents were developed," he said. "At no time was it ever considered to develop a biological offensive weapon." The work was carried out strictly on a "need-to-know" basis. "Dr. Basson should have informed me if the project strayed beyond its defensive parameters."

Yet the scientists involved in the program were under no illusions about what the aim was. Dr. van Rensburg, RRL's head of research, testified that the primary purpose of the company was to develop an "offensive" biological warfare capacity. Most of the company's projects involved developing lethal poisons. "Less than 5 percent of our work was of a protective nature."

More than 500 tailor-made products were manufactured under Project Coast for use by South African agents and assassins. Among the weapons and "poison applicators" produced were walking sticks, umbrellas, bicycle pumps, and screwdrivers tipped with needle units containing lethal poisons; cigarettes and chocolates laced with anthrax spores; shirts and underwear impregnated with organophosphate poisons; packets of sugar contaminated with salmonella; beer bottles containing botulism germs; envelope gums sprinkled with cholera bacteria; soap-powder boxes packed with explosives; and sheet explosives used for letter bombs.

Many of these items were made by Dr. Jan Lourens, a talented bioengineer recruited from the air force by Basson in 1984. Lourens was initially involved in producing low-level technical equipment for military doctors and working on high-performance motor vehicles, fold-up rifles, and a radio network. He then began to design equipment used for animal experimentation at RRL's biological warfare facility north of Pretoria. This equipment included a "restraint chair" into which baboons were strapped for experiments; a transparent "gas chamber" into which the baboon and chair fitted for tests; and a "stimulator and extractor" to obtain semen from baboons. Lourens was also involved in testing a "new generation" of tear gas on caged baboons at RRL.

Lourens then formed his own company, Protechnik, to design and develop items for the defense force. Initially he concentrated on the manufacture of protective clothing against chemical attack, but he soon developed "sidelines" and began designing weaponry. "Poison applicators" were made to order.

> They would say to us, we want to inject 5 ml of watery substance into a body, with other requirements such as that it had to be quiet. [We] would come up with the design. . . .
>
> I was never told what they were for, but it was quite obvious. . . . I was never under any illusion that it was for any purpose other than assassinating human beings. . . . I know that people have been badly hurt, killed, and maimed by [those] mechanisms.

The quantity of equipment and material passed on to the military and the police was substantial. RRL's records showed that in an eight-month period between March and September 1989 the company sold sixty-seven deadly poisons and bacterial agents to the defense force. In September 1989, shortly before the election in neighboring Namibia, RRL handed over sufficient quantities of cholera bacteria to affect the entire population of Namibia.

The impact of this clandestine warfare was difficult to discern. The scientists knew little of the consequences of their work once they had passed it on to the military. An ANC official was known to have died after drinking poisoned beer in a Lusaka nightclub. ANC recruits in camps in Angola and Zambia suffered from outbreaks of mass food poisoning. A platoon of Mozambique troops collapsed from poisonous gas fumes sprayed from reconnaissance aircraft. A Russian advisor to the ANC in Lusaka died from anthrax poisoning. A white conscript thought to be an ANC sympathizer was killed on the Angolan border with simulated snake poison. During a period of unrest in the Eastern Cape in the 1980s, Basson suggested to Dr. van Rensburg that the locals should be "sorted out with cholera."

The most famous incident of poisoning involved the attempted murder of the secretary general of the South African Council of Churches, Frank Chikane, a leading anti-apartheid campaigner. While traveling in northern Namibia in April 1989, Chikane was stricken by what appeared to be gastritis. Two weeks later he recovered sufficiently and was able to fly to the United States, but there he was stricken down once again. Four times he was admitted to the hospital; on one occasion he was put on a respirator when his heart stopped briefly. Doctors eventually found traces of a deadly organophosphate poison in his urine. According to Colonel Eugene de Kock, defense force agents had applied the poison after intercepting Chikane's suitcase at an airport.

What had happened was disclosed nine years later by Dr. Schalk van Rensburg in his testimony to the TRC. He said that five pairs of Chikane's underpants had been contaminated with paraoxyn but not in large enough quantities to kill him outright. Van Rensburg said he had been told the details of the plot by Dr. André Immelman, a RRL toxicologist who served as a liaison with the defense force: "I said to Immelman, 'What the hell have you done?' And he told me, 'Hell, it's a real mess.' And he told me the mistakes they made ... and [that] they wouldn't fail next time." Van Rensburg recalled that senior army officers had been furious that the attempt to assassinate Chikane had failed.

Another scheme involved the possibility of poisoning Nelson Mandela in prison. In its research, the TRC obtained the minutes of a State Security Council meeting in 1986 recommending that Mandela should be released from prison only after he had become too weak to pose a political threat. "Mandela must be in a relatively weak physical condition so that he cannot operate as a leader for long," the minutes recorded. Dr. Goosen testified:

We had long discussions with Basson on Nelson Mandela and Oliver Tambo [the ANC leader in exile]. They were targets, and we were to develop non-traceable ways to deal with them. I had discussions with Basson: If we had to release Mandela it would have been good if we had a disease so he would not be too long a problem.

Dr. van Rensburg testified that André Immelman had also told him of a plan to poison Mandela: "The intention was, as I understood it, to reduce his level of intellectuality and effectiveness through brain damage. I thought it logical that they would use a toxic solution to achieve this aim." Immelman, he said, had been "very confident" that Mandela's mental faculties could be "impaired progressively over time." But the plan was apparently scrapped.

In his explanation for all this, Basson told the TRC that far from plotting to damage Mandela's health he had actually helped save his life. Army chiefs had warned him in the mid-1980s that a radical faction in the ANC planned to kill Mandela because he was too moderate. "The responsibility of Mandela's safety regarding any possible biological and chemical attack on him therefore fell on my shoulders."

To thwart the planned attack, Basson had instructed one of his teams to investigate all possible ways that Mandela could be harmed and another team to work out how to prevent this. He then integrated the two plans into one and handed it to the government. "The fact that Mr. Mandela is alive today can be ascribed to the fact that the political leaders of the time gave instructions that he was to be protected."

Similarly, Basson denied that he had been involved in fertility experiments or any other harmful activity. When the commission's lawyer, Hanif Vally, read out a long list of lethal poisons produced by RRL, Basson claimed they had been used solely for "legitimate training and research purposes." For example, he said, cyanide-laced peppermint chocolates could be used to show undercover agents what they might find on hotel-room pillows. What about poisoned sweets given to laboratory animals? he was asked. "There is no better way for a person to learn to avoid making a mistake than to see the substance tested in front of them," replied Basson.

Like Basson, General Neethling denied any involvement in developing offensive chemical or biological weapons or in supplying poisons used to kill activists. Yet, like Basson, Neethling was renowned in the security establishment for being a master of the tricks of his trade. Dirk Coetzee, the former Vlakplaas commander, disclosed that the security police used to refer to the poisons they collected as *Lothar se Doepa*—Lothar's potions. Coetzee himself had fetched quantities of poison and "knock-out drops" from Neethling's police laboratory to use against ANC activists. The thalium used to poison the Port Elizabeth activist Siphiwo Mtimkulu was thought to have come from Neethling's laboratories.

The chemical business continued to flourish even after de Klerk lifted the ban on the ANC in 1990. In a deal approved by Magnus Malan and Barend du Plessis (the defense minister and the finance minister, respectively) the two front defense force companies— RRL and Delta G. Scientific—were sold for a fraction of their cost in 1990 to a fortunate group of private shareholders. The group included Dr. Philip Mijburgh, the managing director of Delta G. Scientific and a former Special Forces officer who also happened to be Malan's nephew. The companies then signed a lucrative five-year contract with the defense force. When this contract was terminated in 1991, the companies benefited from huge penalty payments.

Other business continued, however. In 1992 Delta G. Scientific received orders from the army to manufacture 1,000 kilograms of the designer drug ecstasy and another 1,000 kilograms of mandrax. The order was requested by Basson and signed by General Knobel. Ostensibly, the drugs were to be used as "incapacitating agents."

The head of research at Delta G. Scientific, Dr. Johan Koekemoer, a former professor of organic chemistry at the Rand Afrikaans
University, told the TRC that between February 1992 and January
1993 he had delivered to Dr. Mijburgh eighty-six drums containing
912 kilograms of ecstasy in pure crystalline form. "I trusted the
people in charge of me were ethical people. I mean, they were medical
doctors and so on," he said.

Koekemoer admitted, however, that he had misgivings about the
project. He did not regard ecstasy as an effective chemical warfare
agent. "It enhances empathy and interpersonal relationships. I told
Dr. Mijburgh I did not want to kiss my enemy." Koekemoer was
also puzzled that chemical warfare agents should be required when
South Africa appeared to be heading toward its first democratic
elections. "I did not understand why, so late in the day, they would
want such a large quantity of this." But Mijburgh urged him to
press on, so he developed a new method to manufacture the drug to
virtually 100 percent purity.

The street value of the ecstasy Koekemoer produced—enough
for a million tablets—was estimated at R100 million. According to
Mijburgh, he handed it all over to Basson. He never discovered
what had happened to it subsequently.

By the end of 1992, however, the glory days of the chemical and
biological warfare programs were coming to an end. In December,
as a result of General Pierre Steyn's investigations into third force
activities, Basson was dismissed from the defense force. The surgeon general, Niel Knobel, was also required to put his house in
order. In January 1993, he issued instructions for the disposal at sea
of two tons of ecstasy, mandrax, and cocaine, entrusting the task to
Basson. In the same year, the Office for Serious Economic Offenses
launched an investigation into the misuse of state funds involving
Project Coast. In January 1997, Basson was arrested in a Pretoria

public park and charged with attempting to sell 1,000 ecstasy tablets. He was subsequently charged with fraud and conspiracy to commit murder. "Medicine is my hobby," he liked to say, "but war is my profession."

I I

The Security Establishment

I N ITS ATTEMPT TO DETERMINE who was ultimately responsible for the government's security policies that had led to so many deaths, the TRC summoned the generals and the politicians who had once run the security establishment and asked them to explain their role. Few were helpful; most were openly hostile.

The first submission by generals from the South African Defense Force (SADF) was so insubstantial that the TRC asked for a second one. The second one, too, was largely irrelevant. "My overall impression is that this submission is breathtaking in its one-sidedness," commented a TRC commissioner, Alex Boraine. "I find it almost unbelievable that in eighty pages there can be no acknowledgment or acceptance that the SADF, in implementing a policy of apartheid, could bear no responsibility for a single death."

In his opening remarks, a former SADF chief, General Constand Viljoen, made no attempt to disguise his contempt for the TRC:

> The former SADF was politically neutral, while your commission is highly politicized. . . . The governing party of the former government did not demonstrate interest in the former SADF. You really erred in your assumption, and the expectations you created in public, that the SADF was guilty of gross violations of human rights on a substantial scale.

When General Magnus Malan appeared before the TRC, he was similarly unhelpful. As a former army commander (1973–1976), a former SADF chief (1976–1980), a former defense minister (1980–1991), and as one of the principal architects of "total strategy," he had been involved more deeply in the military hierarchy than anyone else. Yet he remained evasive.

He opened his submission by accepting political and moral responsibility for the actions of the SADF. "I issued orders, and later as minister of defense I authorized orders, which led to the death of innocent civilians." He said he had approved numerous cross-border raids. "These raids caused bloodshed. As a Christian, I regretted the loss of lives, but unfortunately that is the reality of war." He confirmed his role in setting up the CCB; it had provided the defense force with good covert capability, he said. He admitted he had launched Project Coast, the chemical and biological warfare program. "This project did not have sinister connotations. At no time did I authorize the use of any chemicals developed by Project Coast."

Nor, Malan asserted, had he authorized *any* unlawful action: "The killing of political opponents of the government never formed part of the brief of the SADF. . . . About assassinations, we never discussed things like that. . . . I would never have approved elimination of individuals." Under questioning, he admitted there might have been breaches of discipline:

> During these periods we are talking about, 1980 to 1991, we were fighting a war. I had more than 100,000 troops under training or busy with operations. So we were pretty much busy. We had a front approximately as far as London is from Moscow. It's a big area; it's a lot of people. There's not always the best communications. So things might happen there that are illegal. . . . Where members of the South African Defense Force acted unlawfully during the period I wish to offer my unqualified apologies.

Beyond that, the military gave little away. "The defense force insults us all," said the *Sunday Independent*, irritated by the way army generals had sought to make a mockery of the TRC exercise.

There was, however, one incident that the military was not able to shake off so easily. In 1996, two former security policemen from the Northern Transvaal Security Branch revealed in amnesty applications that the 1986 murders of Fabian Ribeiro, a popular Mamelodi doctor, and his wife had been carried out as a joint operation with SADF Special Forces, which had flown two black Angolan assassins from Namibia to South Africa to do the job. A Special Forces agent, Noel Robey, had driven them to the Ribeiro's house in Mamelodi.

The former commander of Special Forces, General Joep Joubert, was consequently obliged to apply for amnesty too. His version of events, given at the TRC's special hearing on the armed forces in 1997, was that he had received an instruction from the SADF chief, General Jannie Geldenhuys, to "make a plan" to provide support to the security police to combat internal dissent.

Because it had been "a very busy time," Joubert had not been able to secure a formal meeting with Geldenhuys to discuss the plan with him. But he had managed to convey the gist of the plan to Geldenhuys at a social function, and Geldenhuys told him that "it sounded good." Joubert took that comment as authorization to put his plan into action. The consequence was the death of Dr. Ribeiro and his wife, as well as several other murders.

Questioned by the TRC, General Geldenhuys admitted that he had instructed Joubert to draw up a plan but denied that he had authorized the elimination of activists. He conceded, however, that he had known since 1986 of the role of the Special Forces in the Ribeiro murders. He had not taken the matter any further at the time. "I didn't want to meddle because there was already a police investigation. If I had ordered a board of inquiry or a court martial,

that would have amounted to interfering with the judicial process."
When a judicial inquest failed to find anyone responsible, Geldenhuys said he accepted the outcome.

Thus did the head of the SADF account for his involvement in
the criminal cover-up of murder.

THE POLICE GENERALS had a far more difficult task than did the
generals of the defense force. The security police had been
shown to be involved in murder, torture, and bombing on a huge
scale. Two former heads of the security police had been directly
implicated in criminal activity: General Johan Coetzee in the
bombing of the ANC's London offices; and General Johan van der
Merwe in a series of bomb attacks, as well as in incidents like the
cover-up of the murder of Stanza Bopape. A score of generals and
other high-ranking officers had admitted their involvement in murder. Dozens of amnesty applications from policemen had been submitted to the TRC. In one case after another, they had claimed that
their orders had been to "elimineer"; to "neutraliseer"; to "uitwis"
(wipe out); to "maak 'n plan" (make a plan); in other words, to kill.
In its own investigations, the TRC had obtained SSC documents
that used the same language, referring explicitly to the need to
"eliminate" and "neutralize" government opponents. What the
TRC set out to ascertain, therefore, was who was responsible for
these orders and what, exactly, did the orders mean.

In his testimony to the TRC's armed forces hearing, General
Coetzee—head of the security police from 1980 to 1983, police
commissioner from 1983 to 1987, and a former SSC member—
simply stonewalled. Turning to two Afrikaans dictionaries, he said
that "eliminate" meant nothing more than "to remove": "The word

per se does not mean when used in connection with a person that that person should be assassinated. But I agree that it could have been misconstrued." He denied ever having given an unlawful instruction to kill anyone.

General van der Merwe—head of the security police from 1986 to 1988, police commissioner from 1990 to 1995, and a former SSC member—was more forthcoming. As far as he was aware, he said, the SSC had never issued any instruction or given approval "for any action which could be seen as a serious violation of human rights." But he conceded that the government's security policies had created a perception among members of the security forces that they could break the law while combating enemies of the state.

Van der Merwe admitted that the use of words like "eliminate" and "neutralize" in SSC documents was "an unfortunate choice." At a high level, they could have meant arrest or detention or "remove from society." At a lower level, among policemen involved in "a life-or-death struggle every day," they could have meant "kill."

VAN DER MERWE: I have to agree that the message was conveyed that harsher actions should be taken and people should be killed. . . .

COMMISSIONER: Do you then accept that it is one of the possible meanings of those words to say that people may be killed?

VAN DER MERWE: Yes, definitely. If you tell a soldier to eliminate the enemy, depending on the circumstances he will understand that he has to kill. It is not the only meaning, but it is specifically one meaning.

Further down the chain of command, there was no doubt about what such words meant. Brigadier Willem Schoon, former head of the security police antiterrorist division, testified: "Words like 'eliminate' and 'take out' for members on the ground who were in a war situation referred only to killing people."

Brigadier Alfred Oosthuizen, former head of the security police intelligence section, was equally adamant:

QUESTION: How did you understand that terminology, those phrases?

OOSTHUIZEN: It means what it says, to kill, that's clear.

QUESTION: Would you say the same applied at a leadership level within the security police at that time, that perspective?

OOSTHUIZEN: I can only speak from personal experience. I never received an illegal instruction from a general. What did happen was that a matter would be presented to a general, and his answer would be: "You are at the scene, act in the best interest of the community."

The former police spy, Major Craig Williamson, offered a broader perspective. The language used for counterinsurgency operations, he said, had been deliberately "all-encompassing." It was intended "to allow those at the top to avoid having blood on their hands." The government had sought to keep itself at "arm's length" from covert operations so that it could deny responsibility for them.

> It is for this reason that specific so-called chains of responsibility will in many instances be impossible to determine. The operational procedures were designed by people who knew the law, in order to circumvent proof of legal responsibility for the deed by the upper echelon. . . .
>
> With the benefit of hindsight, it appears the upper echelon, especially the politicians, were so keen to be at legal arm's length that

they abdicated their responsibility to exercise close operational control.

Nevertheless, politicians and senior commanders had understood "the full arsenal" available to covert units and what they were used for. And they provided the funds for them.

T HE APEX OF THE SECURITY establishment was the State Security Council (SSC), where senior generals and key politicians met regularly to decide what action to take to crush opposition both at home and abroad. It was here that the policy of "total strategy" was fashioned and that words like "eliminate," "neutralize," and "destroy" were commonly used.

President Botha endowed the SSC with huge powers shortly after he took office in 1978. It became the nerve center of the national security management system he installed in the early 1980s to overcome whatever revolutionary challenge arose. From a network of some 500 offices covering the entire country, security officials were employed to ferret out leading activists, detain them, sabotage their efforts, and mark them out for elimination, if necessary.

As the internal threat increased during the mid-1980s, Botha, in his role as SSC chairman, demanded tougher action. An SSC minute on 18 July 1985, obtained by the TRC, recorded: "The chairman points out that he is convinced that the brain behind the unrest situation is situated inside South Africa, and that it must be found and destroyed. Action thus far has been too reactive, and the security forces must attend to this urgently."

The result of Botha's concern was a far more aggressive strategy carried out under successive states of emergency that gave the security forces powers to act in any manner they deemed appropriate. As an indication of what was expected, SSC documents now referred to the need "to identify and eliminate the revolutionary leaders, especially those with charisma," and recommended "the physical destruction of revolutionary organizations (people, facilities, funds, etc.) by any means, overt and covert."

A new SSC subcommittee was formed in 1986—the Counterrevolutionary Intelligence Task Team, or Trevits—to identify targets. Its aim, according to SSC documents, was "to bring about a solid information base for meaningful counterrevolutionary operational action." The team included representatives from the security police, military intelligence, and the National Intelligence Service and was located in security police headquarters in Pretoria. Military intelligence meanwhile continued to run its own target identification group.

When former members of the SSC appeared before a special TRC hearing, there were the usual denials. General Malan insisted that the SSC had never taken any unlawful action. It was merely an advisory body, he said, with no executive power. Decisions were left to the cabinet. Dr. Niel Barnard, head of the National Intelligence Service and chairman of the SSC's Coordinating Intelligence Committee throughout the 1980s, made the same point and argued that the SSC had made a valuable contribution to the negotiations process:

> The national security management system in the 1980s was well informed and was effective, and it was this system which laid the foundation for the peaceful transition to a democratic political dispensation.
>
> You must not allow the atrocities by individual members of the security forces—which, because of their gruesome nature, had an influence on all—[to] influence your evaluation of the bigger picture.

The response of politicians who had been members of the SSC was little different. All who appeared before the TRC said they were "shocked" to have found out, years later, what had been happening during their tenure of office.

Adriaan Vlok, who served as police minister from 1986 to 1991, denied that either the SSC or the cabinet had ever instructed the security forces to act unlawfully. He admitted that the government had decided to "answer violence with violence" and, in some situations, "to get in the first blow," but their first option had always been to take legal action. Under questioning, however, he agreed that the language commonly used by SSC members—eliminate, neutralize, and destroy—had been open to misinterpretation and misunderstanding:

> I now know it is incontrovertible that people who did not experience the spirit and intention of the [SSC] meetings could very easily have made other conclusions and apparently have indeed done so. . . .
>
> I realize now with shock and dismay that such use of language apparently led to illegal activities by policemen, by which victims were prejudiced.

Vlok also acknowledged that in his public speeches and comments at events like meetings and medal parades, he had used words and expressions that were interpreted by those under his authority as "something other than what I intended—namely, as instructions to act illegally." He said he was prepared to accept moral and political responsibility for the policemen's actions. However, he would not accept responsibility for Vlakplaas policemen who had committed criminal acts: "I personally never knew about the crimes that are now coming to light. I would never have tolerated such things, and I would have acted drastically against them."

Although Vlok had visited Vlakplaas to exhort members to continue their good work, it had since become increasingly clear to him that he had not known "what they were really doing." This was also the case when he had awarded medals to policemen for successful operations that, it now transpired, had been illegal actions all along: "The fact is that I, and probably the police generals, were blissfully unaware of the true facts."

Questioned about how the government could have remained unaware about security force abuses, Vlok replied that the communication system in the line of command was defective. There was no effective mechanism in place to prevent such abuses: "It was a mistake—we could have asked more, we could have delved deeper. . . . It left the door open for people to have done these things."

Vlok admitted that he had never called for an inquiry into allegations of murder and torture, despite deaths in detention. He relied, he said, on reports from the commissioner of police:

> The minister was in an invidious position. He had to react on the basis of information given to him.
>
> In all the reports that found themselves to my desk, there was not a single case in which it was said we tortured a person before he gave us the information. So I could not know about it.

Pik Botha, who was foreign minister for seventeen years and had served on the SSC throughout the 1980s, was more contrite:

> I acknowledge that I could have done more in the State Security Council, in the cabinet, and in parliament to ensure that political opponents were not killed or tortured by government institutions. I could have and should have done more to find out whether the accusations that government institutions were killing and torturing political opponents were true.

Not one of us in the former government can say today that there were no suspicions on our part that members of the South African police were engaged in irregular activities. The decisive question is not whether we, as a cabinet, approved the killing of a specific political opponent. The question is whether we should have done more to ensure that it did not happen. I deeply regret this omission.

Like Pik Botha, a deputy police minister, Roelf Meyer, spoke of his "omission" to rein in the security forces:

The fact that so many transgressions took place over such a lengthy period is an indication that more vigilant action was called for. With hindsight and looking at the embarrassing facts now emerging, one can argue that more stringent steps should have been taken to curb the possibilities of transgressions taking place.

Only one former minister, Leon Wessels, a deputy police minister, acknowledged a wider responsibility for what had happened. It was the politicians, he said, who had progressively eroded the rule of law—by voting for detention without trial, by imposing successive states of emergency, by granting ever more powers to government agencies, by making speeches in parliament and at political rallies giving the impression that any actions were lawful. They must have known the consequences of their own actions.

The framework was that the highest law of the land was the security of the land. . . . It was foreseen that, under those circumstances, people would be detained, people would be tortured. . . . I don't believe I can stand up and say, "Sorry, I didn't know."

12

The Tale of Two Presidents

T WO MEN KNEW MANY of the answers the TRC sought: Botha and de Klerk. For a period of fifteen years they had presided over the massive state machinery used to enforce apartheid and to crush its opponents. They had wielded enormous power and were privy to the innermost secrets of government. What was equally important, they had been leaders of the Afrikaner community, the main protagonists behind the apartheid system. How they accounted for themselves thus had a bearing not only on the past but on the present standing of the Afrikaner community and on the whole process of reconciliation.

Botha, indeed, had been the principal architect of the security apparatus. An authoritarian figure, single-minded, ruthless, and intolerant of opposition, he was often referred to as *die groot krokodil*, feared even by his colleagues for his irascible nature. As defense minister for fourteen years and as SSC chairman for a further twelve years, he had grown close to the military's way of thinking and looked to the military for solutions. He had a fixed and simple view of world politics, believing that they revolved around a struggle between communist and anticommunist forces, with South Africa and its vast mineral resources and maritime facilities as the glittering prize. South Africa, he was convinced, was the target of an internationally organized communist conspiracy to overthrow the government and replace it with a Marxist regime beholden to the Soviet Union. Whatever ills befell South Africa, whether it was domestic unrest, international pressure, or regional threats, Botha attributed ultimately to Moscow's grand design. Every adversity was seen as part of the "total onslaught" that South Africa faced. In this deadly struggle for survival, all methods in defense of South Africa were considered legitimate.

From the outset, Botha made clear his contempt for the TRC, dismissing it as "a circus." Though Archbishop Tutu made every endeavor to persuade him to cooperate, Botha remained hostile. When they met at Botha's home in George in November 1996, Botha handed over a prepared statement expressing his disdain for the whole exercise: "I am not guilty of any deed for which I should apologize or ask for amnesty. I therefore have no intention of doing this. I have nothing to hide."

Botha accused the TRC of being "engaged in a witch-hunt against the Afrikaner and the security forces of previous governments." This hunt, he claimed, was part of a wider attack on the Afrikaner community—"a campaign of revenge," he called it.

> I am . . . deeply concerned about the fierce and unforgiving assault which is being launched against the Afrikaner and his language at all levels of society. In many circles the Afrikaner is being isolated to be punished for all the unfavorable events in the history of South Africa.
>
> The recent conflicts in which we were involved were primarily against Soviet imperialism and colonialism. People who were sympathetic towards the Soviet ideal of world dominance are today members of the present cabinet.

Neither Botha nor his ministers could be expected to respond to all the "unsubstantiated and untested allegations" concerning himself and the security forces.

As a Christian and an Afrikaner I cannot and have never associated myself with blatant murder. It would, however, now appear that there might have been instances during the conflict of the past where individuals have exceeded the limits of their authority.

Such incidents are clearly not limited to members of the security forces. I cannot be expected to take responsibility for the actions of any such individuals.

I stand, however, without any qualification, behind all the thousands of members of the security forces who in the lawful execution of their duties bravely fought against the revolutionary onslaught of Soviet imperialism.

Botha adopted the same tone in an 1,800-page submission he delivered to the TRC a year later, accusing the TRC of being involved "in a transparent attempt to finally discredit the Afrikaner and its former leadership corps."

But in the light of all the evidence it had heard, the TRC was not inclined to deal with Botha leniently. In December 1997 it issued a subpoena requiring Botha to attend a special hearing on the State Security Council. Officials wanted to question him on SSC documents containing references to the need to "eliminate" government opponents—a term that, according to their testimony, police commanders had interpreted to mean "kill." Though not necessarily constituting evidence of Botha's direct involvement in human rights violations, the documents, according to TRC investigators, showed that Botha had "created a climate" where the murder of political opponents could occur. They also wanted to question Botha about cross-border raids and about the government's chemical warfare program.

To make the occasion easier for Botha, Tutu offered to stage the hearing at George and hold it on camera if necessary, pointing out that Botha was eighty-one years old, with a history of heart problems and still recovering from a hip operation. "The commission has gone out of its way to be accommodating to him in view of his age, his health, and his position as a former state president," said Tutu. But he acknowledged: "In showing this consideration for Mr. Botha we have angered many South Africans who have accused us of being spineless for not unceremoniously calling him to account."

But Botha would have none of it. "I am not going to the truth commission. I am not going to repent. I am not going to ask for favors. What I did, I did for my country, for my God, for my people, and for all the people of South Africa. . . . I am not asking for amnesty. I did not authorize murders, and I do not apologize for the struggle against the Marxist revolutionaries."

Botha endeavored to portray himself as a martyr in the Afrikaner cause and to rally right-wing opinion behind him. "The truth," he said, "is that the commission does not bring reconciliation but is trying to tear the Afrikaner and the South African nation apart."

In January 1998, Botha, charged with ignoring the TRC's subpoena, appeared briefly at a magistrate's court in George; afterwards, at an unruly media conference, he gave full vent to the fury he felt in being held to account, railing against all his enemies—the TRC, Mandela's government, the African National Congress, and the communist onslaught. For those familiar with Botha's style of blustering arrogance, it was a vintage performance.

South Africa was on "a dangerous road," he said. He warned Mandela about "waking the tiger in the Afrikaner," for the tiger would fight back if oppressed. "Afrikaners should unite and thereafter join forces with groups of similar convictions so as to oppose that which is wrong in our country." He had told Mandela to his face that "anarchy and the forces of communism and socialism" would destroy him.

When asked whether he did not owe an apology to the thousands of people who had suffered under apartheid, he retorted: "I only apologize for my sins before God." He continued: "I am sick and tired of the hollow parrot-cry of 'apartheid!' I've said many times that the word 'apartheid' means good neighborliness." When a journalist laughed, he swung round, demanding: "Who's laughing?"

Strenuous efforts were made to negotiate a solution. Tutu tried to get Botha to agree to testify before the TRC in return for having the charges against him dropped. Mandela offered to accompany him to the hearing if he agreed to go. Mandela also met Botha's four children to urge them to help prevent what was bound to be a humiliation. Botha's own lawyers worked hard for a settlement. But it was all to no avail. "We have hit a brick wall," said Tutu, after making a last-minute attempt to get Botha to change his mind. "Fundamentally, it stuck in Mr. Botha's gullet to have to appear in front of the commission at all."

Botha gave his own version of that last-minute meeting with Tutu to the Afrikaans Sunday newspaper *Rapport:*

I said to him: "You know that when Christ stood before Herod, he refused to answer questions."

Then he said: "Yes, but Christ replied to questions before Pilate."

I then said: "Yes, but what happened to Pilate?" I said: "I am not Christ, but I am a follower of his." And I said: "You have the truth, and I tell you now: I am prepared to speak with you and President Mandela, but you will not get me to appear before the truth commission. I will not allow myself to be humiliated, because you want to humiliate the Afrikaners who believe in me, like you have already humiliated others."

Then he stood up and left.

At a court hearing in April 1998, Botha argued openly with his lawyers and shouted at the prosecutor, demanding that his trial should be concluded swiftly. As his conduct became increasingly irrational, his supporters in the public gallery drifted away, leaving only his daughter there watching the proceedings, close to tears.

Among the witnesses called to give evidence against him was Tutu. He told the magistrate, Victor Lugaju, an African, that he was appearing "with the greatest possible reluctance" and was "filled with considerable distaste" at the prospect of testifying against Botha. "I believe that this [prosecution] is something that should not have happened." Botha was his "brother," he said, and the day would come when "God will ask me, What did I do to help his child?"

Once again, Tutu made an impassioned appeal to Botha to apologize for his past policies:

> I speak on behalf of people who have suffered grievously as a result of policies carried out by governments, including governments that he headed. I want to appeal to him to take this chance provided by this court to say that he himself may not have intended the suffering to happen to people . . . [but] the governments that he headed caused many of our people deep, deep anguish and pain and suffering. . . .
>
> If Mr. Botha is able to say, "I am sorry the policies of my government caused you so much pain"—just that—that would be a tremendous thing.

Botha, sitting on a chair at the side of the dock, appeared angry and upset by Tutu's remarks but did not react directly. As he was leaving the courtroom, he remarked to reporters: "There are a number of books you people can go and read. I have nothing more to say." His lawyer later explained that he had nothing for which to apologize.

Another witness was the former Vlakplaas commander, Eugene

de Kock, who arrived from prison, where he was serving a sentence of 212 years for murder. It was a poignant moment: Botha, the principal architect of "total strategy," brought face-to-face with his most notorious "foot soldier." Two years earlier de Kock had first exposed Botha's role in the 1988 bombing of Khotso House, headquarters of the South African Council of Churches. Now de Kock had come to show his contempt for him.

Looking straight at Botha, de Kock said that politicians who refused to take responsibility for the illegal actions of their followers were "cowards." "The politicians wanted lamb, but they didn't want to see the blood and guts," he said. "We did the fighting, and I am proud of that. But the politicians have no pride." They had talked much about fighting for *Volk en Vaderland* but had been interested in looking after only a "little incestuous Afrikaner group." They did not have the moral fiber to accept responsibility for the killing. So he, a lowly colonel, had to do so.

In August 1998, Botha was found guilty and fined R10,000, though his conviction was subsequently set aside on a technicality. After watching him in court, the Afrikaner journalist, Antjie Krog, concluded: "He is not senile, or old, or suffering from the effects of a stroke: He is a fool—*n'dwaas*. And we have been governed by this stupidity for decades."

THE BURDEN OF EXPLAINING past government actions thus fell to de Klerk. To his credit, he had dismantled Botha's prized national security management system soon after taking office in 1989; he had released Mandela from prison, lifted the ban on the African National Congress, the Pan-Africanist Congress, and the Communist Party, and opened the way to a negotiated settlement;

and he had removed key parts of the apartheid system on his own initiative. Though his term of office had been marked by some of the worst bouts of violence South Africa had ever experienced, the ANC and Inkatha had been as much to blame as the government's security forces. De Klerk's achievements as president had been duly recognized when he was awarded the Nobel Peace Prize in 1993, along with Nelson Mandela.

What was important about de Klerk's testimony, therefore, was not so much how he explained his own government's record but how far he would go in accepting responsibility for the wider abuses of the apartheid system and the violence it spawned, for de Klerk had been a dedicated disciple of the apartheid system throughout his career. He came from a prominent Afrikaner family at the heart of the political establishment that had ruled South Africa since 1948. His father had served as a cabinet minister under three National Party prime ministers; his uncle by marriage had been prime minister. De Klerk's own progress as a politician had been rapid. After entering parliament in 1972, he had become the youngest member of John Vorster's cabinet in 1978, at the age of forty-two. What had been notable about his political record was his rigid loyalty to the National Party and all that it stood for. He had conformed to every party policy of the time, speaking out adamantly against integrated sports, mixed marriages, trade unions rights for blacks, and black demands for permanent residence rights in urban centers. During the 1980s he had participated in meetings of the State Security Council. De Klerk's involvement in the apartheid establishment thus extended far beyond the years he had served as president.

De Klerk's first submission, on behalf of the National Party, was made in August 1996, before many of the disclosures about security force abuses had come to light. He described the architects of apartheid as "good and honorable men" but admitted that apartheid had caused immense harm and offered a fulsome apology:

> I want to emphasize that it is not my intention to excuse or to gloss over the many unacceptable things that occurred during the period of National Party rule. They happened and caused immeasurable pain and suffering to many. This is starkly illustrated by the evidence placed before the commission at its hearings across the country. Many of the accounts by witnesses are deeply moving.
>
> I should like to express my deepest sympathy with all those on all sides who suffered during the conflict. I, and many other leading figures in our party, have already publicly apologized for the pain and suffering caused by former policies of the National Party. This was accepted and publicly acknowledged by the chairperson of the commission, Archbishop Tutu. I reiterate these apologies today.

But de Klerk refused to accept responsibility for any security force abuses. Although conceding that the government had used "unconventional strategies" to counter the revolutionary threat, he denied that these strategies had involved any approval of illegal action:

> In dealing with the unconventional strategies from the side of the government, I want to make it clear from the outset that within my knowledge and experience they never included the authorization of assassination, murder, torture, rape, assault, or the like.
>
> I have never been part of any decision taken by the cabinet, the State Security Council, or any committee authorizing or instructing the commission of such gross violations of human rights, nor did I individually directly or indirectly ever suggest, order, or authorize any such action.

He acknowledged, however, that security force abuses had occurred:

> The security forces had to operate increasingly within a framework of states of emergency, far-reaching security legislation, underground activities, and unconventional strategies. They had to give operational interpretation to broadly framed decisions aimed at firm and effective action against the insurgency. These circumstances created the environment within which abuses and gross violations of human rights could take place.
>
> However, it would be a serious mistake to adopt a simplistic approach in judging such abuses and violations. Clear distinctions should be drawn between varying situations. In many cases it would be possible to conclude that the perpetrators of certain actions were bona fides in their interpretation of orders and strategies, that they believed that they were acting correctly and with authority.
>
> In other cases it would be possible to make a finding that the bona fides of those involved was there but was clouded by bad judgment, over-zealousness, or negligence. And yet in other cases there is no doubt that there was mala fides which led to abuses, malpractice, and serious violation of human rights.

De Klerk singled out in particular "the rogue elements" he had blamed previously, namely, individuals in the security forces who were opposed to political reform and who had tried to wreck the negotiations process by taking "unauthorized action."

> My colleagues and I were from these sources accused along the grapevine of being soft and even of being traitors. I suspect that many of the unauthorized actions that are now coming to light were at times directed as much against the transformation process as they were directed against the revolutionary threat. It has now become

clear that certain elements misused state funds and were involved in unauthorized operations leading to abuses and violations of human rights.

The National Party government could not be blamed for the activities of these elements, he said.

There was considerable criticism of the limited scope of de Klerk's admissions. "It requires a stretch of the imagination to believe that he did not know that the police were torturing detainees; that the military were assassinating opponents of the state; that vigilante groups, aided by the security forces, were spreading havoc in black townships," commented the Johannesburg *Star*. "We need to hear more from de Klerk and his party."

By the time de Klerk made his second submission in March 1997, the TRC had heard evidence of murder, torture, and brutality on a scale that had shocked and horrified the public at large. Yet de Klerk continued to dismiss it all as the work of "mavericks." He was not prepared, he said, to accept responsibility "for the criminal actions of a handful of operatives of the security forces of which the [National] Party was not aware and which it would never have condoned."

De Klerk seemed more concerned to protest his own innocence than to shoulder any moral responsibility for what had happened: "It is a lie that I knew. It is a lie that I was part of any conspiracy to do these terrible things, that I've ever been part of a decision to assassinate anybody. How many times must I say, it's a lie."

Retreating into defensiveness and denial, de Klerk squabbled with the TRC over terminology and questioned its integrity:

Its investigations have been targeted almost exclusively against those associated with the former government, and its behavior at times appears to be increasingly aggressive. At the same time, comparatively little is said, written, or reported about the abuses perpetrated by those who were opposed to the government.

The TRC's actions and hearings are beginning to create a skewed perception of the conflict, based as they are on the highly emotive testimony of victims who represent predominantly one side of the conflict.

Apartheid, he told the TRC, in answer to questions it had raised, could not be compared to the Nazi Holocaust, the rule of the Russian dictator Joseph Stalin, China's "Great Leap Forward," or the recent genocide in Rwanda. "Without wishing to detract from the humiliation, hardship, and disruption caused by apartheid policies, they are not in any way comparable with these situations."

The international convention that had purported to declare apartheid "a crime against humanity" had been little more than a mobilization exercise by the ANC and "its totalitarian and Third World supporters in the UN General Assembly." He warned that the TRC's whole approach would end up "rekindling racial animosity."

There was one last opportunity for de Klerk to redeem his position: a TRC hearing in Cape Town in May 1997. The hearing opened on a conciliatory note. Tutu began by reminding the audience of de Klerk's contribution to South Africa's negotiated settlement, quoting remarks made by Mandela in a recent newspaper interview: "Whatever mistakes Mr. de Klerk has committed, I do not forget that without him it would not have been possible for us to have this peaceful transformation. . . . I hope everybody who criticizes him will not forget that."

Tutu added his own praise:

Our country escaped from comprehensive and utter disaster. We moved away from the brink of catastrophe, and you, Mr. de Klerk, played a quite crucial role at this most critical hour in our history. And your part, as I have always said, will always be remembered and honored. Your statesmanship and that of Mr. Mandela ensured that the world would behold a veritable miracle unfolding before its very eyes.

De Klerk began in a similar manner:

Let me place once and for all a renewed apology on record. Apartheid was wrong. I apologize in my capacity as leader of the National Party to the millions of South Africans who suffered the wrenching disruption of forced removals in respect of their homes, businesses, and land. Who over the years suffered the shame of being arrested for pass law offenses. Who over the decades and indeed centuries suffered the indignities and humiliation of racial discrimination. Who for so long were prevented from exercising their full democratic rights in the land of their birth. Who were unable to achieve their full potential because of job reservation. And who in any other way suffered as a result of discriminatory legislation and policies. This renewed apology is offered in a spirit of true repentance, in full knowledge of the tremendous harm that apartheid has done to millions of South Africans.

He moved on to the question of security force abuses:

A perception has developed that the National Party is not accepting overall responsibility for its part in the conflict of the past. That National Party politicians are leaving the security forces in the lurch. That we are washing our hands of that which was done in terms of our policies and decisions. Once again this is simply not true. . . .
    Let me state clearly that the National Party and I accept full

responsibility for all our policies, decisions, and actions. We stand by
our security forces who implemented such policies and decisions and
all reasonable interpretations thereof. We accept that our security
legislation and the state of emergency created circumstances which
were conducive to many of the abuses and transgressions against
human rights which forms the basis of the commission's investigation.

We acknowledge that our implementation of unconventional projects and strategies likewise created such an atmosphere. . . . I accept,
without qualification, overall responsibility in respect of the period
of my leadership as state president. But . . . many things happened
which were not authorized, not intended, and of which we were not
aware. The recent information of atrocities I find as shocking and as
abhorrent as anybody else. It came to me as just a shocking revelation
as to anyone else.

During my presidency I went out of my way to get to the bottom
of the truth and to find and prosecute the perpetrators of such dastardly deeds. I have never condoned gross violations of human rights
and reject any insinuation that it was ever the policy of my party or
my government.

Under questioning, de Klerk's mood became increasingly tense
and his explanations increasingly labored. At every turn he sought
to distance himself and the National Party government from the
mountain of abuses and crimes uncovered by the TRC, steadfastly
maintaining that neither he nor his colleagues nor the State Security Council had authorized unlawful acts. Time and again he
fought off suggestions that it was government policy, for which he
was ultimately responsible, that had created the climate for abuses
to occur. It was all the work, said de Klerk, of "a handful of operatives," for whom he was not responsible.

De Klerk was confronted about a series of murders and other

crimes—the Cradock Four, the Pebco Three, the Zero Zero hand grenade incident, Stanza Bopape, Vlakplaas, the Khotso House bombing, Operation Marion, Ruth First's letter bomb, Steve Biko, the torture of detainees—and asked whether those responsible had all acted outside government policy.

His answers remained the same:

> It has never been the policy of the government, of the National Party that people should be murdered, should be assassinated. . . . Such instruction was in conflict with policy. . . . If I, during my presidency, could have ascertained these facts, I would have charged those involved. . . . Murder and assassination cannot be justified.

He acknowledged that "lower ranks" had at times "misinterpreted" government policy and taken their own actions, but he denied that any orders had come "from the top." He had, for example, asked four generals whether they had known about what had been going on at Vlakplaas. "All four of them assured me that they didn't know."

How then, he was asked, did he explain the Zero Zero hand grenade incident, which had led to the death of eight youths and in which a former police commissioner and a minister had been implicated?

QUESTION: Would you classify this as a misinterpretation of policy of what was required or a bona fides instance of overzealous behavior?

DE KLERK: Whoever authorized that was guilty of a very gruesome and totally unacceptable decision. It was wrong. It wasn't part of policy, and whoever authorized it was mala fides and was acting against the interests of South Africa.

He was asked about the torture and death of Stanza Bopape, for which ten amnesty applications had been lodged, including those from three police generals.

QUESTION: Would you say that these are merely a handful of operatives?

DE KLERK: I would firstly like to emphasize that obviously that is absolutely unacceptable. It falls outside the parameters of anything which was ever authorized or intended by government policy, government decisions, or any reasonable interpretation.

He then began to quibble about the meaning of "a handful."

QUESTION: How is it that such senior police officers on so many occasions could so seriously misinterpret government or state policy in this regard?

DE KLERK: Speaking about my presidency first, there is no basis on which any senior police officer or junior police officer could have been under the impression that it was okay in any way to do this type of thing.

Tutu expressed his skepticism about de Klerk's responses: "It becomes difficult how one can sustain a position that it is a few bad eggs, or it is an aberration, or it is not in line with official policy, when the thing extends over a very long period of time."

The questioning moved on to the subject of torture. The TRC, de Klerk was told, had received evidence of nearly 1,200 acts of torture by the security forces. Those responsible ranged from sergeants to generals. Several reports had been published during the 1980s exposing the use of torture. Yet despite the overwhelming evidence, no effective steps had been taken to investigate or stamp out these abuses.

QUESTION: How did the National Party regard these allegations at the time? And is the National Party guilty of tolerating torture?

DE KLERK: The National Party is not supportive of torture. I reject it. It's wrong.

There had been an appropriate system of inspection in place, he said. Steps had been taken to monitor the problem. It was a problem throughout the world.

QUESTION: From amnesty applications from members of the security forces, it appears that they regarded the torture of detainees as standard procedure. How does that fit in with the notion that, from an official point of view, the torture of detainees was actively combated where it was found to exist?

DE KLERK: I don't accept the fact that it was standard practice.

Many of the claims about torture had been made for propaganda reasons.

YASMIN SOOKA: I simply would like to inform you that in the course of our questioning (in closed sessions), very high-ranking officers have informed the commission that in fact torture was widespread, and that in fact it was so widespread that it was not confined only to the security forces; ordinary policemen, each had their own instrument and their own bag of tricks. . . .

DE KLERK: Well that's terrible, that's terrible, and I did say that we were told at times that such propaganda is being spread. I also said that because of the many rumors, steps were taken. With hindsight, I have no problem in saying maybe it wasn't timeous enough and maybe it wasn't strong enough, with the facts now coming to the fore. I'm not saying we were perfect. I am not saying we didn't make mistakes. I am not saying that on such issues, with all these shocking facts coming to the fore, that . . . we should [not] have done more. But what I am saying is that we didn't just lump everything and close our eyes, that there was a process of stepping up measures to prevent that. . . .

SOOKA: Sir, I think the point I want to make is, you are offering us an explanation that in fact these things were committed by a few individuals, and I think in your own submission you talk about a few mavericks. But I think we are faced with insurmountable evidence that it in fact was widespread across the security forces, and I think that's the point that we want to bring home. . . .

DE KLERK: I don't think that when I say that there was a maverick element which was relatively small, which did all these dastardly deeds, that I am not then including in that general practices such as hitting a prisoner with fists, slapping him, kicking him around in order to frighten him to get evidence. That is widespread; and that has been widespread; and it's widespread in all countries. It doesn't make it right, but it's a fact. It's a problem that you have to deal with in each and every police force. But murder and assassination was not, to the best of my experience, something which was widespread.

De Klerk said he had been as shocked as anyone else by the murders, kidnappings, and tortures that had been disclosed by senior police officers in applications for amnesty.

After a five-hour session, de Klerk stood down, leaving a sense of frustration and despair about how he had tried, like a petty politician, to absolve himself and blame instead the generals and the foot soldiers for the government's dirty war. The opportunity for shouldering responsibility for the past, for making the most important gesture an Afrikaner leader could make, had gone. The Johannesburg newspaper, *Business Day*, described de Klerk as "a man who has lost all the vision and moral courage he gave this country seven years ago."

The following day, Tutu was unable to conceal his distress and anger. "I sat there and I was close to tears," he told a TRC briefing in Cape Town. Tutu said that he failed to understand how de Klerk could insist that he had been unaware of apartheid atrocities when Tutu himself and delegations from human rights organizations had gone to him while he was president to tell him. "There was an avalanche of information. To say, I did not know . . . I find that hard to understand. . . . [For him] to make an impassioned apology . . . a handsome apology . . . and then to negate it."

Tutu said that he had struggled to believe that human rights abuses by the security forces could be defined as "aberrations" by individuals acting outside the framework of policy, but that was clearly not the case. "It didn't happen haphazardly. . . . It was a policy that brought about all this suffering. It was a policy that killed people. Not by accident. Deliberately. It was planned."

The episode ended in a flurry of recrimination. De Klerk and the National Party accused Tutu of bias, demanded an apology, instituted legal action, and threatened to withdraw from the whole TRC exercise. Whereas the ANC jeered at de Klerk's performance, the Afrikaner community was all the more convinced that the TRC was nothing more than a witch-hunt against them.

13

In the Name of Liberation

I F THE NATIONAL PARTY personified the past, the African National Congress represented the future. How it accounted for its own involvement in murder, torture, and bombing had an immediate bearing on its fitness for government. The ANC was called upon to answer for the activities not just of MK combatants but also of supporters who had carried out necklace murders and other human rights violations. It also had to account for its role in the internecine conflict with Inkatha, in which thousands had died.

The ANC's military campaign against the government had been largely ineffective. On its own admission, it engaged in little more than "armed propaganda" designed as much to maintain a following among the black population and to raise its morale as to threaten white security or damage the economy.

A number of incidents, however, had seared themselves on the memory and mind-set of the white community. In 1983, a car-bomb attack on Church Street in Pretoria, outside a building housing the administrative headquarters of the air force, killed nineteen people and injured 217, most of them civilians. In 1985, a bomb explosion in a shopping center in Amanzimtoti killed five civilians and injured more than forty others, most of them holidaymakers doing last-minute Christmas shopping. In 1986, a car bomb outside Magoo's Bar on the Durban beachfront killed three whites and injured some seventy others. In 1988, a car bomb exploded near the gate of Ellis Park sports stadium in Johannesburg, killing two and injuring thirty-seven. There had also been a spate of attacks on Wimpy Bars (fast food restaurants) and supermarkets. And in the mid-1980s, the ANC had initiated a land mine campaign in rural areas of the Transvaal in which some thirty people had died.

At TRC hearings, victims of these attacks gave dramatic testimony of their ordeals and of the scars they still bore. In 1985, two Afrikaner families—the van Ecks and the de Neyschens—had been driving on holiday through a game farm near Messina on the northern border of South Africa when their pickup truck struck a land mine. Three women and four children, between the ages of three and nine, died in the blast; there were four survivors. Johannes van Eck, who was severely injured and lost four members of his family, described what happened:

> We were immediately in flames. When I came to myself, I saw my baby boy of eighteen months was still alive. . . . He was lying quite still, but looking at me. Mr. De Neyschen was lying on his steering wheel . . . his hair burning, blood spouting from his forehead.

Van Eck pulled them through the window and looked around for survivors.

> Right behind the vehicle I found my wife and Martie De Neyschen. Both severely maimed and killed outright. I searched further. I came upon little Kobus De Neyschen, who had some life in him. I went back to his father and said: "This child is still alive, but severely maimed and burnt." His father asked there on the scene to let his child go . . . which is what happened. Then I noticed De Neyschen's daughter Lizelda walking towards us out of the veldt. . . . She had a cut across her face and she limped.
>
> Then I searched further for my son of three years but could not

find him. . . . Until today I could not find him. . . . I and my son buried our two family members and the next day our two friends. Since then it has been downhill for me all the way. I sit for days. . . . I simply sit. . . . I lost my business. I am reduced to a poor white.

He spoke directly to the commissioners:

Do you know, you the commissioners, how it feels to be blasted by a land mine? Do you know how it feels to be in a temperature of 6,000 and 8,000 degrees? Do you know how it feels to experience such a blast that is so intense that even the fillings in your teeth are torn out? Do you know what trouble reigns if you survive the blast and . . . must observe the results thereof? Do you know how it feels—how it feels to see crippled loved ones lying and burning? Do you know how it feels to look for your three-year-old child and never, Mr. Chairman, never to see him again and for ever after to wonder where he is? . . . Mr. Chairman, do you know how it feels to try to cheer up a friend while your wife and two children lie dead? Do you know how it feels to leave a baby of eighteen months behind to go and look for help?

Survivors from the urban bombing campaign testified about their experience. A victim of the Church Street bomb in 1983, Marina Geldenhuys, who had only just finished school, spoke of how the explosion had cost her youth and left her permanently disfigured, with head, leg, and internal injuries. "The emotional damage is incalculable," she said. "It was an act of cowardice which was committed, and it damaged and injured more civilians than anything else."

The TRC also heard evidence from victims of the "people's war," conducted during the 1980s by the ANC and its internal ally, the

United Democratic Front. Hundreds of people opposed to the ANC and the UDF had died in this conflict, hunted down by groups of "comrades" whose methods were notoriously brutal. Many victims were local councillors, township policemen, alleged informers, and others deemed to be "collaborators" of the apartheid system. Some victims were ordinary citizens who were simply opposed to the consumer boycotts and school boycotts enforced by the "comrades" and who died after being made to eat soap powder or cooking oil or who were summarily punished by "people's courts."

The "trademark" of the comrades was the "necklace"—a rubber tire thrown over a victim, filled with petrol, and set alight. The necklace method had started in Uitenhage in the Eastern Cape in March 1985 when a group of comrades, enraged because the police had shot and killed twenty-one demonstrators, seized Benjamin Kinikini, a prominent local councillor, and three of his sons and "necklaced" them.

His widow, Nombuzo Kinikini, testified to the commission about what she had heard of the incident:

> I was told that he was stabbed by a spade on his head. Then they stabbed him several times. He was made to drink petrol. They put a tire over him, and then they ignited him. During this time my younger son was hiding under the car. Some of the petrol got to him, and when he was trying to escape somebody saw him. . . .
>
> Silumko was hiding in one of the shops at Mboya. He asked one of the businessmen to hide him under the counter. They took him, and they ignited him alive in front of the shop. I am telling you as it is. They cut his testicles while he was still alive.
>
> Then on Monday at the police station, the doctor told me that he was going to inject me. At that time I had not seen them yet. . . . I will not be able to tell you about the head of my husband.

The necklace method subsequently spread to other areas of the country. Over the next five years, at least 400 people died this way.

The ANC's war against Inkatha also came under scrutiny. TRC investigations showed the ANC/UDF to be clearly responsible for the murder of at least seventy-six Inkatha officials. There was further evidence that the ANC's self-defense units, set up to protect its supporters from Inkatha attacks, had often been involved in indiscriminate warfare against Inkatha supporters. Some had broken up into factions and engaged in their own form of territorial warfare; others had developed into criminal gangs notorious for extortion, rape, and murder.

The most damaging testimony of all came from within the ANC itself. For years, the ANC had been dogged by accounts of murder and torture in its guerrilla camps in Angola and elsewhere in Africa. Its own investigations confirmed that numerous abuses had occurred, often sparked by "spy scares." Suspected agents had been tortured to make confessions, then tried by tribunals without any legal defense, then summarily executed. Others had been held for years in detention, maltreated by guards, and given starvation rations. Several mutinies had been brutally suppressed.

A former MK commander, Diliza Mthembu, told the TRC how he had been detained for more than four years in Quatro Camp in Angola and subjected to various forms of torture, including electric shocks; being suffocated with gas masks; hit with broomsticks; beaten on the buttocks continuously for a whole day; and forced at gunpoint to simulate sexual intercourse with a tree.

Other witnesses gave similar accounts. Many were deeply bitter about what they saw as the ANC's betrayal of its own supporters.

A long-standing ANC member, Joseph Seremane, who had once been imprisoned on Robben Island, asked the TRC to find out the truth about what had happened in Angola to his brother, "Chief"

Timothy. He had heard in 1994 that his brother had been "brutally disfigured" before being shot at Quatro in 1982, but his efforts to find out more had been thwarted.

> I want somebody to come and tell me what my younger brother actually did that he deserved to be shot like an animal being put down after being brutally disfigured so that his best friends could not recognize him.
>
> Why do you cheat me of my brother's bones? Why do you think that my contribution is worth nothing? Why do you think we ran and volunteered to risk our lives, calling for your return home, for justice, for supporting you in your call to be treated under the Geneva conventions, and you couldn't treat your own that way?
>
> Suddenly, nobody has ever come across this young man, Seremane [Chief Timothy]. Suddenly, nobody has ever known him. Suddenly, nobody has a record to show what kind of trial he had, he faced. Was he defended or was he not defended? And where was the accountability that you couldn't account to his people and say he is dead? . . .
>
> I have been on the [Robben] Island. I have gone through hell. I have been tortured, nearly lost my life. . . . I have seen what it means to be tortured. But when I think of Chief Timothy and compare the way he died to my suffering, my suffering is nothing.

THE POSITION THE ANC adopted from the outset was that there was little for which it had to answer. The ANC, said Deputy President Thabo Mbeki at his first appearance before the TRC in August 1996, had been engaged in "a just war of liberation." It had resorted to violence as a "last resort" only after the apartheid regime had blocked all possibilities of nonviolent resistance. Its armed struggle had been only one aspect of its overall strategy. It had set out deliberately to avoid civilian casualties, despite the ease with which it could have attacked white schools, churches, and other "soft" targets.

> We made a determined and sustained effort to ensure that we conducted an irregular war as closely as possible according to international conventions governing the humanitarian conduct of warfare. . . .
>
> The overwhelming majority of the actions carried out in the context of [a] just war of national liberation do not constitute gross violations of human rights within the meaning of the act establishing and mandating the commission.

Some actions by MK members and by ANC/UDF supporters might have occurred "outside of the established norms," Mbeki said, but they had to be understood in the context of irregular warfare. In any event, the ANC's leadership was ready "to accept collective responsibility for all operations of its properly constituted offensive structures," including acts that fell outside "established norms." Therefore, Mbeki said, the ANC "will not be making any representation about those activities in its conduct of the struggle for liberation which constitute legitimate actions carried out during a just and irregular war for national liberation."

Mbeki argued that it was the brutal activities of the security forces in the mid-1980s that had inevitably led the ANC to deviate from its fundamental policy of avoiding civilian casualties and to broaden its range of targets: "The risk of civilians being caught in the crossfire . . . could no longer be allowed to prevent the urgently needed all-round intensification of the armed struggle."

A number of attacks on targets with no apparent connection to the apartheid state had been made, he said. "In some cases these attacks were the result of the gray areas caused by anger and/or misunderstanding of ANC policy. The ANC has acknowledged that in a number of instances breaches in policy did occur and deeply regrets civilian casualties."

As an example of an attack precipitated by government actions, Mbeki cited the bomb explosion at the Amanzimtoti shopping center in which five people died. The MK member who planted the bomb, Andrew Zondo, had been searching for a government installation in Amanzimtoti to attack, when he went into a restaurant in the shopping center for a meal. At his trial for murder, Zondo had explained what had happened:

> While I was eating I saw people reading a newspaper which carried a picture of a woman shot in Lesotho, the mother of a nine-month-old baby. I bought the newspaper myself. On returning home, I decided to go and put a mine in the center. The decision I took that day was racial in character because I had seen that the area had a lot of white people. Before placing the mine, I debated over it, but on Monday I decided to do it, racial as it was. I knew the people were innocent and had nothing to do with the government. I hoped it would not injure them, but I hoped it would bring the government to its senses.

Asked whether he had anything to say before sentence of death was passed, Zondo had replied: "I wish to say this to the people who might have lost their friends and kids and families, that I am sorry."

Zondo had carried out the attack, said Mbeki, even though he knew it was contrary to ANC policy. "With regard to those attacks on soft targets for which MK personnel were responsible, the ANC does not seek to justify such attacks but insists that the context in which they occurred is relevant."

Because the ANC had been engaged in a "just war" against an

evil system of government, it would be "morally wrong and legally incorrect" to equate resistance to apartheid with defense of it.

Though the ANC's submission in August 1996 was only a preliminary account, its penchant for self-exoneration was to surface again and again, causing the TRC serious difficulty. In November, when senior ANC officials declared that ANC members need not seek amnesty for bombings, shootings, and killings on the grounds that their fight against apartheid had been part of a "just war," Tutu threatened to resign. "If this position is accepted as ANC policy, we will have to look for another chairperson," he said. "If parties are able to grant themselves amnesty, what is the point of having a truth commission?"

The legislation setting up the TRC was quite clear, he said. It made no provision for a moral distinction between gross violations of human rights. "A gross violation is a gross violation, whoever commits it and for whatever reason. There is thus legal equivalence between all perpetrators. Their political affiliation is irrelevant."

> A venerable tradition holds that those who use force to overthrow or even to oppose an unjust system occupy the moral high ground over those who use force to sustain that same system. That is when the criteria of the so-called just war come into play. . . . This does not mean that those who hold the moral high ground have carte blanche as to the methods they use.

The TRC would continue to act with evenhandedness in accordance with its mandate. "We have said clearly to the ANC that we will not accept their position," said Tutu. "To talk about 'a just war' is to introduce irrelevancies."

In its second submission in May 1997, the ANC was notably more forthcoming. Mbeki was accompanied by a large ANC delegation that included senior officials directly responsible for the armed struggle. The ANC listed thirty pages of military actions in an attempt to clarify its definition of legitimate targets. The air force headquarters building on Church Street in Pretoria, it said, was clearly a legitimate military target; eight of those killed were military personnel; the civilian casualties had been unavoidable. However, the bombing of the Ellis Park stadium in Johannesburg contravened ANC instructions not to hit purely civilian targets. Civilian casualties had also been caused by poor reconnaissance, faulty intelligence, faulty equipment, and the "blurring of the lines" between military and civilian targets in the mid-1980s. Some of its orders to intensify the armed struggle "may have given the impression to some cadres that they should totally disregard the possibility of civilian casualties in the course of their operations."

Out of 600 armed operations, the ANC was unsure about the origin of about 100 of them, including a number of attacks on "soft" targets like restaurants and hotels. In some cases, the incidents had gone unrecorded because of the disappearance of MK operatives and commanders. In others, the incidents may have been "false flag" operations carried out by the security forces to discredit their opponents.

Whatever the circumstances, the ANC regretted the deaths and injuries to civilians and accepted full responsibility for attacks carried out by its operatives, whether or not they had been in accordance with ANC policy.

Mbeki described how the ANC had resisted demands from within its own ranks to select "soft" white targets.

> There were many instances when people said: "When are we going to abandon this policy? . . . You have white school children who travel in a bus on a morning to go to a white school. It's an easy target. . . . Why don't we just hit these things? Let the white population feel the pain."

Any number of times these matters would come up, and people would argue this, and we would always say: "No, no, no, no. It can never be done because it's wrong."

The ANC justified its use of land mines by arguing that they had been laid in border areas patrolled regularly by security forces. Since white farmers in these areas had been integrated into the security force system, they too were considered legitimate targets. Only anti-tank land mines had been used, not anti-personnel mines. When it became clear that many of the victims were civilians, the land mine campaign was halted.

The ANC admitted that abuses had taken place in its guerrilla camps but claimed they had occurred largely as a result of spy scares and mutinies. Tribunals set up to judge informers and mutineers had used confessions obtained under torture without offering the accused the right to legal representation. Between 1982 and 1985, twenty-two prisoners had been executed on the orders of such tribunals; some of them had been falsely accused of spying. Other ill-treatment had occurred. Women recruits were frequently subjected to sexual abuse. The ANC denied, however, that there had been any systematic brutality in its camps. "We should avoid the danger whereby concentrating on these particular and exceptional acts of the liberation movement, which could be deemed as constituting gross human rights violations, we convey the impression that the struggle for liberation was itself a gross violation of human rights," said Mbeki.

In answering questions about "necklacing," the ANC was more ambivalent. Its official position was that the ANC leadership "strongly disapproved" of necklacing. But the TRC's lawyer, Hanif Vally, insisted on probing deeper. He quoted remarks made in 1986 by two prominent ANC leaders, Winnie Mandela and Alfred Nzo. "Together with our boxes of matches and our necklaces we shall liberate this country," Winnie Mandela had said. "Whatever the people decide to use to eliminate those enemy elements is their decision. If they decide to use necklacing, we support it," Alfred Nzo had said.

Furthermore, Vally pointed out that the ANC leadership had waited for more than a year before it spoke out officially against necklacing, during which time its supporters carried out scores of necklace murders. The effect, said Vally, was to create a climate in which necklacing was thought to be permissible. To illustrate his point, he quoted from an amnesty application that the TRC had received from a necklace perpetrator: "As beginners in the struggle against apartheid we had a copycat mind, whereby we used acts which were used by other comrades in the late 1980s, acts of necklacing, when we thought it was the right way of dealing with culprits."

Vally pressed his point with Mac Maharaj.

HANIF VALLY: Why did it take the ANC so long to condemn the practice of necklacing?

MAC MAHARAJ: On hindsight, if we delayed, in the judgment of any person, too long in appealing for the end of this practice and to condemn it, then on hindsight, yes, we made a mistake. We should have done it earlier. But the question arises again about the realities in which we were struggling.

First, said Maharaj, the ANC had needed to understand what was happening on the ground.

It would be an extremely foolhardy leader of the ANC in 1984–1985—1985, I think, is the period of the first necklacing—to have stood up and said, "This is wrong, out with it." I know some people had the courage, but we had to balance the need for that understanding with a proper appreciation of what was happening at home, and we were always mindful that being so far from home needed for us to temper our judgments by a better understanding of what was happening on the ground. . . .

So that's the explanation I have. And I think it is an explanation that allows for us to say that if some people say our condemnation was made too late, we can say, in all honesty, that, yes, it is possible to make that judgment from hindsight, but it would not be a judgment that would be very wisely made, and should not be made too lightly.

It was left to a former UDF leader, Patrick Lekota, at a separate hearing in 1998, to tackle the issue of necklacing more adequately. His explanation was that government acts of brutality and the systematic detention and banning of UDF leaders had created the space for uncontrolled acts of violence by angry mobs. During successive states of emergency, most of the leadership had been detained. "This severely hampered the ability of the UDF to moderate, prevent, or curtail the activities of angry activists and supporters of boycotts and work stoppages."

Lekota concluded:

We accept political and moral responsibility. We cannot say these people have nothing to do with us. We organized them; we led them. When we were taken into prisons, they were left without leadership, and many of them, angry even at our arrest, did things which were irrational.

When it came to dealing with its internecine warfare with Inkatha, the ANC evaded virtually all responsibility. Mbeki delivered a long, rambling explanation notable for its misleading answers. Even when Hanif Vally read out inflammatory statements made by ANC leaders attacking Buthelezi as "the enemy" and demanding retribution, Mbeki continued to dodge the issue. His explanation for the conflict in which thousands of Inkatha and ANC supporters died was that it was all the work of the security forces and "the third force."

MBEKI: We did not regard the IFP, its members, as legitimate military targets. Therefore at no stage were any decisions taken to attack the IFP as IFP. . . .

COMMISSIONER: Much as we accept that there was an element of the third force, I just want to look at whether there are any other factors which might have contributed to this which the ANC should have control over, like the culture of intolerance within the organization, lack of a human rights culture. I just want us to look internally at what else might have contributed to an escalation of violence over years between these two parties besides the third force.

MBEKI: I don't know if there is anything besides a third force. . . .

The most that Mbeki was prepared to admit to was a plan by an MK unit to assassinate Buthelezi, which headquarters had stopped once they learned of it. He also admitted that "things had gone wrong" with the ANC's self-defense units. "An attempt was made to keep an eye on them by the national leadership. There were instances where we had to intervene when there were all sorts of crazy things."

The reception accorded to Mbeki and his colleagues by the TRC was notably more friendly than that accorded to de Klerk. The ANC was openly regarded as the moral victor. The questions they faced were far less persistent. But even under those favorable circumstances, many of the answers they gave were as self-serving as those given by de Klerk. What was clear was that the ANC fully expected those answers to satisfy the TRC. At the end of it all, Mbeki declared triumphantly that he had won his round with the truth commissioners. But therein lay the seeds of future conflict.

A MORE DETAILED PICTURE OF ANC military operations came during a series of amnesty hearings held in 1998. Among the applicants was Aboobaker Ismail, former head of MK's Special Operations Unit, which was responsible for thirteen major acts of sabotage that killed twenty people and injured some 350 others. The targets had included oil refineries, government buildings, and the air force headquarters on Church Street in Pretoria.

The Church Street target had been chosen, said Ismail, to avenge a cross-border raid into Lesotho by South African security forces. The intention had been to kill military personnel, but it was fully understood by the ANC's president, Oliver Tambo, who authorized the attack, that civilian casualties in the center of Pretoria were inevitable. Quoting Tambo, Ismail explained: "The policy of the ANC was that we could not for the sake of a few civilians be prevented from striking at the power of the state, the apartheid state."

The objective had been to instill fear into the white community by carrying out "a highly visible attack against large numbers of military personnel in uniform, so that the security forces could not hide it." It was also to show blacks that MK had the capability to strike at the very heart of white power. "We wanted to show it was not only MK soldiers who bled. We knew the only way we could rip the apartheid war machine open was to hit the soft underbelly."

Ismail was challenged by Louis Visser, an advocate representing victims of the bombing, who said that the Church Street building was clearly a "soft military target"; the victims had been overwhelmingly civilian. "Victims find it hard to understand how they were considered part of the military machine if they were mere typists and telephonists." Ismail contended that all members of the security forces were targets. "No military machine will work without its administrative personnel. They are part of the whole, and the whole was targeted."

Ismail said he regretted the deaths of innocent civilians, but he praised the work of his comrades. "I am proud of the bravery, discipline, and selfless sacrifices of the cadres of special operations who operated under my command," he said. "Many of them laid down their lives in the pursuit of freedom for all in South Africa."

His remarks infuriated much of the white community. "We do not see how anyone can be proud of acts in which civilians were killed," said *The Citizen*, a Johannesburg newspaper. "The idea is sickening."

The amnesty hearing, however, provided the occasion for one of the most memorable acts of reconciliation the TRC was to witness—an encounter between Aboobaker Ismail, the master bomber, and one of his victims, Neville Clarence, an air force officer who had lost his sight in the Church Street bombing.

Ismail was close to tears as he came face-to-face with Clarence and apologized for the hurt he had caused. "This is very difficult," he said. "I am sorry about what happened to you." Clarence replied: "I do not hold any grudges." Afterwards he told reporters:

I came here today partially out of curiosity and hoping to meet Mr. Ismail. I wanted to express the feeling that I never held any grudges or bitterness against him. It was a wonderful experience.

Reconciliation does not just come from one side, it comes from both sides. I was on the one side, and he was on the other. In this instance though, I came off second best. . . .

I could read so many subconscious things in our handshake. There was so much sincerity and willingness to put this behind us.

14

The Trial of Winnie Mandela

There was one episode from the past from which the ANC had struggled to escape but that had returned to haunt it again and again. The scandal of Winnie Mandela's role as the head of a notorious criminal gang that had terrorized parts of Soweto during the 1980s had severely damaged the reputation of both Nelson Mandela and the ANC. The issue surfaced again during TRC victim hearings held in Soweto in 1996. In an endeavor to gain a clearer picture of what had happened, the TRC decided to hold a separate hearing in 1997. The official title of the hearing was "A Human Rights Violation Hearing into the Activities of the Mandela United Football Club"; but it was known popularly as "the Winnie hearing." And what it amounted to in effect was a trial of Winnie Mandela.

Winnie Mandela had once been an icon of the liberation struggle, bravely keeping alive the Mandela name while her husband endured twenty-seven years of imprisonment. For years she had been persecuted by the security police. Banished to a remote township near Brandfort in the Orange Free State, she had become as much a symbol of defiance against the apartheid regime as Nelson Mandela. Reveling in the international attention she attracted, she styled herself "Mother of the Nation." But as she became embroiled in one scandal after another, the title turned into an object of derision. She was renowned for her extravagant lifestyle, for her succession of lovers, and for dubious business deals. But by far the worst scandal involved the Mandela United Football Club.

Though several of her former associates in the club were serving long prison sentences for murder, assault, arson, and abduction, the only penalty Winnie had paid was a R15,000 fine for ordering the kidnapping of a fourteen-year-old boy, Stompie Moeketsi, who was subsequently murdered by the club's coach. Despite an avalanche of allegations against her, Winnie had otherwise survived unscathed. She seemed untouchable.

Fear of Winnie still prevailed. As the hearing commenced, a Johannesburg newspaper reported that in Orlando, the area of Soweto where the football club used to operate and where Winnie still lived, witnesses it had interviewed wept and trembled as they recalled the terrible events of those times. No one was willing to testify before the commission. "Soweto is still a haunted community," reported the *Sunday Times*, "where many who were involved live in fear of the resurrection of past deeds."

During its own investigations, the commission had compiled a dossier of eighteen crimes, including eight murders, about which it wanted to cross-examine Winnie. Allegations it had heard cast her as a cruel, violent, and sadistic bully. One official said the subpoena summoning her before the commission read like "a script from a horror movie."

What added particular significance to the hearing was Winnie's relentless drive for high office. Despite her divorce from Nelson Mandela in 1996 and her ignominious dismissal as a junior minister from his government the year before, she had recently launched a campaign to win the post of deputy president of the African National Congress in elections due to be held later in the year. If she succeeded, she would become a leading contender for the job of deputy president in the post–Mandela era in 1999 and thus only a heartbeat away from the presidency itself.

The commission's hearing therefore had as much bearing on the future as on the past. It was also a crucial test of how the new political establishment dealt with gruesome events from its own history. Some government ministers had already made their own views clear. "You cannot compare the allegations against Winnie Madikizela-Mandela with the crimes of apartheid in their nature, scale, or quantity," proclaimed Dullah Omar, the justice minister, a few days before the hearing started.

Winnie's response to the barrage of accusations was to deny everything and to assert that it was all part of a campaign by her political enemies to destroy her reputation before the ANC elections and to eliminate her from the political arena. "They have tried so hard for decades and failed," she said. "This time they will fail forever." When asked whether she would apply for amnesty, she retorted: "For what? I am not apologetic to anyone on my contribution to the struggle." She insisted that her testimony be given in public, not behind closed doors as the commission had initially intended, believing that it would help clear her name.

Accompanied by bodyguards, she arrived at the Johannesburg recreation hall that had been hired by the commission for the occasion; she was wearing a stylish white and blue two-piece suit, three strings of pearls, her customary bejeweled glasses, and an assortment of rings and bangles. At the age of sixty-three, she remained an imposing figure, tall and still physically attractive, with an aura of menace. She brought with her her two daughters, Zenani and Zindzi, who smiled their way through days of grim testimony, passing sweets along their row as though they were watching a movie. Zindzi herself had been fully involved in the club's activities.

"I intend to bare my soul to the scrutiny of my country," declared Winnie. "I beg that these issues be tested by the vigilance of the public."

THE FOOTBALL CLUB HAD been started for township youths in 1986, a year after Winnie had returned from banishment in Brandfort to live in her own home in Orlando West. Forming football teams in the name of popular political leaders was a fashionable pursuit at the time. Winnie allowed them to stay in rooms at the back of her house and provided them with track suits and money. She acquired a "coach," a thirty-eight-year-old local man named Jerry Richardson, a skilled football player but someone with limited intelligence, a meager education, and a reputation as a police informer.

From its origins as a football club, Mandela United rapidly descended into a world of brutal crime. Winnie used it initially as a personal bodyguard, to accompany her to rallies and funerals and to guard her house. Its members were subject to her own strict rules. They were required to return home by a certain time each night, signing in and out of the house in a special register. Failure to sign the register meant a whipping from Winnie as well as from other youths. Looking for more recruits, club members roamed the township, accusing those who did not want to join them of being police informers or "sellouts." Many who were coerced into joining subsequently found it difficult to leave. No one could resign voluntarily from the club. Stories began to circulate of youths being taken to Winnie's house and never seen again.

Mandela United soon began operating as a vigilante gang. Victims accused of theft and other crimes or of being police informers were brought to Winnie's house for interrogation by a "disciplinary committee" and for whatever punishment it decided to order. Punishment varied according to the offense but included kicking, punching, whipping, and beating. A favorite form of punishment was known as "breakdown," in which victims were thrown high into the air and left to hit the floor. Other forms of torture were also used.

In May 1987, a teenage youth, Peter Makanda, was abducted along with his brother by members of Mandela United, who accused them of being informers. They were taken to Winnie's house and beaten savagely. Makanda was hung by the neck with a plastic rope from a rafter until it broke. Both brothers were tortured with knives. A large "M" for Mandela was carved on Makanda's chest, and the words "Viva ANC" were sliced down the length of one of his thighs. Battery acid was smeared into the wounds. The brothers claimed that Winnie put in an appearance soon after they were first beaten, returning a few hours afterwards. They later managed to escape from a garage.

When the Makanda brothers reported their ordeal to the police, three members of Mandela United were arrested. But Winnie herself was never charged in connection with the crime; nor was she called as a witness or even questioned. The police were keen to avoid being seen persecuting her any more. The activities of her gang of vigilantes were no different from those of scores of others that had sprung up during the township revolts of the 1980s. Kangaroo courts like the one she was running in Orlando were relatively common. She thus enjoyed a kind of immunity that not only induced greater fear of her but increased her own sense of power.

In previous accounts of the club's activities, Winnie's own involvement in the beatings that went on at her Orlando home had always been a matter of dispute. But in a dramatic start to the commission's nine days of hearings, a new witness came forward with a personal account that left little room for doubt.

Phumzile Dlamini, a single mother from Soweto, described how, when she was three months pregnant, she had been beaten savagely for five hours by Winnie and members of the football club. Her child had subsequently been born with apparent brain damage.

The reason for the beating, she said, was that Winnie had taken a liking to her boyfriend, "Shakes," a club member. Shakes had told her how "Winnie had come to him in the middle of the night and got under the blanket with him"; and he had warned her that if Winnie found out about their own relationship there would be trouble.

Winnie did find out, arrived at Phumzile's home, and questioned her about her relationship with Shakes. Phumzile denied there was one, but Winnie told her not to lie and began hitting her. "She slapped me in the face and hit me with her fists over all my body and my stomach."

A few days later, Winnie returned in a minibus accompanied by club members. "She spoke to my mother and said they wanted to see me. And my mother asked as to where they were taking me. Winnie said: 'I'll bring her back just now. I just need to talk to her.' And my mother said: 'Please bring my child back. Do not kill her.'"

On the way to Winnie's house, Winnie assaulted her again. "When we got to Winnie's house, Winnie said: 'Guys, see what you can do with this one.' . . . They started assaulting me and kicking me in accordance with Winnie's instructions, and I think this continued for about five hours."

Eventually, Winnie's daughter Zindzi came to ask what was happening and pleaded with them to stop assaulting Phumzile.

I wanted to lay a charge, but my brother said the football team will burn our house. . . . People were scared to air their views. They loved Winnie and trusted Winnie as a mother of the community. . . . After all that, I changed my views completely. I did not even want to hear people refer to her as "the Mother of the Nation."

The first glimpse that the outside world had of what was going on in Soweto was in July 1988 when a crowd of teenage pupils from the Daliwonga High School marched on Winnie's house, smashed the doors and windows, and then set fire to it. Their attack was launched in revenge for the detention of a group of Daliwonga students who had been accused of rape, found guilty, and then beaten up in the back rooms of Winnie's house. All the Mandela family records, their photographs, letters, and gifts, even a slice of wedding cake that Winnie had been saving for Mandela's release were destroyed in the fire. As local residents gathered to watch, none of them ventured to help. They watched in silence as the house burned down.

Informed of these events in prison, Nelson Mandela told Winnie to disband her football team. And to limit further damage, he asked a group of influential community leaders, including the Reverend Frank Chikane of the South African Council of Churches, Sydney Mufamadi, a prominent trade unionist, and Aubrey Mokoena, national coordinator of the Release Mandela Committee, to form a "crisis committee" to take control of the matter.

But Winnie refused to disband Mandela United. While the house in Orlando was being rebuilt, she moved into a house in Diepkloof Extension in another part of Soweto, taking members of Mandela United with her. The crisis committee was soon to admit that Winnie was out of control.

In November 1988, Winnie asked the club's coach, Jerry Richardson, to hide two ANC insurgents in his house in Soweto. Richardson, a police informer, promptly told the police they were there, and in an ensuing gunfight, the two insurgents were killed. Just before the shooting started, Richardson, who was in the garden, raised his arms in the air, surrendered to the police, and was taken away.

At Winnie's house, the finger of suspicion was pointed not at Richardson but at two young activists, Lolo Sono and Siboniso

Tshabalala, who had been friendly with the two insurgents and who had been seen at Richardson's house shortly before the gunfight started. They were summoned to Winnie's house.

Lolo's father, Nicodemus Sono, testified to the commission as to what happened shortly afterwards. A successful businessman, he owned a small fleet of minibuses; he was also an underground ANC operative, providing insurgents with transport and safe houses. On the evening of 13 November, Nicodemus Sono was told by one of Winnie's drivers, Michael Siyakamela, that she was waiting outside in the street in a kombi—a minibus—and wanted to see him.

When I opened the slide door, the light in the kombi went on and I could see Lolo at the back. He was beaten up; his face was bruised; it was actually pulped. He was like, you know, thick, as if somebody had beaten him up and crushed him against the wall. . . .

When Lolo tried to speak, he was told to shut up by Mrs. Mandela. . . . Mrs. Mandela explained to me that Lolo is a spy and it was for that reason that the two comrades at Richardson's house were killed. They had been sold out by Lolo. And I denied that. I tried to explain to her that Lolo is not a spy. In fact Lolo was helping Peter and Sipho [the two insurgents] when they were around. He had done quite a lot for them. . . .

But she raised her voice, speaking very loud. "I cannot leave him with you. He is a spy!" So I tried to plead with her. She told the driver to pull off. . . . We went right round the block and stopped again in front of my house.

When I looked at Lolo he was in a terrible state; he was shaking. Then I asked her that I may please get a jersey for Lolo because by then I thought he's feeling cold. . . . She agreed that we must get a jersey for Lolo.

When we alighted from the kombi, me and Lolo, there was this tall, hefty young man who had Lolo on the collar of his shirt and pushed him towards the gate. He had a gun.

Lolo's mother, Caroline, brought him a jersey. Lolo asked a friend who was standing by to fetch an envelope containing photographs from his room and then climbed back into the minibus sitting between two men. His father took the front seat. "I sat there, and I started pleading again with Mrs. Mandela. 'Please won't you leave my son with me because he's already been beaten? If you leave him with me, I'll see what to do from here.' And she totally refused that. 'This is a spy!'"

Winnie told the driver to move off. "As we went down I pleaded with her until she said to me, 'I am taking this dog away. The movement will see what to do.'" Nicodemus Sono got out of the minibus. "That was the last time I saw my son Lolo, in the company of Mrs. Mandela and some young men."

Asked why he thought Winnie would have brought Lolo to him, Sono replied that he could only assume that his son had told her that she could find something of use at his house. "I think Lolo could have led Mrs. Mandela and the boys to my house so that I can be able to rescue him," he said. "I failed."

Sono had subsequently hoped that Lolo had been taken to an ANC camp in Zambia. After two months of hearing no news about him, he summoned up the courage to ask Winnie, but she was hostile and evasive. He reported Lolo's disappearance to the police, telling them he had last seen him in Winnie's minibus, but he heard nothing more.

At the hearing, Sono was followed by Nomsa Tshabalala, the widowed mother of the other youth, who accused Winnie outright of the murder of her son and demanded to be given his remains. Nomsa said that at the time she had been too terrified of Winnie to ask her about his disappearance. "We were warned not to approach her. Winnie has got bodyguards. . . . I used to see her scaring other people or threatening other people. . . . I'm scared of her even now. The same fate that befell Siboniso might have possibly befallen us."

Winnie sat listening to the testimony, fanning herself with paper and sipping iced water.

Evidence about what had happened to the two youths came later from the club coach, Jerry Richardson, who was brought to the hearing from prison, where he was serving a life sentence for the murder of Stompie Moeketsi. Richardson had once idolized Winnie, invariably referring to her as "Mummy." "I loved Mummy with all my heart. I would have done anything to please her," he told the commission. But in prison he had changed his mind. "She never came to visit. I have woken up."

An unstable man, he toyed with a miniature football throughout his testimony and caused derisive laughter in the audience by claiming he was a "soccer star." He admitted that he was a police informer who had betrayed the two ANC insurgents killed in his house. After being detained by the police for two weeks after the gunfight, he had been released. Even though this aroused much suspicion within the football club, Winnie allowed him to stay at her house.

He later saw Lolo Sono and Siboniso Tshabalala there, badly beaten, tied hand and foot. There was a discussion about what to do with them, said Richardson. A decision was made to "dump" them. "Mummy was the one who gave the go-ahead or the green light for anything to happen," said Richardson. "Mummy was the main decisionmaker."

With other members of the football club, Richardson took the two youths to a wasteland where they were "slaughtered like goats," and then he returned to give "Mummy" a "report back."

The commission knew of one other witness who possessed significant evidence about the disappearance of the two youths: Winnie's driver, Michael Siyakamela. But during the course of their hearing, the commissioners discovered to what lengths Winnie would go to impede the proceedings. The commission had hoped that Siyakamela would give evidence about driving Lolo from Winnie's house to the Sono's house and back in the minibus, thus corroborating Nicodemus Sono's testimony. He had assured a commission investigator, Piers Pigou, that he would testify willingly. But shortly before he was due to appear, he refused to cooperate further, telling Pigou that "Mummy had contacted him."

In December 1988 there were further murders. Kuki Zwane, a twenty-three-year-old activist, was a close friend of Winnie's daughter Zindzi. Kuki spent much time at the Mandela household in the company of club members, but she fell out of favor with Winnie. According to Richardson, Winnie said to him: "Richardson, Kuki is disturbing me, she's bothering me." Winnie claimed that she was a police informer.

Richardson duly made a plan to get rid of her. With other club members, he took her to a stretch of wasteland near a school, then stabbed her and slit her throat.

> I reported to Mummy: "Mummy, I have now carried out your orders. I have killed Kuki." And she said, the following day, she wanted me to show her where I had dumped Kuki's body. We got into the car. . . . I pointed out at a distance the place. . . . She pointed out that the school kids will discover the body very quickly. I made a mistake by dumping the body at such a spot.

The corpse was discovered on 18 December, but it remained unidentified, consigned to a pauper's grave, until Richardson confessed to the murder while in prison.

Two weeks later, the murder of fourteen-year-old "Stompie" Moeketsi Seipei created a scandal from which Winnie was never able to escape. It not only exposed her as a common criminal but contaminated the whole reputation of the African National Congress at a time when it was anxious to prove its credentials for responsible leadership.

Stompie was an obstreperous and boastful youth with a reputation for being both a fervent activist and a police informer who had "cracked" in detention. Along with other homeless youths, he had found lodgings in a church manse in Orlando East; the church was run by a white Methodist minister, Paul Verryn, who was highly respected in the neighborhood for his commitment to helping the local community.

On 29 December 1988, shortly after Winnie returned home from a Christmas visit to Nelson Mandela in Victor Verster Prison, she ordered the abduction of four occupants of the Methodist manse, including Stompie. Winnie had been told by another occupant of the manse, Xoliswa Falati, a troublesome thirty-five-year-old woman who had quarreled with Stompie and with Verryn, that Verryn had engaged in homosexual practices at the manse. The victims were brought to Winnie's house at Diepkloof Extension, where Falati repeated her accusations about homosexuality and claimed that Stompie was an informer. All four victims were then interrogated and beaten mercilessly to extract confessions.

The three survivors said later that Winnie, who had been drinking and who was in a foul mood, had led the assaults, punching and slapping each of the victims. "You are not fit to be alive," she told them. Members of Mandela United joined in, throwing their victims in the air, shouting "breakdown" as they did. Winnie, according to one of the victims, Kenny Kgase, watched "with a look of satisfaction." She called for a sjambok—a rawhide whip—to be brought and, humming a freedom song, lashed the victims. Stompie, deemed to be a "sellout," came in for especially brutal treatment, and eventually he confessed to being a police informer. The following day, he was beaten again and again. On 1 January, he was taken away.

News of the abductions spread quickly around Soweto. On 4 January, Aubrey Mokoena, a member of the crisis committee and a close friend of Winnie's, questioned her about the missing youths, but she denied that any of them were at her home. On 6 January, when Dr. Nthatho Motlana, an old friend of the Mandela family, went to see Winnie, she admitted that they were at her home but refused to allow him to see them.

Then on 7 January, one of the kidnap victims, Kenny Kgase, managed to escape. He immediately alerted Methodist Church elders about what had happened to him and the three others. Led by Bishop Peter Storey, the Methodist Church now played a central role in trying to free the missing youths, coordinating its efforts with the crisis committee but avoiding contact with the police to minimize complications.

On 11 January, three members of the crisis committee— Mufamadi, Mokoena, and Sister Bernard Ncube—went to Winnie's house. At the TRC's special hearing, they testified about the difficulties they encountered in dealing with Winnie, but they seemed as nervous about antagonizing her in front of the commission as they had been at the time of their visit, even though at the time of the hearing Mufamadi was a government minister and the two others were members of parliament. None of them was willing to criticize Winnie for holding the youths. Mokoena, an argumentative man, went so far as to claim that "Mama," as he called Winnie, had been "overcome by altruism" in wanting to protect them.

> We approached Winnie who promised to give us access to the kids so that we could see them for ourselves. She immediately asserted that they came to her house voluntarily because they were tired of

being sodomized by the priest who was giving them sanctuary. She promised that the kids would confirm that to us when we see them.

At the meeting, however, Zindzi Mandela had let slip the fact that one of the youths had "escaped." The committee members did not pursue the matter further, though they noted her use of the word "escape."

The following day, the committee members were finally allowed to see two kidnap victims, Pelo Mekgwe and Thabiso Mono. They were accompanied by another youth, Katiza Cebekhulu. Both Mekgwe and Mono had obvious wounds but claimed they were staying at Winnie's house of their own free will and had gone there to seek protection from Verryn's sexual advances. Their injuries, they said, had been sustained when they fell from trees at Verryn's mission house.

But Katiza told a different story.

Katiza, finding himself alone with the committee, broke down under questioning and admitted that they were being held against their will and they were going to tell the story of the sexual advances. He said: "I am going to die anyway so I may as well tell the truth."

Katiza's version was that all four kidnap victims had been brutally assaulted. He himself had participated in the assault. He said he suspected that Stompie was dead. But the committee decided not to enquire about the whereabouts of Stompie. "We didn't deem it prudent at that stage to confront Mrs. Mandela with what Katiza told us," Mufamadi told the commission.

The committee members then met Bishop Storey. Having consulted Fink Haysom, a prominent human rights lawyer, Storey suggested that the best way forward was for the crisis committee to obtain a writ of habeas corpus. But the committee refused. Mokoena argued that they had "no mandate."

"The crisis committee, having refused to assist in a habeas corpus operation, left us really in great difficulty about how to proceed," Bishop Storey told the commission. "We actually were in a hostage negotiation." When the commission asked, "Who was the hostage-taker?" Storey replied: "There was no doubt in my mind that the person we were negotiating with was Mrs. Mandela."

To help resolve the issue, the Methodist Church and the crisis committee sought assistance from Oliver Tambo—the ANC president based in Lusaka, Zambia—and from Nelson Mandela in Victor Verster Prison. Fink Haysom flew to Lusaka to brief Tambo. As he listened to Haysom's account, Tambo, appalled, threw up his hands and covered his face. "What must I do?" he exclaimed. "We can't control her. The ANC can't control her. We tried to control her, that's why we formed the crisis committee. You must tell the crisis committee they must do more."

In Victor Verster, after being informed of the details by his lawyer, Ismail Ayob, on 14 January, Mandela issued an instruction that the two youths should be released. After further prevarication from Winnie, they were set free on 16 January and handed over to Bishop Storey. There was, however, still no word of the whereabouts of Stompie.

That evening, the crisis committee convened a meeting of community leaders in a church hall in Dobsonville, a suburb at the opposite end of Soweto from Winnie's house in Diepkloof; the site had been chosen for safety reasons. In all, there were about 150 participants, representing civic movements, trade unions, and church organizations. Bishop Storey took along the two kidnap victims, Mono and Mekgwe.

In the car, the two of them volunteered the following information: that they never wanted to go back to the Mandela house; that they were badly beaten, and the phrase that sticks with me is the phrase: "Our eyes could not see for a week." They were worried about Stompie, and they had been told to accuse Paul Verryn or be killed. They were also assaulted by Mrs. Mandela herself.

Mono and Mekgwe gave the meeting their account of what had happened: They described how Winnie had assaulted them and denied allegations that Verryn had sodomized them. While they were telling their story, into the hall strode Winnie's lawyer, Krish Naidoo, together with Katiza Cebekhulu and a member of the football club. "I have never seen such terror on people's faces," Storey testified.

There was discussion about whether the meeting should be abandoned, but the participants decided to press on. Katiza was asked to give his account. Storey continued:

> He admitted that he had participated in the beatings that took place. . . . Asked why, he said, "Well, they were being beaten and I also felt like beating them. . . . "
>
> He was also asked to describe Stompie's injuries, and he said he was "soft" on one side of his head, and had been beaten so that he could not see out of his eyes, and had been picked up and dropped on the floor, and that he couldn't walk. Asked where Stompie went, he said he didn't know. "When I came back to the house, Stompie was missing." Asked whether he thought Stompie was dead, he answered: "Yes."

Storey then asked the meeting at large if anyone knew of any misconduct on the part of Verryn. About a dozen residents from the manse were present, but no one spoke against him. He was given a unanimous vote of confidence. The meeting agreed that Winnie was using allegations of homosexuality as a smoke screen.

Another victim of the football club, Lerotodi Ikaneng, stepped forward. A wound across his neck was still raw and livid. Shudders of consternation ran through the audience. A former member of the club himself, he described how he had decided to quit despite being accused by Zindzi Mandela of being a "sellout." On 3 January, only two weeks before, Jerry Richardson and other members of the gang had tried to murder him using a pair of garden shears, leaving him for dead.

The meeting concluded by agreeing that Winnie should be ostracized, that "all progressive organizations should no longer give her a platform," and that she should "desist from creating an impression that she speaks on behalf of the people." They also resolved "that Winnie be approached and be instructed to produce Stompie."

A report sent by the crisis committee to Tambo described what happened next:

> When Winnie was informed about the decisions of the meeting, her immediate response was to demand a list of all the people who were at the meeting.
>
> She seems to think that she is above the community! She shows utter contempt for both the crisis committee and the community.

The committee ended their report with a pitiful plea: "Help us map out the way forward."

No news of these events had yet been reported in the press. Neither the local press nor the foreign press delved too closely into Winnie's activities for fear that their reports would be used by the government for propaganda purposes and serve only to discredit the anti-apartheid struggle. They were also concerned that rumors about Winnie and Mandela United might have been manufactured by the government in the first place. It was not until 27 January that the first tentative reports appeared, based on the Dobsonville meeting.

Then suddenly the crisis erupted further. On 27 January, a popular Indian doctor, Abu-Baker Asvat, was murdered in his surgery in Soweto. Asvat had been a close friend of Winnie, always ready to respond to her requests for help. He was a prominent political activist involved not with pro-ANC organizations but with the black-consciousness movement. Members of his family had noticed in recent weeks that he had become increasingly troubled and anxious. Their first reaction to the murder was to assume that he had been killed for political reasons. But other possibilities soon emerged.

The crisis committee knew that Asvat had been called to Winnie's house on 31 December to examine Stompie. He had found Stompie to be brain damaged and had urged that he should be taken to the hospital. Asvat subsequently reported his findings to members of the crisis committee. He was therefore a key witness to the circumstances surrounding Stompie's disappearance.

Asvat had also been involved in the case as a result of a visit that Winnie had paid to his surgery with Katiza Cebekhulu. After joining in the assaults of the four kidnap victims, he had become distraught. Winnie's explanation was that he had been sexually abused by Verryn. Asvat examined Katiza; he found no evidence of sexual abuse but noted on Katiza's medical record that he was mentally confused and occasionally hysterical. According to the record book and the medical card completed in Asvat's surgery, Winnie brought Katiza to see Asvat on 30 December, the day after the abduction had taken place. This evidence of Winnie's whereabouts on 30 December was to assume considerable significance at a later stage.

On 26 January, shortly after a Johannesburg newspaper had asked Krish Naidoo, Winnie's lawyer, to comment on an article about the abductions that it intended to publish the following day, Winnie ordered Katiza to accompany Naidoo to the Orlando police station to make a statement alleging he had been raped by Verryn. The police duly opened a docket and told Katiza to get a doctor's certificate.

That same evening, Asvat was visited in his surgery by a new patient, Jerry Richardson. Richardson said he had been referred by Winnie and complained of an abscess. Asvat made a note in red on Richardson's patient card: "Sent by Winnie." He found little wrong with Richardson but told him to return the next morning for a penicillin injection. Friends and family members who met Asvat later that day described him as being tense and frightened. Richardson duly arrived the next morning. In the afternoon, two Zulu youths arrived at the surgery, shot Asvat dead, and escaped.

Winnie's conduct following the murder was strange. Late that night, she arrived at Asvat's house in the company of Richardson and Zindzi, went straight up to Asvat's widow, Zhora, and asked: "Who do you think did this?" Then she sat silently on the floor.

The following day she gave a press interview claiming that Asvat had been murdered because he possessed evidence of Verryn's sexual misconduct, drawing attention for the first time to a possible link between the kidnapping at the Methodist manse and Asvat's murder. The implication was that the Methodist Church was involved in Asvat's murder.

"Dr. Asvat was the only professional witness to back my story that the boys, alleged to have been kept against their will in my house, were in fact victims of abuse," she told the Johannesburg *Sunday Times*. "I gave them shelter as is my duty as a social worker." It was "uncanny," she added, that an important witness who may have been able to help one of his own patients was dead.

Bishop Storey told the commission:

It was so utterly bizarre even to suggest that the church could be colluding with some murderer in order to get rid of evidence that might embarrass the church; it was so absurd; it made us very, very angry, and by the end of that day we had met and decided to open a defamation action against the *Sunday Times*.

But Winnie pursued her vendetta against Verryn with a vengeance. In a television interview with NBC News on 1 February, she gave a detailed account of what she said had really happened:

> The tragedy is that the Reverend Paul Verryn has a medical problem which needs to be addressed by responsible leaders. It's a psychological problem. I don't understand how a man of his standing and a Christian continues to sodomize black children. There is clear evidence that he has fallen victim to a medical problem which should be addressed quietly with his doctors. He brutalizes these youths who are with him because one youth would not give into his sexual advances. . . .
>
> It is well known in church circles and [among] those who have been working with him. . . . He is continuing with these activities with the full knowledge of some of the top members of the church. My responsibility as a mother is to draw attention to this problem. . . . There is a gigantic cover-up by the church.

The press was by now in full pursuit of the story. Local newspapers obtained statements from a host of civic associations. The statements supported the Methodist Church and the decision that had been made at the Dobsonville meeting to condemn Winnie. But to Storey's immense frustration, the crisis committee intervened to try to prevent the publication of these statements.

COMMISSION LAWYER: What was your response to this? Initially you wanted to bring a court application, a habeas corpus application for Mr. Seipei's release. Now press information was being blocked. What was your response?

BISHOP STOREY: I realized that there were two things running here. There was an attempt to find out the truth about Stompie and, possibly, still save his life. . . .

On the other hand, there was a political agenda running here. There were people with deep political concerns and fears. I was aware of that. I'm not a politician myself, but it was quite clear to me that the crisis committee was involved in damage control, as well as trying to get to the bottom of this.

And when damage control, politically, took the upper hand, then they would move in a certain way, and when the moral essence of assault and possible murder took the upper hand, then they would move in another way. I think they were really in a deep dilemma.

. . . It was a reality of the time, and that frustrated me deeply.

Despite the press attention, the activities of Mandela United still continued. On 11 February, a club member known as Dodo rushed to tell a local community activist, Dudu Chili, that she and her son Siboniso, were in danger. "You could see that he was scared," Mrs. Chili told the commission. "He had this fear." Winnie, Dodo blurted out, had just finished chairing a meeting at her office in Soweto at which it had been decided that Mrs. Chili and her son should be killed. "They have become too problematic," Winnie had said, according to Dodo.

Dudu Chili had been involved in a long-standing feud with Winnie over the football club. Alarmed by its increasingly brutal activities, she had told her three sons to steer clear of it. When the football club began to harass them, she went to Winnie to ask why.

"She just said that if my children didn't join the football club, then they were sell-outs." In conjunction with Albertina Sisulu, another respected community leader and the wife of Nelson Mandela's close colleague, Walter Sisulu, Mrs. Chili helped set up an escape route for club members wanting to run away. When the Dobsonville meeting had been called in January, she had been one of the organizers. "At the beginning, we all regarded her as the Mother of the Nation because she was Nelson Mandela's wife, not realizing that we were building up a monster with the help of the rest of the world."

On 13 February, Sibusiso Chili was intercepted by two Mandela United members, but the alarm was raised, and, in the ensuing fracas, it was one of the club members, Maxwell Madondo, who died. In retaliation, club members attacked Mrs. Chili's house, setting it on fire and shooting dead her thirteen-year-old niece, Finkie Msomi.

The end of Mandela United, however, was nigh. On 15 February, two forensic pathologists, alerted by press reports about Stompie's disappearance, identified his body in the mortuary at Diepkloof. The body, with knife wounds, had been found lying on an open stretch of wasteland on 6 January by a local woman and had been in the mortuary unidentified ever since. Stompie's mother, Joyce Seipei, confirmed the body's identity.

Now that they had a body, the police began to round up suspects, acting on information from the three kidnap victims, Kgase, Mono, and Mekgwe. Richardson and other members of the club were arrested. Winnie's house in Diepkloof Extension was raided. In one of the rooms there, police found a handwritten hit list with eleven names on it, including those of the three Chili brothers; Lerotodi Ikaneng, who had given evidence at the Dobsonville meeting; and two of Albertina Sisulu's sons. Police also arrested two illiterate youths in connection with the murder of Dr. Asvat.

Winnie herself remained curiously immune from police interrogation. She was questioned about the sjamboks found on her premises, but she denied any knowledge of them. She was not required to make a statement in connection with either Stompie's death or Asvat's murder. A statement made by one of the two youths charged with Asvat's murder clearly implicated her. He claimed that his accomplice had said, "Look, I've been bought by Winnie Mandela and I must go and shoot Asvat dead." But the statement was never produced in court. The official motive for the murder was said to be robbery.

A group of senior figures in the liberation movement were by now so appalled at Winnie's conduct and the damage it was causing that they resolved to denounce her in public. One of them was Azar Cachalia, then treasurer of the United Democratic Front and at the time of the hearing a senior official in the police ministry. His testimony to the commission, unlike that given by members of the crisis committee, was unequivocal. He described Mandela United as "a gang of thugs" often directed by Winnie herself.

The football club often dispensed their frightening brand of justice, which included vicious assaults in cases ranging from domestic disputes to those who crossed their paths and were branded as informers.

Perhaps the most sickening case to my memory involved the abduction of two youths who were brought to the Mandela home, where they were accused of being informers. On one of them the letter "M" was sliced into his chest with a penknife and the words "Viva ANC" were carved down his thigh. Battery acid was then poured over his open wounds. The second youth also had the words "Viva ANC" carved on his back.

In none of these cases was Mrs. Mandela charged or called as a witness, and this of course fueled some of the rumors around her.

The rumors included Winnie's relationship with the police.

Some members of the community held the view that Mrs. Mandela herself was working with the police. This was because just about everyone seemed to be aware that there were guerrillas and arms in the Mandela home. Some of them had been involved in armed incidents in the township, some even ended up being arrested.

Cachalia went on to list facts about the Stompie episode that were evident at the time.

Firstly, four males, including Stompie, were forcibly removed from the manse to the Mandela home. Secondly, they were viciously beaten at the Mandela home, where they were kept against their will. Third, one young man, Kenneth Kgase, had escaped on 7 January and reported his ordeal. Four, Stompie was not only tortured at the house but then subsequently murdered in a savage fashion.

[Five], at best, Mrs. Mandela was aware and encouraged this criminal activity. At worst, she directed it and actively participated in the assaults.

Six, Paul Verryn was framed. And seven, all reasonable efforts by the church, community leaders, Mr. Mandela, and President Oliver Tambo to disband the gang of thugs by trying to secure Mrs. Mandela's cooperation had failed.

By 15 February 1989, we were really at the end of our tether. . . . The crisis committee had become ineffective in the face of Mrs. Mandela's obstinacy. Stompie's body had been positively identified, and our worst fears had now materialized. The community anger was at boiling point. . . . The national leadership of the UDF realized we had to do something.

Murphy Morobe, then the UDF's publicity secretary and at the time of the hearings a senior government official, testified how he had returned from a trip abroad in late January to find "the air in Soweto thick with tension." On 16 February, the day after Stompie's body had been identified, Morobe read out a statement in the name of the Mass Democratic Movement (MDM)—an umbrella organization representing a huge array of community associations and trade unions—censuring Winnie for criminal activity.

> We have now reached the state where we have no option but to speak publicly on what is a very sensitive and painful matter. In recent years, Mrs. Mandela's actions have increasingly led her into conflict with various sections of the oppressed people and with the Mass Democratic Movement as a whole. The recent conflict in the community has centered largely around the conduct of her so-called football club, which has been widely condemned by the community. In particular, we are outraged by the reign of terror that the team has been associated with. Not only is Mrs. Mandela associated with the team, in fact it is her creation.

Morobe then directly linked Winnie to Stompie's death.

> We are outraged at Mrs. Mandela's obvious complicity in the recent abductions. Had Stompie and his colleagues not been abducted by Mrs. Mandela's "football team," he would have been alive today. . . .
>   We are not prepared to remain silent where those who are violating human rights claim to be doing so in the name of the struggle against apartheid.

Winnie, he continued, had "abused the trust and confidence" of the community. Because of her conduct, "the Mass Democratic

Movement hereby distances itself from Mrs. Mandela and her actions."

Cachalia testified:

> It was one of the most difficult decisions I have ever made, but I think it was also one of the proudest moments that I can remember. As time went on I have often over the last nine years had cause to reflect on that decision. I hope that if I am ever confronted with having to make a similar decision that I will have the moral courage to do it again.

There was, however, a price paid by those who spoke out against Winnie:

> Unfortunately, upon President Mandela's release from prison, for Mrs. Mandela the time had come to settle old scores. She telephoned me one evening at my law firm after I had presided over a press conference at which Mr. Mandela was present. She warned me to stay away from Mandela.

Other adversaries of Winnie also received threatening phone calls.

In his testimony, Bishop Storey referred to the "integrity, moral courage, and political courage" of those activists behind the MDM statement:

> Nobody will ever know how much it cost them to do that and how hard it was for them to do that. I've the greatest admiration for the courage which they displayed, and if only their courage had been upheld by other members of the movement, we wouldn't be sitting here today.

With Winnie sitting only a few yards from him, Storey concluded his testimony with one of the most powerful indictments the commission had heard in two years:

> I really hope and pray that these hearings will give us the truth, because throughout this saga I believe the truth has been trimmed to prevailing political whims by politicians, very often by people with political interests. Or the truth has been suppressed because people have vanished and feared for their lives.
>
> I really believe that to dispel this suffocating fog of silence and lies is very important for the future of this country.

He recalled words he had used in his address at Stompie's funeral in February 1989, referring to the deep hidden wounds the years of conflict had carved into people's souls—"the erosion of conscience, the devaluing of human life, the evasion of truth, and the reckless resort to violence."

> The primary cancer may be, and was, will always be the apartheid oppression, but the secondary infection has touched many of apartheid's opponents and eroded their knowledge of good and evil.
>
> One of the tragedies of life is it is possible to become like that which we hate most, and I have a feeling that this drama is an example of that. And unless this fact is recognized, then all the truth will not have been told, and we will never admit to what really happened in this case.
>
> And that's why I thought the kidnapping and the murder of Stompie Seipei were important beyond the normal horror we should feel, because at one level they may have been common-law crimes, but they are also about the ruthless abuse of power. Even given the latitude of a time of struggle, they resemble far too closely the abuses of

apartheid itself. We have got a right to know that we've left that era behind.

Storey paid tribute to Paul Verryn for the resilience he had shown in facing such virulent abuse from Winnie. For eight years, whenever his name had been mentioned in the press, he had always been associated with the idea of sodomy.

> To my knowledge, everybody who has publicly accused him of these dreadful misdemeanors has withdrawn those words—except one. It is my hope that before these hearings are ended, that last remaining accuser will use this opportunity to withdraw her words and to take back the accusations that she made against him.

Paul Verryn—now a bishop—took the stand, impressing all who heard him with the strength of his Christian beliefs. He blamed himself for not doing enough to protect Stompie once he had become aware of rumors that he was a police spy. He turned to Stompie's mother, Joyce Seipei, breaking into sobs as he asked for her forgiveness.

> I see that Mrs. Seipei is in the audience here today, and the thing that has been most difficult for me is that, having heard the allegations, I did not remove him from the mission house and get him to a place where he could be safe. And I think that if I had acted in another way he could be alive today. And so I want to apologize to Mrs. Seipei for my part in that.

Many in the audience also wept.

He next turned to Winnie, who was looking distinctly uncomfortable.

I don't know Mrs. Mandela really. We've met face-to-face briefly in my mission house once, and my feelings about her have taken me in many directions, as you can imagine. I long for our reconciliation. I have been profoundly, profoundly affected by some of the things that you have said about me, that have hurt me and cut me to the quick.

I have had to struggle to come to some place of learning to forgive, even if you do not want forgiveness or even think that I deserve to offer that to you. I struggle to find a way in which we can be reconciled for the sake of this nation and for the people that I believe God loves so deeply.

Winnie was asked whether she wanted to make any public response. She declined, saying through her lawyer that she preferred to "communicate" in private. She never did.

A FEW DAYS AFTER Morobe read the MDM's censure of Winnie, a new twist was added to the Stompie saga. Facing outright condemnation by the black political establishment, Winnie tried to divert attention by claiming in media interviews that Stompie was still alive and by disputing Joyce Seipei's identification of the corpse. "I am convinced Stompie has not been killed," she told a television station on 19 February. "That poor mother is being forced into admitting that is the corpse of her son." Winnie appealed to Stompie to "come forward," asserting that he had escaped from her house on New Year's Eve.

Joyce Seipei rejected Winnie's claim the next day. "Stompie is dead. I have seen the evidence. I have seen his body. I have seen his clothes. He is dead." Any claims to the contrary, she said, were lies.

But, stirred up by Winnie and her supporters, rumors persisted that Stompie was still alive. Even at his funeral on 25 February, there were murmurs in the crowd that the body in the coffin was not Stompie's.

The commission heard how Winnie had tried to cover up Stompie's murder by instructing one of her henchmen, Themba Mabotha, to spread reports from neighboring Botswana that Stompie was in a refugee camp there.

Mabotha had led a checkered life. An ANC-trained insurgent, he had defected to the police counterinsurgency unit at Vlakplaas and then absconded into the black underworld, ending up in Winnie's household in Soweto, where, he subsequently claimed, he had become her "sex slave." Police tapping Winnie's phones at her home and her office recorded several "love conversations" between them. In his testimony to the commission, Anton Pretorius, a former security police captain based in Soweto, described Mabotha as "a man of Olympic standards in that respect who left no women unsatisfied."

On 20 February, the police intercepted a phone call that Mabotha made to Winnie from Marble Hall, a village in Northern Transvaal; Mabotha said he needed money to return to Soweto and asked Winnie to telegraph money to the local post office. When arrested by police, he was found with several documents and the names and telephone numbers of Johannesburg newspapers. One of the documents related to Stompie. It contained a message that Winnie had told him to pass on to the media.

"I had to travel to Botswana on 18 February until the 20th and to phone from Botswana to tell the media that Stompie is in a refugee camp in Botswana," he told the police shortly after his arrest. "I also had to discredit the security police by saying that Stompie was running away from the police. However, I did not perform this instruction of Winnie Mandela."

Nevertheless, he did telephone newspapers from inside South Africa. The *Sowetan* reported on 22 February that it had received four calls in two days from Mabotha claiming that Stompie was in a refugee camp in Botswana. The *City Press* received similar calls.

After spending six months in police detention, Mabotha was executed by members of the police counterinsurgency unit.

I N ALL THE MEDIA INTERVIEWS Winnie gave during this period, denying any involvement in the kidnapping and assaults, not once did she mention she had been absent from Soweto at the time. Eighteen months later, however, when Jerry Richardson was put on trial for the murder of Stompie, a new version emerged. Winnie now claimed that she had been on a visit to Brandfort at the time, driving there before the assaults took place.

Richardson was the only person accused of the murder, but six others were charged on four counts of kidnapping and four counts of assault with intent to cause grievous bodily harm. Winnie was not among them. State prosecutors planned to bring charges against her only if the case against Richardson resulted in a conviction.

In their evidence, the three kidnap victims—Kenny Kgase, Thabiso Mono, and Pelo Mekgwe—related how Winnie had told them they were not fit to be alive; how she had accused Stompie of being a sellout; how she had beat them using her fists and then whips; and how members of the football team had joined in afterwards.

Richardson, for his part, denied killing Stompie. He also denied that Winnie had been present on 29 December 1988, when Stompie and the other kidnap victims were brought to her home.

The question of whether or not Winnie had been present during the beatings at her house was obviously crucial. Both the defense and the prosecution in the Richardson trial asked the court to make a finding on the matter.

On 24 May 1990, in the Rand Supreme Court, Justice O'Donovan found Richardson guilty of the murder of Stompie and guilty of kidnapping, assault, and attempted murder. He was sentenced to death but subsequently received a life sentence. The judge also ruled on Winnie's involvement: "The court finding on this issue is that Mrs. Mandela was present on 29 December for at least part of the time."

On 17 September 1990, Winnie was duly charged with four counts of kidnapping and four charges of assault with intent to cause grievous bodily harm, making her the eighth accused in the Stompie murder case.

Her trial opened on 4 February 1991 in the Rand Supreme Court in Johannesburg. From the start, it was marked by one drama after another. Four of the eight accused, including Katiza Cebekhulu, jumped bail and failed to appear. One of the three key state witnesses, Pelo Mekgwe, also went missing. At first it was thought he had been abducted, but he subsequently surfaced in Lusaka, saying that he had left South Africa with the help of ANC officials and alleging that he had been bribed by Winnie not to testify. Mekgwe's disappearance so frightened the two remaining key witnesses, Kenny Kgase and Thabiso Mono, that they refused to testify. Without their testimony, the trial would inevitably have collapsed. After a spell in the police cells, Kgase and Mono changed their mind, and the trial proceeded.

Winnie's defense was to deny everything. She claimed that the football club had ceased to exist by the time of the incident. She knew nothing about any of the "boys in the back" living on her premises. Nor had she met any of the four kidnap victims there. She produced two witnesses to corroborate her claim that on the evening of 29 December 1988 she had already left Soweto for Brandfort. Her remaining codefendants, including Xoliswa Falati and John Morgan, her driver, also denied she had been present.

Judge Stegmann's judgment on 13 May 1991 contained a devastating indictment of Winnie's character. He described her as "a calm, composed, deliberate, and unblushing liar." He was in no doubt that Winnie had masterminded the kidnapping of the four youths. But he was uncertain about her involvement in the beatings. The prosecution had failed to prove that her alibi in Brandfort was false, so there remained a reasonable possibility that she had gone there before the assaults began, as she had claimed. Nevertheless, she must have known about the kidnappings and beatings subsequently, but she willfully ignored the victims' plight. When pressed by Soweto leaders to release the youths, she refused to free them. By continuing to hold them for twenty days and by giving accommodation to those who had committed the assault, she had associated herself with the crime. At the very least, Stegmann concluded, Winnie was an accessory after the fact to all that had happened. He found her guilty on four counts of kidnapping and of being an accessory to the assaults; he sentenced her to a prison term of five years on the kidnapping charge and to an additional year for her role as an accessory to the assaults.

On appeal two years later, Winnie's six-year term was reduced to a two-year suspended sentence and payment of a fine of R15,000. The chief justice, Michael Corbett, although agreeing with the trial judge in finding Winnie guilty of kidnapping, accepted Winnie's claim that she had been far from her home during the beatings and consequently found her not guilty of being an accessory to the assaults. Winnie was now free to pursue her political ambitions.

Her codefendants, however, fared less well. Xoliswa Falati lost her appeal and was given a sentence of two years in prison. After serving eight months, she emerged threatening revenge against Winnie, claiming that she had lied at her trial to protect her. Winnie's driver, John Morgan, admitted that he too had lied to cover up for Winnie.

The facade behind which Winnie had sheltered for so long was beginning to crumble. Now she faced an array of accusers determined to pull it down further.

O N THE FIRST DAY of the TRC hearing, John Morgan took the stand. He described how Winnie had instructed him to take her bus—and Richardson, Katiza Cebekhulu, Falati, and Falati's daughter—to collect the four youths from Verryn's manse. They were taken to a room at the back of Winnie's house next to the Jacuzzi.

"The first person who started assaulting was Winnie Mandela." She singled out Stompie. "The others followed as well, assaulting the rest. . . . They would throw these boys in the air and let go of them so they would bounce back on the floor." Morgan said he himself did not participate in the assaults.

QUESTION: Did you see Stompie again?

MORGAN: Yes, the following day I saw him. I found him in a deformed state. His face was as round as a football. I tried to help him drink some coffee and fed him bread, as he was not in a position to help himself. And I felt pity for the boy.

QUESTION: And when was the next time you saw Stompie?

MORGAN: I saw him on the third day, and I found that he was in a critical condition. . . . Mrs. Mandela asked Asvat to assist him medically, and Asvat refused and said: "The boy should be sent to hospital."

On the fourth day, when he arrived at Winnie's house, she pointed to Stompie's prostrate body and told him "to pick up the dog and dump him." He refused. "I told Winnie I would never do something like that."

When Morgan was asked why he had previously lied about all this, he replied: "I was trying to protect Mrs. Mandela because she was my superior, she was my employer."

On the second day of the hearing, Falati took the stand. She too testified that Winnie had led the assaults.

QUESTION: Why did you agree to give false evidence to protect her?

FALATI: That was our culture, to protect our leaders. That is number one. And number two, I was scared of seeing how people were brutally beaten. I never knew that Mrs. Mandela was taking these hard drinks, and she is aggressive when she is taking that. She gives you orders. You don't reply. You are not to reason. You are to do and die. You have to take orders or die.

With her bulging eyes darting constantly around the hall, Falati became increasingly emotional and incoherent. Her testimony soon degenerated into a diatribe against Winnie:

She dehumanizes a person. She reduces a person to nothing. She regards herself as a demigod. She regards herself as a super being. She wants everybody to cover her up by all means. . . .

My hands are not dripping with the blood of African children. I've never compromised my comrades. I've never even compromised her. I went to prison for her as my leader. . . . She was so much ungrateful!

Some of Falati's accusations drew laughter from the audience. Winnie, looking glamorous in gold necklaces and an elegant silk suit, made the most of it, shaking her head, laughing, and indicating with a circular movement of her hand that Falati was a lunatic.

"She's busy indicating that I'm mad. She's pointing at me that I'm crazy," Falati complained to the chairman, Archbishop Tutu. The proceedings were in danger of descending into farce.

Falati was followed by Katiza Cebekhulu, another unstable character. He had told his story on several previous occasions, most recently in a book entitled *Katiza's Journey*, written by the journalist Fred Bridgland. But his various accounts of what had happened were inconsistent in places. After fleeing from South Africa with the help of Winnie and the ANC, Katiza had ended up in a Zambian prison before being rescued by a British member of parliament, Emma Nicholson, who had since appointed herself as his guardian and provided a refuge for him in exile.

Nicholson saw herself as a major player in the Winnie saga and wrote a foreword to *Katiza's Journey*, describing in melodramatic fashion, how, when she first heard Katiza tell his story, it was as though a window on South Africa's murky past had unexpectedly opened.

> The curtain drew back and we stared, horrified, into the inner turmoil of the bloody struggle by the African National Congress movement against apartheid. The mesmeric beauty of Winnie Mandela, wife of the imprisoned leader, Nelson Mandela, was lit up for a brief moment. Then her heroic public image crumbled to dust and ashes before us as the self-styled Mother of the Nation was revealed as the black mamba of the ANC. She turned into a witch as we listened.

Newly appointed to Britain's House of Lords, Nicholson arrived at the commission with Katiza in tow, rather like a colonial madam seeking to impose some sort of propriety on the fickle natives. Dressed in a canary yellow jacket, she sat with Katiza beside her, a saintly smile on her face.

On his own admission, Katiza was a petty thief who had unwittingly become caught up in the activities of Mandela United and had participated in the beatings of Stompie and the other kidnap victims.

Winnie, he said, had been the first to start whipping Stompie with a sjambok. "She had a heavy whip in her right hand which she was hitting him with again and again." The assaults lasted for about forty-five minutes, by which time Stompie's head had "gone soft." He described how Asvat had been called and had said Stompie should be taken to hospital.

But he then added a new allegation: Under a midnight moon on 31 December, he said, he had gone out into the garden of Winnie's home and by chance witnessed Winnie stabbing Stompie's prostrate body, with Richardson beside her. As Winnie looked on, he brought his arm down twice on a table to demonstrate the motion. And, pointing a finger at her, he barked: "I saw her kill Stompie." This was a piece of evidence that not even Richardson was prepared to support. In other evidence he gave, Katiza contradicted himself and appeared at times vague and evasive.

Outside the commission hearing, Nicholson continued her private war against Winnie. After meeting Joyce Seipei, Nicholson announced she would act on her behalf in helping to bring a private prosecution against Winnie. "The commission is not a court of law," she pronounced, posing with Mrs. Seipei at a photo call, "and murder demands a court of law." Then she flew off to England.

Richardson, in his testimony, added further detail. "I think we threw Stompie about seven times in the air and he fell to the ground. He was tortured so severely that at some stage I could see that he would ultimately die. . . . We did a lot of things. We kicked him. We just kicked him like a ball." Winnie, he said, joined in the assaults with sjambok and fists, but she also sat and watched.

From the audience, there came an anguished cry, a deep moan of agony, as Joyce Seipei, distraught at hearing the blunt details of Stompie's torture, broke down in tears. She was led from the hall, weeping.

Continuing his account, Richardson said that Stompie eventually confessed to being a "sellout," pleaded for mercy, and asked to be taken home. The next day, though "Stompie was in a very bad shape"; he was assaulted again and again. When it became obvious that Stompie was dying, Winnie ordered Richardson to kill him.

While members of the football club sang liberation songs to Winnie, Richardson and "Sledge," another member, took Stompie away. "I had to help Stompie along, because he was very ill, very weak, and he looked quite delirious. We dragged Stompie along."

They went to a piece of wasteland near a railway line, taking with them a pair of garden shears. "We made him lay on his back, and I put garden shears through his neck. . . . I slaughtered him. I slaughtered him like a goat." They then went back to "Mummy's house" and put the shears back in her garage.

"I killed Stompie under the instructions of Mummy," said Richardson. "Mummy never killed anyone but used us to kill a lot of people. She does not even visit us in prison! She used us!"

T HE EVIDENCE PLACING Winnie at the center of the assaults in December 1988 was overwhelming. Not a single witness testifying before the commission supported the alibi that had saved her from a prison sentence. Two kidnap victims—Thabiso Mono and Pelo Mekgwe—confirmed her involvement in the beatings.

The security police monitoring phone calls at her house also knew that her alibi was false. A former police captain, Daniel Bosman, told the commission that transcripts of her calls showed that she had been in Soweto between the evening of 29 December and 31 December, not in Brandfort as she claimed. The wiretap evidence had been withheld during Winnie's trial, he said, because it had been "too sensitive to use." The transcripts had subsequently been destroyed in the general purge of secret government documents before the 1994 elections. But Bosman was certain about what they proved.

One further piece of evidence that demolished Winnie's alibi but was never used during her 1991 trial was the medical record showing that she had brought Katiza to Asvat's surgery on 30 December. According to Winnie, her visit to the surgery had taken place on 29 December, before she left for Brandfort. Now a copy of the medical record was produced in public for the first time. But this led to an unexpected twist in the drama.

Asvat's nurse was Albertina Sisulu, long revered for her steadfast defiance of apartheid and widely trusted in the Soweto community. Her persecution at the hands of the security police had been as great as Winnie's, but throughout her ordeal she had remained rock solid. Though the friendship between the Sisulu and the Mandela families had lasted for years, Albertina had come to dislike and distrust Winnie's ruthless ambition and had fallen out with her over the activities of the football club. The names of Albertina's sons had been found on a hit list seized by police in Winnie's house.

Albertina had been particularly close to Dr. Asvat, regarding him almost as a son. For years she had remained silent in public about the football club. But she accepted an invitation to appear before

the truth commission, and in a rare television interview broadcast a
few weeks beforehand, she had identified her handwriting on a copy
of the medical record placing Winnie in Soweto on 29 December.

Her appearance before the commission on the sixth day of the
hearing was thus a crucial moment. With a few choice words, she
could have demolished Winnie's reputation. She certainly knew
enough. Even her own home had once been attacked by club members.

Yet suddenly this stalwart figure in the liberation movement
seemed uncertain and evasive. When the commission's lawyer,
Hanif Vally, handed her a copy of the medical record, she denied
the writing on it was hers. Vally was stunned.

VALLY: Now I know that is a bad copy, but are you sure that it is not
   your handwriting?

ALBERTINA: No. I don't write like this.

VALLY: I am sorry. I wasn't expecting this, Archbishop.

When he took her through a transcript of her television interview, Albertina stuck to her denial but was unable to explain the dis-
crepancy. One of the commissioners, Dumisa Ntsebeza, was bold
enough to challenge her:

My impression is that you are trying your very best to say as little as
possible about anything that might implicate Mrs. Mandela. . . . Can
it be that it is because she is your comrade? The Mandelas and the
Sisulus have come a very long way. And is it because for that very reason you wouldn't like to be the one who should be identified in South
African history as having dared to speak about your comrade in
terms that seem to suggest that she was involved in something like
the death of Dr. Asvat?

"I don't think it would be proper for me to come and tell lies," retorted Albertina indignantly. But her testimony descended into a rambling and tearful account of her suffering under apartheid. Not once did she utter a word of reproach.

Two days later, the Asvat family's lawyer helped restore for her a semblance of dignity by graciously announcing that after examining the medical card he had found the handwriting on it to be different from Albertina's. But the overall result was to leave a fine reputation tarnished. When Winnie walked across to embrace her after her testimony was over, Albertina hissed: "*Hayi, suka wena!*"—"Get away!"

The commission's inquiry into the murder of Asvat produced further revelations. It also brought the commissioners face-to-face with the methods of intimidation that Winnie habitually practiced. When the two Zulu men convicted of murdering Asvat arrived from prison to testify about Winnie's involvement, a group of eight men dressed in military fatigues and red berets were seen prowling around the hall. One of the convicts, Cyril Mbatha, immediately told his lawyer, Peter Soller, that he was afraid of testifying because of what might happen to his family. Soller asked the commission to provide protection for the family. He also disclosed that he himself, within forty-eight hours of agreeing to represent Mbatha, had received death threats. The commission's lawyer, Hanif Vally, then stepped in to complain that he knew of at least three instances where Winnie had interfered with witnesses, as in the case of Siyakamela.

Archbishop Tutu expressed his concern. "There is no doubt that some people are feeling intimidated," he said. Addressing Winnie's lawyer, Ishmael Semenya, Tutu said: "It may not emanate from your client, but it is clear there is a miasma covering some of the people who have come here and who might come here."

In his testimony, Cyril Mbatha said that during a meeting at her house Winnie had offered him and his accomplice, Thulani

Dlamini, the sum of R20,000 to kill Asvat. She then asked Katiza Cebekhulu to show them the way to the surgery, as Katiza himself had confirmed earlier. When they arrived there, Katiza pointed out Asvat to them, as he was passing from one building to another, dressed in a white safari suit. The next day, after making an appointment, Mbatha shot Asvat dead in his own room. Dlamini told the same story. Shortly after his arrest in 1989, Dlamini had given this account to the police, but they withheld the evidence.

Mbatha now turned sobbing to face Asvat's brother, Ebrahim: "All that I have done, I did it because I was tempted by a very clever person who was older than me. . . . I want the Asvat family to forgive. This is from the depth of my heart because I am the killer you have seen. I'm the first and the last."

Sitting directly across from Mbatha, Ebrahim Asvat was stricken with emotion, his genial face crumbling, until he held his head in his hands; his body shook, and the tears ran down his face.

As members of the Asvat family sat weeping together, Winnie, elegant as ever in a pillar-box red suit, smiled across the hall as a government minister, Mathews Phosa, came toward her, kissed her in greeting, and took her hand.

A FTER EIGHT DAYS of damning testimony against her, Winnie took the stand. Her strategy was to deny everything. She maintained that she had no knowledge of what went on in her backyard. She claimed she had disbanded the football club in 1987 after Nelson Mandela had told her to do so. She knew nothing about a disciplinary committee. She knew of no reason why her house had been burned down in 1988. She denied being present during the assaults on Stompie and the others. She denied all involvement in murder.

Her lawyer, Ishmael Semenya, took her briskly through the list of allegations.

SEMENYA: Jerry Richardson says you ordered the killing of Stompie.

MANDELA: That is ludicrous and the worst lunacy.

. . .

SEMENYA: Richardson says he killed [Lolo Sono and Siboniso Tshabalala] on your instructions.

MANDELA: That is ridiculous.

. . .

SEMENYA: There was evidence by Phumzile Dlamini that you assaulted her. What is your response?

MANDELA: I regard that statement as totally ludicrous.

. . .

SEMENYA: Mr. Nicodemus Sono said the last time he saw his son, he was in a vehicle, in a kombi, wherein you were a passenger. What is your reaction to this?

MANDELA: It is true that he last saw his son with me in that kombi when I went to collect him.

SEMENYA: He states that at the time Lolo Sono was injured.

MANDELA: I have no idea why he is making up that fabrication, save to say, I suppose, he is on this band wagon to lead these false fabrications.

. . .

SEMENYA: Did you order anybody to burn the house of Mrs. Chili?

MANDELA: Why would I order the burning of the house of Dudu Chili? I had absolutely nothing against her. I hadn't seen her for years.

.   .   .

SEMENYA: Do you know anything about a decision to kill her son
because he is refusing to play for the Mandela United Football
Club?

MANDELA: That logically sounds very ridiculous to me. I know nothing about it, and I don't know of incidents where boys were forced to
join the club. That was not my understanding of how they func-
tioned.

.   .   .

SEMENYA: Katiza [Cebekhulu] described how you made an ultimatum
to him that if he did not leave the country, you would kill him. What
is your response to this?

MANDELA: As far as I am concerned, Katiza is a mental patient and he
would have hallucinated like that. That is pure fabrication on his
part.

Under cross-examination, Winnie maintained the same ploy,
denying everything. She even denied she had accused Paul Verryn
of sodomizing African children. "I made no allegation against Paul
Verryn." The commission's lawyer, Hanif Vally, soon showed his
impatience:

VALLY: Mrs. Madikizela-Mandela, please don't play around.

MANDELA: I am not playing around. And I will not tolerate you speaking to me like that! I will not!

Despite Tutu's earlier slap on the wrist regarding the intimidation of witnesses, there was now another blatant example. During a
tea break, Joyce Seipei, who had sat solemnly through days of har-

rowing evidence, was threatened in the public lavatories by two members of Winnie Mandela's Women's League.

Tutu expressed his shock. "It is reprehensible conduct which I condemn in the strongest possible terms," he said. "It is disgraceful for people who claim to be mothers to subject her to the kind of treatment that I learn Mrs. Seipei was subjected to."

Winnie shrugged off the incident:

> Mr. Chairman, I think that this is a very grave allegation. We, as Women's League, regret very much, and we would request that we be given details of that information. We cannot believe that any mother, let alone members of the Women's League, would be involved in that kind of conduct.

The evasion and the lies continued. Winnie was asked to explain the meaning of a notorious speech she had made in April 1986 endorsing the necklace method of killing by which several hundred people had died. "Together, hand in hand, with our boxes of matches and our necklaces we shall liberate this country," Winnie had told her supporters.

Her answer now was that she was not exhorting her supporters to violence but merely giving "a description of the events of the time." Pressed on the point, she snapped: "I gave you my answer. I told you I was describing the situation at the time. If you don't like it, too bad."

Asked about the statement by the Mass Democratic Movement, read out by Murphy Morobe, urging the black community to shun her, she replied with a racist smear, saying it was all the work of a "cabal"—a name she used for her Indian opponents. "Azar Cachalia is part of the cabal. I learned later that they call Murphy Morobe 'Murphy Patel.' They were all part of the cabal."

Every piece of evidence implicating her, she dismissed as the work of her opponents and adversaries. Her accusers were either lunatics or liars or pawns of the security police. "Such fabrications are absolutely unbelievable. I do not know what you are talking about. None of these things took place whatsoever. . . . Really, for me to have [to] sit here and answer those ridiculous allegations, it is a source of great pain to me."

One of the commissioners, Yasmin Sooka, observed caustically: "If we believe your evidence, everyone else is lying."

"Yes," replied Winnie, "it's true."

But when lawyers pursued her relentlessly over her Brandfort alibi, she began to flounder. Time and again she was questioned about the medical record showing she had been in Soweto, but she could offer no plausible explanation.

DENIS KUNY: Your alibi is false, is that not so?

MANDELA: That is ludicrous.

DENIS KUNY: What I want to put to you is that if you look at the evidence that is presented before this commission, that the truth, in your hands, is putty which you can simply mold to suit your own ends.

MANDELA: That is a preposterous statement. I beg you not to talk to me like that.

At this crucial juncture, as Winnie began to look vulnerable, Archbishop Tutu intervened. As the lawyers looked on in exasperation, he suddenly invited Winnie's victims and members of their families to come forward for reconciliation. "Mrs. Seipei, could you please come up here, and others?" urged Tutu. "Where is Mrs. Seipei?"

In a grotesque climax to the hearing, Mrs. Seipei came forward to be embraced by Winnie. The gesture was hollow, a fake event made only for the cameras, and it reduced the hearing to a charade. Winnie beamed triumphantly. Mrs. Seipei returned to her seat, looking lost and alone. The rest of the questioning that followed was devoid of all purpose.

The hearing ended in further ignominy. In an emotional summary, Tutu praised Winnie as "a tremendous stalwart of our struggle, an icon of liberation":

> We can never forget her outstanding contribution to the struggle and her indomitable spirit. . . . She was an incredible inspiration. Many, many love you. Many, many say you should have been where you ought to be, the first lady of this country.

Seeing only the need to get the sinner to repent, Tutu pleaded with her to give some sign of contrition.

> There are people out there who want to embrace you. I still embrace you because I love you, and I love you very deeply. There are many out there who would have wanted to do so if you were able to bring yourself to say something went wrong. . . .
>
> I beg you, I beg you, I beg you, please. I have not made any particular finding from what has happened here. I speak as someone who has lived in this community. You are a great person, and you don't know how your greatness would be enhanced if you were to say: "Sorry, things went wrong, forgive me. I beg you."

Winnie's reply was terse:

> I will take this opportunity to say to the family of Dr. Asvat how deeply sorry I am. To Stompie's mother, how deeply sorry I am. I

have said so to her before a few years back, when the heat was very hot.

I am saying it is true, things went horribly wrong. I fully agree with that and for that part of those painful years when things went horribly wrong . . . for that I am deeply sorry.

On that false note, the hearing ended. Outside the hall, Caroline Sono, Lolo's mother, shouted: "She's the woman who murdered our children! I will not rest until I find my son's remains!" Nomsa Tshabalala, Siboniso's mother, described the hearing as "a complete sham."

Winnie meanwhile stood amid a crowd of supporters, laughing heartily until a motorcade whisked her away.

15

Operation Great Storm

L IKE THE ANC, the Pan-Africanist Congress (PAC) declared an armed struggle against the apartheid regime, but its efforts were insignificant. Only during the early 1990s, when negotiations for a political settlement were underway, did it make an impact by launching Operation Great Storm, a campaign against white targets.

The PAC was started in 1959 by a group of "Africanists" determined to break with the ANC's commitment to a multiracial struggle; the goal was to establish a purely African leadership to regain control of "the land" from white settlers. The PAC formed an armed wing, the Azanian People's Liberation Army (Apla), but for most of its existence it was consumed with its own internal squabbles.

When the ANC suspended its armed struggle in 1990, the PAC declared that it would fight on, and it launched the slogan "One Settler, One Bullet!" Little more was heard for the next three years, until a group of Apla members attacked the golf club in King William's Town in November 1992, killing four whites.

Apla's chief commander, Sabelo Phama, subsequently confirmed that he had authorized the attack and declared that 1993 would be "The Year of the Great Storm." A series of attacks on white farmers and on other white targets such as hotels, restaurants, and bars followed. In a television interview in April 1993, Phama was quite specific about his objective. He would aim his guns at children, he said, "to hurt whites where it hurts most."

Two incidents from this period gained worldwide attention. One was an attack on a church congregation in Cape Town in July 1993. The other was the death of an American exchange student, Amy Biehl, in Cape Town a month later.

There were about one thousand people attending a Sunday evening service at St. James Church in Kenilworth when two gunmen burst in through the door carrying automatic rifles and hand grenades. The congregation included a mixture of races, about half of them white, and a large contingent of Russian seamen who were regular visitors. The first gunman to enter opened fire with his automatic rifle. The other threw hand grenades coated with nails and then joined in the firing. Eleven people died and fifty-eight were injured, their bodies strewn amid the pews. Four of the dead were Russian seamen.

The order for the attack had been given by Apla's director of operations, Letlapa Mphalele. An Apla commander, Sichumiso Nonxuba, led the attack and subsequently died in a car accident. His main accomplice, Gcinikhya Makoma, a seventeen-year-old youth, was caught, tried, and given a twenty-three-year prison sentence. Two other youths—Bassie Mkhumbuzi and Thobela Mlambisi—had waited outside the church in a getaway car and were also caught.

Makoma, Mkhumbuzi, and Mlambisi applied for amnesty, claiming that their actions were politically motivated and inspired by Apla's quest for the land to be returned to the African people. At an amnesty hearing in July 1997, their testimony consisted mainly of PAC slogans and propaganda; they showed little understanding of the conflict they were caught up in. The only reasons they gave for targeting a church were that whites had used the church to oppress black people and that targeting whites would bring attention to their political aim of getting the land back.

"Whites were using churches to oppress blacks. They took our country using churches and bibles," said Mkhumbuzi. "The country was ruled by a white minority government regarded as illegitimate. The St. James churchgoers were regarded as part of the white minority."

When told that the church was used by many people other than whites, Mkhumbuzi apologized to the "non-whites" who were in the church at the time of the attack. "You have to understand how quickly things happen. . . . We could not differentiate between whites and coloreds."

The amnesty application was opposed by three members of the congregation, including Dawie Ackermann, a church official whose wife had died in the attack. Ackermann argued that there could be no justification for the attackers' claim that St. James Church was a legitimate political target; it was well known, he said, that the church was a place of worship for all races. "There is no reasonable link between the slaughter of a racially mixed congregation and any defined political goal," his lawyer told the TRC.

In his testimony to the amnesty committee, Ackermann described how he had had to step over the bodies of Russian seamen and through pools of blood to reach his wife, Marita, who had been sitting near the door. "I went forward to my wife, saw her sitting upright. I thought she might have survived, but she had not."

As he spoke of the devastating effect the incident had had on him and on his family, he broke into uncontrollable sobs. Pointing to the three perpetrators, he said:

> I find it impossible to be angry with them. I should have anger, but instead I am angry with my own family members. It is very difficult for me to say this, but I have a need to say it. I want them to hear it. I fight more with my children now than what I ever did before, and we fight about stupid things. I have never cried over the death of my

wife, other than . . . silent cries, but I have never had an emotional crying outburst.

While Mr. Makoma was testifying, . . . he talked about his tortures and [said] he was suicidal; I could identify with that. I thought to myself, and I wrote you a note to bring your cross-examination to an end, because what are we doing here? The truth, yes, but I looked at the way in which he answered you and his anger. How on earth are we going to be reconciled?

May I add one thing? I am sorry, while it is in my mind now. I went on record after the event to say that I hold no personal grudge, that I do not hate them, and I stand by that. I also held out reconciliation to them, and I believe with all my heart—because I've experienced reconciliation with God, through Jesus Christ—that it is available to everybody, including to them. And I held that out to them at the time, and I still do so now.

Ackermann was asked whether he thought the attack could be justified in the circumstances.

ACKERMANN: It is difficult for me to answer that because I am so subjectively close to the happening.

In retrospect I can see now that the apartheid government was an evil government, that in some respects that the opposition to it was legitimate.

I must tell you that, in my own personal opinion, I think that the gravity of the attack and the fact that it was a defenseless church, people at worship, that I cannot under any circumstances condone that in terms of an armed struggle, and I must stand with that answer.

QUESTION: Is there anything else you would like to say to the committee at this stage, Mr. Ackermann?

ACKERMANN: Yes. May I address the applicants? May I ask the applicants to turn around and to face me?

The three men turned around slowly to face him.

ACKERMANN: This is the first opportunity we've had to look each other in the eye and talk. I want to ask Mr. Makoma, who actually entered the church—my wife was sitting right at the door when you came in; she was wearing a long, blue coat; can you remember if you shot her?

MAKOMA: I do remember that I fired some shots, but I couldn't identify; I don't know whom did I shoot or not, but my gun pointed at the people.

ACKERMANN: It is important for me to know if it is possible, as much as it is important for your people who suffered, to know who killed. I don't know why it is so important for me, but it just is.

His voice trailed off.

ACKERMANN: If you don't remember, I will accept that. I have heard you through your attorney say, and into the microphone, "[We] apologize." . . . I would like to hear from each one of you, as you look me in the face, that you are sorry for what you have done, that you regret it and that you want to be personally reconciled.

MAKOMA: We are sorry for what we have done. It was the situation in South Africa. Although people died during that struggle, we didn't do that out of our own will. It is the situation that we were living under.

We are asking from you, please do forgive us. All that we did, we can see the effects today.

The other two responded with similar apologies, and then Ack-ermann said: "I want you to know that I forgive you uncondition-ally. I do that because I am a Christian, and I can forgive you for the hurt that you have caused me, but I cannot forgive you the sin that you have done. Only God can forgive you for that."

L IKE THE ST. JAMES MASSACRE, the death of Amy Biehl con-cerned the killing of the innocent. A twenty-six-year-old Ful-bright scholar, she had come to Cape Town to work on a research project at the University of the Western Cape, relishing the pros-pect of witnessing South Africa's transition to democracy. She was fully aware of how difficult the transition would be. In a letter to the editor of the *Cape Times* in June 1993, two months before she died, she wrote: "Racism in South Africa has been a painful experience for blacks and whites, and reconciliation may be equally painful. However, the most important vehicle towards reconciliation is open and honest dialogue."

At the end of a successful visit, she was preparing to return home to the United States. A farewell party was to be held for her that night. Though friends had warned her that the mood in the town-ships was ugly, in the afternoon she decided to give three black friends a lift home to Gugulethu. As she was approaching a service station in Gugulethu, she ran into a mob of youths throwing stones at passing traffic.

The youths had spent the afternoon at a meeting of the Pan-Africanist Student Organization (Paso), the PAC's student wing, lis-tening to speeches urging them to join the war against the whites and shouting slogans like "One Settler, One Bullet!"

"The order was, we should make South Africa ungovernable,

burn down government vehicles—and every white person we came across was an enemy," said one of the youths, Ntobeko Peni.

When a brick shattered her car window, striking her on the head, Amy Biehl got out and stumbled, bleeding, across the road to the service station. Her friends shouted that she was "a comrade," but the mob ignored them, pelting her with stones. Mongezi Manquina testified:

> We chased after her, and I tripped her, and she fell down next to a box with the name "Caltex" on it. I asked one of the persons in the crowd for a knife . . . and moved toward [her] as she was sitting down in front of the box facing us. I took the knife and stabbed her once. . . .
>
> I stabbed Amy Biehl because I saw her as a "target," a "settler."

Four youths—Manquina, Peni, Mzikhona Nofemela, and Vusumzi Ntamo—were convicted of Biehl's murder and sentenced to eighteen years' imprisonment each. All four applied for amnesty, arguing that they were furthering the aims of Operation Great Storm to make the country ungovernable and to "kill, maim, or injure settlers."

Their amnesty hearing was held in July 1997, in the same week as the St. James massacre hearing. It was attended by Amy's parents, Peter and Linda Biehl, who told the amnesty committee that they would not oppose amnesty. "It is your process, not ours. We cannot, therefore, oppose amnesty if it is granted on the merits. In the truest sense it is for the community in South Africa to forgive its own. . . . Amnesty is clearly not for Linda and Peter Biehl to grant."

Manquina told the TRC that he had stabbed Biehl because, the way he saw it then, "She was white. She was an oppressor." The political motivation for killing her was that "that would make us proud, and the government would respond to the demands of the people."

"Isn't it [the case] that you were involved in a mindless savage attack on this young woman and that it was not politically motivated?" Judge Andrew Wilson asked Peni. Peni replied: "Our killing Amy Biehl had everything to do with politics—the unrest at the time and international attention helped bring South Africa to where we are today." He had not heard Biehl's friends pleading for her to be left alone, as she was a comrade, but even if he had, he would not have acted differently—"A white person was a white person in our eyes."

"During those days we were told to assist Apla," said Nofemela. "If you were killing a white person, it's how we were going to get our land back." A TRC lawyer, Robin Brink, argued that the attack could not have been politically motivated; it was rather an act of "wanton brutality, like a pack of sharks smelling blood." Nofemela replied: "No. That's not true. We are not such things. . . . It's because she came to Gugulethu at a wrong moment. . . . That day we were very emotional and we find Amy in our location."

All four men contended that killing whites would help to achieve the PAC's aim of reclaiming the land for the African people. Yet under questioning, none of them could explain what that meant beyond quoting party slogans, nor could they explain how the killing of an innocent white women would advance their cause. Each applicant, however, made a perfunctory apology. "When I look closely at what I did," said Peni, "I realize it was bad. We took part in killing someone we could have used to achieve our own aims. I ask Amy's parents, friends, relatives—I ask them to forgive me."

T HREE MONTHS LATER, in October 1997, at a TRC hearing on
armed forces, Apla leaders were called upon to justify their
policies. They made it clear that they regarded all whites as "the
enemy" and hence as legitimate targets. The militarization of white
society had made all whites, even those who were formally noncom-
batants, members of the security establishment, said Dan Mofo-
keng, a former Apla commander and at the time of the hearing a
brigadier in the new national army.

> It would be a fallacy in the context of white South Africa to talk about
> innocent civilians. . . . In all honesty, the term soft or hard target did
> not exist in our vocabulary, and it was a foreign concept. All that mat-
> tered were the political and psychological benefits that the organiza-
> tion would derive from such military operations.

The decision to launch attacks against white civilians was "aimed
at carrying out legitimate reprisals in forcing the regime to end the
killings of African people by intensifying the armed struggle."

> This was done both in reprisal and self-defense, and it must be
> understood that the war of liberation, as seen by the Azanian People's
> Liberation Army, was a war of self-defense.
> The only requirement was proportionality. It should therefore
> not surprise anyone that targets like St. James Church, King
> William's Town golf club, Heidelberg Tavern, et cetera . . . were
> selected.

Apla forces that had carried out such operations had followed the
orders of their commanders, and their orders had come from the
highest echelons of the military leadership: "We do not, therefore,
regret that such operations took place, and there is therefore noth-

ing to apologize for, because we believe in the justness of our war and the correctness of our struggle."

Letlapa Mphalele, who had ordered the St. James Church attack, added his own gloss:

> We did not attack white civilians, but we destroyed European invaders, dispossessors, criminals. . . .
>
> He who benefits by crime is guilty of that crime and every white person in this country benefited from the crime of dispossession, benefited from the crime of colonialism, benefited from the crime of apartheid.

Mphalele ended with an attack on the TRC:

> This whole farce, this whole circus is doomed for failure for obvious reasons, because you cannot reconcile the dispossessed and the dispossessor, you cannot reconcile the oppressor and the oppressed, and the fact of the matter is that the whites are still firmly in power, the whites are still calling the shots.

At an amnesty hearing in Bloemfontein in 1997 for Apla members who had taken part in the killing of white farmers as part of Operation Great Storm, Mphalele, who was then serving in the new national defense force as a brigadier, held a media conference acknowledging his involvement in the planning and execution of the operation. His "proudest moment," he said, "was seeing whites dying in the killing fields."

IN JUNE 1998, the TRC's amnesty committee announced that it had decided to grant an amnesty to the three Apla members involved in the St. James Church massacre. It accepted that they believed "they were advancing the struggle of the PAC which was waging a war against the National Party–led government." Therefore, they met the criteria for acting with a political objective.

A month later, the TRC's amnesty committee granted amnesty to the killers of Amy Biehl. It explained:

> One of the applicants said during evidence that they all submitted to the slogan "One Settler, One Bullet." To them this meant every white person was an enemy of the black people.
>
> At that moment, to them, Amy Biehl was a representative of the white community. They believed that by killing white civilians Apla was sending a serious political message to the government.

Apla believed that by intensifying activity, the political pressure on the government would increase, demoralizing it and compelling it to hand over power to the masses: "When the conduct of the applicants is viewed in that light, it must be accepted that their crime was related to a political objective."

16

Findings

A FTER TWO AND A HALF YEARS of endeavor, the TRC was
ready to produce its report. It had traveled farther than it had
once thought possible, traversing a landscape littered with shattered
lives, reaching hidden areas of the past it never knew existed. From
every corner of the country, it had heard tales of murder, torture,
and brutality on a scale it never expected to find. In a relentless rep-
etition of horror, some 21,000 victims had come forward to testify
about their own ordeals or about the plight of others. Many more
tales were never told.

The TRC had listened to politicians and generals, bombers and
torturers, spies and saboteurs. It had heard testimony from every
part of the political spectrum, from extremist Afrikaners on one
hand to extremist Africanists on the other. It had held special hearings for businessmen, for churchmen, for the legal profession, for
the media, seeking to ascertain their degree of complicity in the
apartheid system. It had searched through reams of government
records, launched investigations into secret burial grounds and
chemical and biological warfare projects, and examined everything
from the activities of vigilante groups to necklacing.

Even so, the TRC acknowledged that the picture it had gained
was far from complete. In some places it had barely scratched at the
surface. Much more remained buried than had been exhumed. It
cited in particular the fact that the destruction of tons of government records relating to the police, the defense force, and the

national intelligence agencies had left gaping holes in its reconstruction of the past.

> The former government deliberately and systematically destroyed a
> huge body of state records. . . . The urge to destroy gained momen-
> tum in the 1980s. . . . By the 1990s the process of destruction of
> records and documents had become a coordinated endeavor, sanc-
> tioned by the cabinet, with the aim of denying a new government
> access to incriminating evidence and [of] sanitizing the history of the
> apartheid era.

The destruction of records by the security establishment had
continued even after a new democratic government had been
installed in 1994. The National Intelligence Agency was still
destroying records systematically as late as November 1996, in defiance of government instructions. The defense force had been particularly unhelpful about releasing documents.

> The destruction of state documentation probably did more to under-
> mine the investigative work of the commission than any other single
> factor. . . .
>   Numerous investigations of gross violations of human rights were
> severely hampered by the absence of documentation.

The submissions made by former officials from the police and
the defense force were often intended to be of little assistance.

> The usefulness of these submissions varied widely, but they were
> generally disappointing and did little to further the work of the com-
> mission. Frequently, they consisted of little more than recitations of
> the policies under which these groups operated and [of] often uncon-
> vincing apologies for excesses committed.

The TRC cited in particular its disappointment with de Klerk's contribution.

> As one who had done so much to turn the tide of South African history, his evasiveness and unwillingness candidly to acknowledge the full burden of the [National Party's] responsibility seemed to the commission to be a missed opportunity to take the reconciliation process forward.

The white community in general had shown similar disdain.

> The white community often seemed either indifferent or plainly hostile to the work of the commission, and certain media [the Afrikaans press] appear to have actively sought to sustain this indifference and hostility.
>
> With rare individual exceptions, the response of the former state, its leaders, institutions, and the predominant organs of civil society of that era, was to hedge and obfuscate. Few grasped the olive branch of full disclosure.
>
> Even when political leaders and institutional spokespersons of the former state claimed to take full responsibility for the actions of the past, these sometimes seemed to take the form of ritualized platitudes rather than genuine expressions of remorse.
>
> Often, it seemed to the commission, there was no real appreciation of the enormity of the violations of which these leaders and those under them were accused, or of the massive degree of hurt and pain their actions had caused.

Nevertheless, despite the gaps in its information, the TRC was confident about the findings it had made. It started by concurring with a number of UN decisions that had declared apartheid "a crime against humanity." It made this finding, it said, not with the intention of calling for prosecution but with the intention of recognizing the finding as "a fundamental starting point for reconciliation in South Africa."

> The recognition of apartheid as an oppressive and inhuman system of social engineering is a crucial point of departure for the promotion and protection and the advancement of reconciliation in South Africa.

This verdict, it said, was supported by testimony it had heard from key quarters of the white community. De Klerk himself, in his appearance before the TRC in May 1997, had described apartheid as a system that caused great suffering to millions of people. Five senior judges, in their submissions on behalf of the judiciary past and present, had declared that apartheid was, in itself, a gross violation of human rights. Four former National Party cabinet ministers, when testifying about the workings of the State Security Council, had acknowledged that apartheid had no moral base. Furthermore, the Dutch Reformed Church, which for years had provided biblical cover for apartheid, now admitted that it was neither scripturally nor morally justified.

The TRC acknowledged that there were whites at the time who sincerely believed that apartheid—or "separate development," as they preferred to call it—was a defensible policy intended to solve complex racial issues. Archbishop Tutu, in his foreword to the TRC report, summed up his own view:

> I cannot be asked to be neutral about apartheid. It is an evil system. But I *am* even-handed, in that I will let an apartheid supporter tell me what . . . sincerely moved him or her, and what his or her insights and perspectives were; and I will take these seriously into account in making my finding.

I do believe that there were those who supported apartheid who genuinely believed that it offered the best solution to the complexities of a multiracial land with citizens at very different levels of economic, social, and educational development.

I do not doubt that many who supported apartheid believed that it was the best policy in the circumstances to preserve their identity, language, and culture, and those of other peoples as well.

I do believe such people were not driven by malicious motives. Many believed God had given them a calling to help civilize benighted natives.

I do not for a single moment question the sincerity of those who believed that they were defending their country and what they understood to be its Western Christian values against the atheistic communist onslaught.

No, I do not call their motives into question. I do, however, condemn the policy they applied.

The TRC took particular note of the "virulent form of anticommunism"' that had taken root in South Africa after the National Party's election victory in 1948. By the 1960s, virtually all opposition to the government was labeled "communist." All forms of conflict and instability were seen as "avenues for Soviet involvement." Many whites genuinely believed that what they were caught up in was a deadly struggle for survival against the communist threat in which any actions taken against their adversaries were justified.

As examples, the TRC quoted excerpts from testimony it had heard. One example was from the former police minister, Adriaan Vlok:

The mother organizations of the liberation movement, the ANC/PAC, were seen with justification as fronts and tools of the Marxist-communist threat against the country. . . . I believed and still believe that if the forces of communism and Marxism since the 1950s were allowed to take over South Africa, our country would today be destroyed, impoverished, and a backward country with an atheist communist ideology as the government policy. . . . I saw it as part of my duty to fight against such thoughts, programs, or initiatives and to ensure that these objectives were not successful.

Craig Williamson, the former intelligence officer and bomber, went a stage further:

[The] South African security forces gave very little cognizance to the political motivation of the . . . liberation movements, beyond regarding them as part and parcel of the Soviet onslaught against the civilized/free/democratic Western world. This fact, I believe, made it easier for the most violent actions to be taken against the liberation movements and their supporters, because such violence was not aimed at our own people, but at a "foreign" enemy.

"Soviet expansion," de Klerk had told the TRC, "was as real as the sun in the sky." Tutu acknowledged that Soviet communism had played a "central, indeed pivotal" role in the geopolitics of the apartheid era. Nations had defined themselves in terms of their relationship to communism. They had decided who their allies were, what their defense budgets should be, and which surrogate states to support on that basis. The communist threat was seen to be so serious, said Tutu, that it led prominent democracies, like the United States, to support some of the world's worst dictatorships, such as Pinochet's government in Chile. Similarly, the United States had been willing to subvert democratically elected governments by supporting internal dissidents merely because the governments were communist-influenced. "The West did not seem to care much about the human rights records of their surrogates." The South African government, then, in its own crusade against "communism," was far from being an exception.

But after taking into account all these factors, the TRC was in no doubt about the central issue: "At the heart of the conflict stood an illegal, oppressive, and inhuman system imposed on the majority without their consent." Therefore, those who fought against the apartheid system were clearly fighting for a just cause.

Over many decades, anti-apartheid activists had tried to bring about change by nonviolent means but to no avail. Only when peaceful methods had failed did they resort to armed resistance. Their activities in seeking to oppose and remove apartheid could not be morally equated with those seeking to sustain and uphold it.

Nevertheless, although their cause was just, this did not mean that all acts carried out in order to destroy apartheid were necessarily legal, moral, and acceptable.

> Just war does not legitimate the perpetration of gross violation of human rights in pursuit of a just end. . . .
>
> Violations committed in the cause of a just war should be subjected to the same rigorous scrutiny as violations committed by the former state. . . .
>
> A just cause does not exempt an organization from pursuing its goals through just means.

The TRC made one further distinction between the government and its opponents:

> The measures used to assess the actions of a legally constituted and elected government cannot be the same as those used in the case of a voluntary grouping of individuals who come together in pursuit of

certain commonly agreed goals. A state has powers, resources, obligations, responsibilities, and privileges that are much greater than
those of any group within that state. It must therefore be held to a
higher standard of moral and political conduct than are voluntary
associations operating within its political terrain—particularly where
they operate underground with limited communication and less-
developed structures of accountability.

H AVING LAID DOWN its criteria on accountability, the TRC
delivered its verdict on the principal protagonists.

It was Botha's government in the late 1970s, the TRC declared,
that had entered "the realm of criminal misconduct." Previous governments had ruled by repression. But Botha's government had
adopted a policy of killing its opponents. It was also responsible for
the widespread use of torture, abduction, arson, and sabotage. At
meetings of the State Security Council, leading members—including Botha, Malan, Vlok, and the heads of the security forces—had
used terminology like "eliminate," "take out," and "wipe out,"
knowing full well that this would result in the killing of political
opponents.

> This rhetoric made no distinction between persons engaged in mili-
> tary operations or acts of terrorism and those who opposed apartheid
> by lawful or peaceful means. The word "terrorist" was used con-
> stantly but never defined. Nor was a distinction drawn between
> activists and those who only supported or associated with them. All
> were lumped together as one target—a single category of persons to
> be killed. . . .
>
> In the opinion of the commission, the kind of rhetoric employed

by politicians and SSC functionaries was reckless, inflammatory, and an incitement to unlawful acts.

SSC documents had been phrased deliberately to allow for "plausible deniability." But, said the TRC, it rejected such attempts by politicians to ensure that their subordinates took responsibility for "acts of which politicians are the intellectual authors."

Botha was specifically found responsible for ordering Vlok and the former police commissioner, van der Merwe, to destroy Khotso House in Johannesburg in 1988. This decision, said the TRC, "greatly enhanced the prevailing culture of impunity and facilitated the further gross violations of human rights by senior members of the security forces."

The TRC's final verdict on Botha was that "by virtue of his position as head of state and chairperson of the SSC, [he] contributed to and facilitated a climate in which . . . gross violations of human rights could and did occur, and as such is accountable for such violations."

THE "REALM OF CRIMINAL MISCONDUCT" extended into de Klerk's period in office. The TRC was highly critical of de Klerk's failure to tackle the problem of the "third force"—the network of security force members and right-wing groups seeking to wreck any transition that would lead to an ANC government. Though it acknowledged that de Klerk had taken steps to dismantle the national security management system he had inherited from Botha, the TRC said he had made "little obvious attempt" to curb third force activities and had ignored pleas from senior officers like General Steyn, the defense force chief of staff, to institute a thorough investigation. He had failed to take action, concluded the TRC, "either deliberately or by omission."

The TRC cited testimony it had heard that "de Klerk was aware that his commissioner of police [van der Merwe] had been involved in illegal activity regarding the bombing of Khotso House"; and yet, despite this, "he continued to retain his position as the most senior policeman in the country." Similarly, despite allegations that had emerged from General Steyn's investigation into third force activities implicating the chief of the defense force and the chief of the army, de Klerk had assigned them the task of deciding what action should be taken.

> While . . . de Klerk may well have been constrained by the delicate balance within the security forces and a fear that firmer action could lead to a schism between the [National Party's] agenda and disgruntled security force members, the commission notes that no such constraint applied at the time that . . . de Klerk made his submission to the commission. De Klerk made no attempt to take the commission into his confidence and to explain the very real dilemmas and difficulties that he faced at the time.
>
> It was precisely this seeming unwillingness to take more significant action against individual security force members and structures that led to a public perception that the violence, if not part of an NP agenda, was in some way in its interest.

De Klerk's testimony, said the TRC, had "lacked candor," He was "morally accountable for concealing the truth from the country when he, as executive head of government, was under an obligation not to do so."

> The commission finds that F. W. de Klerk failed to make full disclosure to the commission of gross human rights violations committed

by senior members of government and senior members of the South African police despite being given the opportunity to do so.

The commission finds that his failure to do so constitutes a material nondisclosure, thus rendering him an accessory to the commission of gross human rights violations.

T HE TRC THEN TURNED its attention to Inkatha (IFP) and Buthelezi. It depicted Buthelezi as a fervent ally of the apartheid government, as determined as Botha and de Klerk to crush the ANC. "During the latter half of the 1980s, Inkatha began to draw increasingly upon the support of the South African government," said the report. "The South African government not only welcomed but actively promoted this covert alliance with Inkatha, as it fell squarely into its response to what it saw as the total revolutionary onslaught against it."

At a time when it portrayed itself nationally and abroad as a liberation movement, the IFP, through the intervention of its senior members, was receiving direct financial and logistical assistance from the highest levels of the apartheid state's security apparatus.

By the latter half of the 1980s, said the TRC, government and Inkatha had "united against a common enemy, the UDF/ANC and their affiliates." An early example of their collaboration was the pact by the defense force to train Inkatha "hit squads" in the Caprivi Strip under the plan known as Operation Marion. The activities of these hit squads subsequently became widespread in KwaZulu and Natal. Those whom the TRC found accountable for hit squad activity included Botha, Malan, and Buthelezi.

The statistics it had compiled, said the TRC, provided "the most devastating indictment" of the role of the IFP in political violence. The statistics showed that for a period of twelve years, from 1982 to 1994, Inkatha had been involved in a "systematic pattern" of violence against its ANC/UDF opponents.

During the 1990–1994 period, when the conflict with the ANC was at its peak, the IFP was "the foremost perpetrator" of gross human rights violations in KwaZulu and Natal. IFP violations constituted about half of all violations reported to the TRC's Durban office for this period, and over one-third of the total number of violations committed during the thirty-four-year period of the TRC's mandate.

The statistics showed that Inkatha was responsible, in the mandate period, for some 3,800 killings in the Natal and KwaZulu area, compared with some 1,100 attributed to the ANC and some 700 to the police. On a national scale, Inkatha was also "the major perpetrator of killings"; it was responsible for more than 4,500 deaths, compared to 2,700 attributed to the police and 1,300 to the ANC.

The TRC held Buthelezi responsible for making speeches "which had the effect of inciting supporters of [Inkatha] to commit acts of violence." He was also held responsible for authorizing a paramilitary training program in 1993–1994 that was intended to enable Inkatha "to prevent by force the holding of elections." In sum, said the TRC, Buthelezi—in his capacity as president of Inkatha, as chief minister in the KwaZulu government, and as police minister for thirteen years—was accountable for the commission of numerous human rights violations, including murder.

T HE TRC DEALT WITH the ANC in an equally forthright manner. During its armed struggle, said the TRC, the ANC had engaged in bombing and land mine campaigns resulting in civilian casualties. In fact, the TRC pointed out, MK operations "ended up killing fewer security force members than civilians." The TRC accepted that targeting civilians was not ANC policy. Nevertheless:

> Whatever the justification given by the ANC for such acts—misin-
> terpretation of policy, poor surveillance, anger, or differing interpre-
> tations of what constituted a "legitimate military target"—the people
> who were killed or injured by such explosions are all victims of gross
> violations of human rights perpetrated by the ANC.

These violations included such actions as the 1983 bombing of the air force headquarters in Church Street, Pretoria; the bombing of the Amanzimtoti shopping center; the bombing of Magoo's Bar in Durban; and the land mine campaign.

The TRC also censured the ANC for regarding state informers, state witnesses, and askaris as legitimate targets for assassination. Their killing, it said, constituted gross violations of human rights.

Furthermore, the ANC was held "morally and politically accountable" for creating a climate during the armed struggle that allowed its supporters inside the country to regard violence against opponents as a legitimate part of a "people's war."

> Violations, including killings, attempted killings, and severe ill-treat-
> ment, were committed by ANC supporters against urban councillors
> and rural headmen, members of the IFP, and other people perceived
> to be collaborators of the system or enemies of the ANC.

During the period from 1990 to 1994, the ANC was responsible for the death and injury of hundreds of its opponents. Although there was no evidence to support Inkatha's claims that the ANC had set out to kill IFP officials by the hundreds, the TRC nevertheless found the ANC and UDF to be responsible for the death of seventy-six of them. "The killings of the IFP office-bearers amount to a systematic pattern of abuse, entailing deliberate planning."

The ANC had also contributed to the spiral of violence in the 1990s by creating and arming self-defense units that, uncontrolled and unaccountable, "took the law into their own hands" and committed atrocities.

Furthermore, the ANC was guilty of serious abuses in its camps in Angola and elsewhere. "Suspected agents" had been routinely subjected to torture and other forms of severe ill-treatment. Some had been executed without proper legal procedure. Adequate steps had not been taken against perpetrators, some of whom were senior officials.

The TRC took the UDF and its leadership to task for failing to exert political and moral authority over supporters who were involved in UDF campaigns and who resorted to violent attacks on their opponents, including the practice of necklacing.

THE VERDICT ON WINNIE MANDELA was damning. She was found to be the central figure in the Mandela United Football Club, and she was held personally responsible for the outbreak of killing, torture, assaults, and arson in Soweto during the late 1980s. Though started with good intentions, the club had developed into her private vigilante unit. Club members had been involved in at least eighteen murders. Many of the club's operations that led to the killings were launched from her home. Winnie not only sanctioned the club's criminal activities but in some cases participated in them. Those who opposed her and the club were branded as informers, hunted down, and killed.

The TRC examined a number of crimes in which Winnie had been implicated and delivered judgments on several of them. It found that she had participated in the abduction of Lolo Sono and Siboniso Tshabalala, both of whom were subsequently assumed to have been murdered. It said she was involved in and responsible for the attempted murder of Lerotodi Ikaneng.

Of particular significance, the TRC found that Winnie had initiated the assaults on Stompie Seipei and three other youths abducted from the Methodist manse on her orders. It dismissed the alibi she had produced during her trial, which claimed that she had been in Brandfort and not at home when the assaults took place—the one factor that had enabled her to escape a prison sentence during her appeal.

"In all probability," said the TRC, "she was aware of Seipei's condition"—that he was close to death after being severely injured during the assaults at her house. "The commission finds . . . that she failed to act responsibly in taking the necessary action required to avert his death."

T HE VERDICT ON THE Pan-Africanist Congress was short but sharp. The TRC lambasted PAC leaders for the "flimsiness and lack of coherence" of their submission. "The PAC offered very little by way of information on any of its activities." The TRC found that although the PAC claimed to be involved in a military struggle, the primary targets of its operations were civilians—white civilians in general, and white farmers in particular. It rejected the PAC's explanation that its killing of white farmers constituted acts of war.

The commission finds PAC action directed towards both civilians
and whites to have been a gross violation of human rights for which

the PAC and Apla leadership are held to be morally and politically responsible and accountable.

T WO MONTHS BEFORE its report was due to be published in October 1998, the TRC, in accordance with its statutory obligations, sent summaries of its findings to some 200 individuals and organizations that it had named in connection with human rights abuses. The list included Botha, de Klerk, Malan, Vlok, Buthelezi, several prominent ANC figures, and Winnie Mandela. Their reaction was uniformly hostile.

De Klerk was livid that he had been named "an accessory to gross human rights violations." He vehemently denied being involved in any cover-up of the bombing of Khotso House in 1988 and demanded changes to the TRC's findings against him; he was concerned above all, as before, about his personal reputation. When the TRC refused to oblige, de Klerk applied to the High Court on 26 October for an interdict preventing publication of a thirty-line passage referring to him; he succeeded in forcing the TRC to remove the passage from its report "temporarily," pending a further court hearing in 1999.

Far more of a shock was the ANC's reaction. Outraged that it had been roundly condemned for war crimes, the ANC insisted on a meeting with the TRC, intending to get it to rewrite its findings. The TRC invited the ANC to make a written submission but refused a meeting. The ANC retaliated by accusing the TRC of "criminalizing" the anti-apartheid struggle. Its findings were "capricious and arbitrary." The TRC had "grossly misdirected itself."

Whatever the efforts to besmirch our struggle by denouncing it as gross violation of human rights, the ANC, Umkhonto we Sizwe

[MK], and the millions of people who were part of this struggle
will always be proud of what they did to ensure that, in the process
of the destruction of a vile system, they did not themselves resort to
vile methods of struggle on the basis that the means justified the
ends.

The abuses for which the ANC was said to be politically and
morally accountable were inseparable from the consequences of the
legitimate struggle. By making findings that in effect delegitimized
the struggle against apartheid, the TRC was according legitimacy
to real gross violations of human rights.

On 28 October, the day before the TRC's report was due to be
handed to President Mandela at a public ceremony in Pretoria and
published simultaneously, the ANC applied to the Cape High
Court for an urgent interdict to block its publication. The decision
to apply for the interdict was made by Thabo Mbeki, the ANC's
president and Mandela's designated successor as head of state; Mandela himself took no part in it.

In the early morning of 29 October, while a High Court judge in
Cape Town listened to the ANC's lawyers make their case to halt
publication, Archbishop Tutu in Pretoria was unable to conceal his
anger and frustration. At an impromptu press conference on the
pavement outside the State Theater, he warned of the dangers of a
new tyranny.

I have struggled against a tyranny. I did not do that to substitute
another, and I will be me if there is another tyranny and an abuse of
power. Let them know that I will oppose them with every fiber of my
being. That is who I am. . . .

I didn't struggle in order to remove one set of those who thought
they were tin gods and replace them with others who are tempted to
think they are.

In one media interview after another, he pursued the same theme: "We can't assume that yesterday's oppressed will not become tomorrow's oppressors. We have seen it happen all over the world, and we shouldn't be surprised if it happens here." Tutu urged all South Africans to be on their guard against government abuse and corruption.

> We so easily jettison the ideals we had when we were struggling. It is important that we retain the vigor of our civil society organs that were part of the struggle. . . . We've got to retain the same capacity to smell out corruption, the abuse of power. . . .
>
> If they [the government] are the true democrats which we hope they are, they will say: "Those are in fact our true friends—the ones who tell us when things are not right."

Describing himself as "devastated" by the ANC's action, Tutu went off for a meeting with Mandela in his Pretoria residence. He entered "with a long face," he said later, but came out "with a smile."

Later that morning, the High Court threw out the ANC's application, enabling the presentation ceremony in Pretoria to proceed as planned. The ANC had gained nothing from its ill-fated attempt to muzzle the commission, other than severe damage to its own reputation.

Press comment was uniformly damning. *Business Day* observed:

> What the African National Congress will come to regret most about the truth commission's final report is not anything said about the party itself but rather its own ill-advised attempt to delay publication. Instead of sharing in the achievement of a vast undertaking by a commission it helped set up, the ANC will be perceived as autocratic, mean-spirited and seeking just the opposite of truth and reconciliation.

The *Sunday Times* pointed to lessons for the future:

The ANC's belief that its human rights abuses were somehow more justifiable than those of others shows again the corrupting influence of power.

We have now learnt the starkest lesson of the truth commission—that the moral compass must not be held by those in power, but by those with integrity outside the state.

It is the duty, as Tutu has so eloquently put it, of every South African, of every institution in civil society, of every church, to ensure that we do not repeat the past. We must now ensure that the commission's report, with all its flaws, becomes part of our popular memory.

The presentation of the TRC's five-volume report, three hours after the court's decision, was a somber occasion, overshadowed not only by the ANC's wrecking maneuver but by boycotts by the National Party, Inkatha, and the Afrikaner opposition party, the Freedom Front. Tutu, in presenting the report, and Mandela, in accepting it, seemed almost like voices in a wilderness of anger.

"Many will be upset by this report," Tutu acknowledged.

Some have sought to discredit it preemptively. Even if they were to succeed, what is that to the point? It won't change the fact that they killed Stanza Bopape, that they bombed Khotso House, that they tortured their own people in their camps in Tanzania, that they necklaced people.

That is what the perpetrators told us—not an invention by the commission.

No, dear fellow South Africans, accept this report as a way, an indispensable way to healing. Let the waters of healing flow from Pretoria today as they flowed from the altar in Ezekiel's vision, to cleanse our land, its people, and to bring unity and reconciliation.

We will have looked the beast in the eye. We will have come to
terms with our horrendous past, and it will no longer keep us
hostage. We will cast off its shackles, and, holding hands together,
black and white will stride into the future, the glorious future God
holds out before us—we who are the rainbow people of God—and
looking at our past we will commit ourselves: "Never again! *Nooit
weer*!"

Mandela, in reply, made clear his support for the TRC and its
work, distancing himself from the ANC's response. "I accept this
report as it is, with all its imperfections." He continued:

The commission was not required to muster a definitive and comprehensive history of the past three decades. Nor was it expected to
conjure up instant reconciliation. . . .

Yet we are confident that it has contributed to the work in
progress of laying the foundation of the edifice of reconciliation.
The further construction of that house of peace needs my hand. It
needs your hand.

A cacophony of contrary voices was heard. "They [the TRC] are
wrong," declared Mbeki, the ANC leader, "wrong and misguided."
The TRC process, said the National Party, was "an expensive disaster"—"fatally flawed and divisive." De Klerk accused the TRC of
seeking vengeance not reconciliation. "I fear the TRC report has
left our communities more divided than at any time since the inau-
guration of the government of national unity [in 1994]." The TRC,
said the Freedom Front, was no more than a witch-hunt aimed at
developing a burden of guilt among Afrikaners in order to press for
compensation. Its report was based on sob stories—*traanstories*—
and should be taken with a pinch of salt.

Buthelezi fired off letters to newspapers and bought advertisement space to denounce the TRC's work. "The truth commission report remains at best a collection of hearsay, meaningless anecdotes and clichés of propaganda that ignore the reality of the black-on-black conflict." Inkatha, he said, had been one of the main targets of the ANC's campaign to make the country ungovernable. The TRC had failed to understand that.

> My hands are clean. I have never ordered, authorized, ratified, condoned, or failed to prosecute any gross violation of human rights.
>
> I presided over the erstwhile KwaZulu government and the IFP for over twenty-five years, and no violation of human rights was ever brought to my attention, which leads me to believe that the TRC's findings are the product of blind bias, incompetence, and the flawed structure and composition of that commission.

Thus the TRC ended its task, assailed from all sides, praised by few. Tutu remained hopeful that in time more South Africans would come to recognize the value of dealing openly with the past, as the TRC had tried to do. The pain of facing the truth about past horrors was an unavoidable price to pay for reconciliation, he said. "Now we are facing it. It is going to be horrible. But maybe the worst is already past."

17

In the Fullness of Time

I N HIS POEM about the war between the Boer Republics and the British Empire from 1899 to 1902, William Plomer wrote:

Out of that bungled, unwise war, an alp of unforgiveness grew.

One hundred years later, reverberations from the Anglo–Boer war still affect South Africa. The war had been fought by Britain to establish British supremacy throughout southern Africa, and by the Boers to preserve the independence of their republics. It left a legacy of bitterness among the Boers that endured for generations. The loss of their republics; the memories of British "concentration camps," where some 26,000 women and children died from disease and malnutrition; the effects of Britain's "scorched earth" policy, in which Boer villages were razed to the ground and thousands of Boer farms were destroyed, reducing the Boers to an impoverished, destitute people; all became part of a Boer heritage passed in anger from one generation to the next, inspiring a virulent Afrikaner nationalism that eventually took hold of South Africa. One hundred years later, the bitterness is still discernible.

In his prison cell on Robben Island, Nelson Mandela well understood this tormented past of the Afrikaners. He made an effort both to learn the Afrikaans language and to study Afrikaner history. During his first encounter with President Botha in 1989, when Mandela was taken secretly from prison to the president's office in Cape Town, their only point of common interest came during a polite exchange about Afrikaner history. Mandela mentioned that he had recently read an article in an Afrikaans magazine about the 1914 Afrikaner rebellion, and he drew parallels between their rival nationalisms. The African nationalist struggle, he said, was not unlike the 1914 Afrikaner rebellion: the one pitted Afrikaner brother against brother; the other was a struggle "between brothers who happened to be different colors." Botha, who had hitherto denounced Mandela as a "communist terrorist," was unfailingly courteous, poured the tea, but was not convinced.

Released from prison after twenty-seven years, Mandela set an example of reconciliation that had a profound impact on white South Africa. Not once did he express bitterness toward the white community for his ordeal, only against the system they imposed. His generosity of spirit earned him measures of trust and confidence among his white adversaries that became a crucial factor in making a political settlement attainable.

Yet though the birth of democracy in South Africa in 1994 was accompanied by much goodwill on all sides, the legacies of apartheid remained deep-rooted. As president, Mandela turned the pursuit of national reconciliation into a personal crusade, but the mountain of division and resentment he faced was daunting. This became Mandela's alp, his final task of seeking to overcome the bitterness of the past before it festered, as it had done one hundred years before.

There was always a risk that setting up a truth commission would exacerbate divisions rather than heal them. The white community would have preferred to let the past slip by into amnesia. Many members of the old white establishment sought to thwart the commission's work, claiming that it was merely an attempt to exact revenge. The Afrikaans press, notably *Rapport* and *Die Burger*, led the field in denouncing the TRC contemptuously as the *Biegbank*—the *Lieg-en-biegkommissie*, the Lying and Confessing Commission; or as the *Waarheids-en-voorsieningskommissie*, the Truth and Provision Commission.

White critics pointed to the background of the seventeen commissioners as evidence of the TRC's built-in bias. Only two members were *wit Afrikaners*, and neither of those represented true Afrikaner interests. The rest were either "struggle" people or English-speaking liberals. They compared the friendly reception the commissioners accorded the ANC's delegation to the grilling that de Klerk received the day before, aimed, they said, at humiliating him. They cited the way Botha had been "hounded," a sick, old man dragged through the courts, and contrasted this treatment with the deferential attitude Tutu had adopted in handling Winnie Mandela, a personal friend whom, despite her record as a common criminal, he had lauded as "a great person."

Few whites attended TRC hearings, watched them on television, or listened to radio broadcasts. What most heard were mere fragments of evidence. Many whites were genuinely shocked when they learned of the activities of death squads and other atrocities, but they believed them to be no more than one part of the picture, the part on which the TRC was concentrating. The more shocking the disclosures became, the more they felt able to distance themselves from them.

Most whites held firmly to the view that what had taken place was a war against communism in which there was no moral difference between one side or the other and in which the other side's atrocities—the bombing of civilian targets, necklacing, torture in the camps—were far more numerous than theirs. "There is no doubt that the liberation side has committed more atrocities," said General Constand Viljoen, the Freedom Front leader. "Naturally, I have to say there are some aggravating conditions on one side because they were in government and were supposed to apply the law equally. But in numbers, there is no doubt in my mind that the Afrikaners have not been responsible for more atrocities than the other side."

A number of judgments made by the amnesty committee further convinced the white community of the TRC's bias. In 1997, the TRC's amnesty committee granted a blanket amnesty to thirty-seven ANC leaders, including Thabo Mbeki, without requiring them to make any disclosure of their offenses, in clear contravention of the TRC's legal procedures and with no explanation. The decision, made by three judges, caused uproar in the white community.

Although the amnesty committee operated independently of the main body of the TRC, the whole exercise was called into question. The TRC itself quickly took steps to challenge the amnesty decision, but the damage done was immense. In many white eyes, the TRC lost all credibility.

There was further outrage when Archbishop Tutu's son, Trevor Tutu, was granted an amnesty for a bomb hoax at an airport, which many saw as a stupid prank but which the amnesty committee decided to dignify as a political act. Another questionable decision concerned an amnesty granted to a necklace murderer.

But the deepest sense of revulsion came when the amnesty committee freed the culprits who had carried out the St. James Church massacre and the murder of Amy Biehl. White critics questioned how the massacre of a church congregation fitted any notion of "proportionality," one of the key criteria on which amnesties were supposed to be based, or how the murder of Amy Biehl could be seen as anything other than an example of mob violence.

Opinion polls consistently showed white distrust and resentment about the TRC. In a survey carried out in July 1998, some 72 percent of whites felt that the TRC had made race relations worse; almost 70 percent felt that the TRC would not help South Africans to live together more harmoniously in the future; and some 83 percent of Afrikaners and 71 percent of English-speaking whites believed the TRC to be biased. In effect, it was a massive vote of no confidence.

By contrast, the black community followed the proceedings of the TRC with avid interest. Writing in the *Sowetan* at the end of the exercise, Mathatha Tsedu recalled:

> We were moved by the testimony, the fears, the sobs and the wailing of survivors and relatives who could not take the memories and the revelations. We cried a little too in our own homes.
>
> We also sat glued to the radio and television screens as killers of our patriots spoke of the murders they committed to defend white hegemony.
>
> We hissed as the men, with no visible remorse, spoke of the pyres and burning of human bodies alongside the lamb chops and steak barbecues on the banks of various rivers of our land.
>
> We got even more angry as the men walked away scot-free after such testimony.

Indeed, the work of the TRC provoked as much anger in parts of the black community as it did among the whites, particularly over the way that security force operatives responsible for heinous crimes were given freedom in exchange for a bit of truth-telling, while victims and their families were denied access to the courts. What many wanted more than the truth was justice—prosecution in the courts and prison sentences. Whereas whites were aggrieved by the release of the St. James Church murderers, blacks pointed angrily to amnesties granted to individuals like Dirk Coetzee, the former

Vlakplaas commander; Brian Mitchell, the Trust Feed killer; and Jeffrey Benzien, the police torturer. Though the security policemen involved in Steve Biko's death were denied an amnesty, the prospect of them facing prosecution was remote.

Tutu tried to answer such anger by arguing that trials were not necessarily an effective way of establishing either the truth or guilt. They required proof beyond reasonable doubt, something that was difficult to obtain. The "Malan" trial was a case in point. The investigation had taken thirty detectives nine months to complete; the trial had lasted nine months; the cost had exceeded R12 million; and the result had been an acquittal.

"The criminal justice system is not the best way to arrive at the truth," said Tutu. "There is no incentive for perpetrators to tell the truth, and often the court must decide between the word of a victim against the evidence of many perpetrators. Such legal proceedings are also harrowing experiences for victims, who are invariably put through extensive cross-examination." Tutu claimed that the commission had contributed more to uncovering the truth about the past "than all the court cases in the history of apartheid."

Moreover, South Africa could not afford a lengthy series of trials, not only because it did not possess sufficient resources in terms of money and personnel but also because of their disruptive effect: "It would have rocked the boat massively and for too long."

He quoted a passage from *Out of the Shadows of the Night*, Judge Marvin Frankel's book about the struggle for international human rights:

> The call to punish human rights criminals can present complex and agonising problems that have no single or simple solution. While the debate over the Nuremberg trials still goes on, that episode—trials of war criminals of a defeated nation—was simplicity itself as com-

pared to the subtle and dangerous issues that can divide a country when it undertakes to punish its own violators.

A nation divided during a repressive regime does not emerge suddenly when the time of repression has passed. The human rights criminals are fellow citizens, living alongside everyone else, and they may be very powerful and dangerous. . . . If they are treated too harshly—or if the net of punishment is cast too widely—there may be a backlash.

Answering criticism about the amnesty process, Tutu acknowledged that it was bound to cause outrage. "Amnesty is not meant for nice people. It is intended for perpetrators." He accepted that it was "a heavy price to pay," but that was the price that politicians seeking a negotiated settlement to a terrible conflict had decided was worth paying.

Tutu denied that the amnesty process, by sacrificing justice, encouraged impunity and allowed perpetrators to get off "scot-free." Amnesty applicants, he pointed out, had to admit responsibility for their crimes and account for them in open hearings in the full glare of publicity.

Let us imagine what this means. Often this is the first time that an applicant's family and community learn that an apparently decent man was, for instance, a callous torturer or a member of a ruthless death squad that assassinated many opponents of the previous regime. There is, therefore, a price to be paid. Public disclosure results in public shaming, and sometimes a marriage may be a sad casualty as well.

In any case, the number of applicants granted amnesty, he said, was relatively small. Out of some 7,000 applications, only about 150

had been granted; some 4,500 had been refused; most of them common criminals; and some 2,000 more awaited an outcome."This
can hardly be described as an avalanche of reckless decisions."

Moreover, there was more than one aspect to justice. "Certainly
amnesty cannot be viewed as justice if we think of justice only as re-
tributive and punitive in nature," said Tutu. "However, there is
another kind of justice—a restorative justice which is concerned not
so much with punishment as with correcting imbalances, restoring
broken relationships—with healing, harmony and reconciliation."

But black anger was not confined to the amnesty process and the
denial of justice it entailed. Many objected to the way the TRC concentrated on perpetrators and victims rather than on the wider
injustices of the apartheid system that had ruined so many lives.
Some opposed the whole reconciliation "project."

In an open letter addressed to President Mandela and Archbishop Tutu in April 1998, a magazine editor, Jon Qwelane, asked:

> Is it not simply amazing that black South Africans are the only people
> in the entire history of humankind expected to hug and kiss their
> oppressors, and to love them unconditionally like brothers and sisters,
> while the new-found family members give nothing in return except
> scorn, derision and absolute contempt for our dignity as a people?

Qwelane made what he called "an agonized and anguished cry"
to Mandela and Tutu "to stop your one-sided brand of 'reconciliation' before it causes irreparable damage to the psyche of the black
people of this country."

Opinion polls reflected nearly as much disillusionment with the
work of the TRC among the black population as among the white
community. The survey carried out in July 1998 showed that
though a majority of blacks—60 percent—believed that the TRC
had been fair to all sides, some 62 percent thought its work had

made race relations worse. Significantly, however, blacks were more optimistic than whites about the future: Nearly 80 percent felt that as a result of the TRC's work people in South Africa would now live together more harmoniously.

The TRC's critics nevertheless pointed out gleefully that the responses of whites and blacks in the July 1998 survey, when combined, showed that nearly 80 percent of the people felt that the commission's hearings had worsened race relations.

Angered by the glee, Tutu retorted in the Johannesburg *Star*:

> How utterly pathetic. It surely would have been odd in the extreme had people not been incensed at the atrocities that have been revealed. What did we expect? Surely not that the Bopape family would dance with joy to hear that their son was tortured to death and that his body was fed to crocodiles—while police engaged in an elaborate and macabre cover-up?
>
> What is breathtaking . . . is that nearly 80 percent of blacks, the ones who suffered most under apartheid, are ready to make a go of working for reconciliation.

He said the TRC had witnessed many inspiring examples of forgiveness and reconciliation. He cited the examples of Beth Savage, a white victim of the attack on the King William's Town golf club who had sought a meeting with the gunman she had seen in the doorway; of Hennie Smit, the father of an eight-year-old boy killed by the bomb in the Amanzimtoti shopping center, who spoke of how his son had died for the cause of freedom; of Neville Clarence, the air force officer blinded by the Church Street bomb who had welcomed a meeting with the ANC's chief bomber, Aboobaker Ismail; and of Amy Biehl's family, who publicly forgave her killers.

What was missing, said Tutu, was a proper response from the leaders of the white community.

Is there no leader of some stature and some integrity in the white community who won't try to be too smart, who is not trying to see how much he can get away with, but who will say quite simply: "We had a bad policy that had evil consequences. We are sorry. Please forgive us." And then not qualify it to death?

That would help to close the chapter on our horrendous past and enable us to move forward into the future with confidence, absolved, forgiving and forgiven.

It fell to de Klerk, on behalf of the white community, to make the magnanimous gesture that Tutu sought and that he believed would contribute so much to healing the divisions of the past. That de Klerk failed to do so showed him to be a small-minded politician but was no more than a reflection of what much of the white community felt. For those whites hoping for a moment of catharsis, there was only bitter disappointment. For blacks, it was nothing more than they had expected.

WHEN THE TRC finally ended its assignment, there was as much a sense of relief as of achievement. Dealing with the past had been a painful business. Yet its achievements were considerable. It had uncovered far more about South Africa's violent past than had been thought possible when it started its work.

It had established beyond all doubt that death squads operated not as aberrations but as part and parcel of the system of government repression; that torture was used systematically and in effect condoned as official practice; that violence between rival black factions was officially encouraged, supported, and financed; that offensive chemical and biological warfare projects had been set in motion.

It had established the chain of command leading directly to the highest levels of government, to the politicians and generals who ran the State Security Council and conducted the government's dirty war against apartheid's opponents.

It had helped to solve many of the murders and disappearances that for so long had troubled so many families—the Pebco Three, the Cradock Four, the Nietverdiend Nine, the fate of Siphiwo Mtimkulu, of Stanza Bopape, of Sizwe Kondile, of Phila Ndwandwe.

It had confronted the liberation movements with their own crimes of murder, torture, and necklacing, refusing to judge these crimes any differently than government crimes.

It had provided a hearing for thousands of victims and their families, affording many people relief from their burden of suffering and grief for the first time. As Lukas Sikwepere, a victim blinded by police gunfire, summed up the experience: "I feel that what has been making me sick all the time is the fact that I couldn't tell my story. But now it feels like I got my sight back by coming here and telling you the story."

A high price had been paid for all this—amnesty. It was the guarantee of amnesty that had made a negotiated settlement of the conflict over apartheid possible in the first place. It was the amnesty process, moreover, that had persuaded many perpetrators to come forward, throwing light on past atrocities. But the disturbing consequence was that guilty men who had been seen and heard to confess to appalling crimes then walked entirely free.

In its report, the TRC argued that trials were never really a feasible alternative:

> Even if the South African transition had occurred without any amnesty agreement, even if criminal prosecution had been politically feasible, the successful prosecution of more than a fraction of those responsible for gross violations of human rights would have been impossible in practice.

The justice system in South Africa could not have coped with more than a fraction of cases. The police, the prosecutors, the courts, and the judges were already stretched to the limit with the normal flow of business and had limited capacity to deal with complex political crimes committed by highly skilled operatives who were trained to conceal crimes and destroy evidence.

> The issue is not, therefore, a straight trade-off between amnesty and criminal or civil trials. What is at stake, rather, is a choice between more or less full disclosure; the option of hearing as many cases as possible against the possibility of a small number of trials revealing, at best, information only directly relevant to specific charges.

Despite this statement, the TRC proceeded to recommend the prosecution of any individual linked to gross human rights violations who had not applied for amnesty. "The commission will make available to the appropriate authorities information in its possession concerning serious allegations against individuals." Among those placed in this category were Botha, Malan, Buthelezi, and Winnie Mandela. Scores of other names were mentioned, including army and police generals.

There seemed little prospect that any of them would ever face prosecution. Mandela's justice minister, Dullah Omar, said that any decision to prosecute would have to take into account "the national interest." The process, he suggested, could last for a decade. Nor would any of these individuals face lustration—disqualification from holding public office—a sanction the TRC decided not to recommend.

Nevertheless, even if they escaped prosecution, many of those held responsible for gross violations of human rights had been named. And that itself was a form of justice.

There were few signs, however, that the cause of reconciliation had been advanced. Apart from individual examples of reconciliation, little had changed at a national level. "The truth is often divisive," explained Tutu. "Reconciliation is not about being cozy; it is not about pretending that things were other than they were. Reconciliation based on falsehood, on not facing up to reality, is not true reconciliation and will not last."

But, Tutu argued, though truth might not always lead to reconciliation, there could be no genuine reconciliation without truth. Hence, South Africa had to go through the painful process of facing the truth about the past before the business of reconciliation could commence. A single initiative, like the Truth and Reconciliation Commission, could not expect to overcome the deep wounds caused by years of conflict, but it could lay the foundation for a common understanding of the past, enabling reconciliation to proceed. That, at least, was the hope.

There was, however, an even greater legacy of the past to overcome. The apartheid years had left the white community largely prosperous and the black community largely impoverished. Even after five years of Mandela's government, the gap remained as wide as before. It will take generations for this great divide to change; and in the meantime the two communities will continue to inhabit different worlds.

AFTERWORD

Confronting the Painful Past

TINA ROSENBERG

A COUNTRY LIKE SOUTH AFRICA, wishing to move from dicta-torship to democracy or from war to peace, has a double set of obligations. It has a responsibility to do as much as possible to heal its victims. The nation also has a responsibility to its own future—to analyze how war or dictatorship came to pass and to change its political culture so that it does not happen again.

Governments have a variety of ways to try to reach these goals. A brief catalogue includes trials in an international or national court of law, truth commissions, official apologies, the opening of secret-police files to victims, administrative purges, the payment of repara-tions, affirmative action, civic education programs, and reform of the institutions complicit in dictatorship—for example, the judicial system.

In what follows, I examine the failures and the successes of the various methods that governments have chosen to deal with the past and to plan for the future. I draw on my conversations about this issue with victims and perpetrators in Latin America, eastern and central Europe, South Africa, and Bosnia over more than ten years. This essay includes much reporting and analysis from my previous books and articles but also much that is new. Ideas about how to deal with the past are shifting rapidly, and I attempt to put even previously reported material into a new context and to draw new conclusions.

The first part of the essay will look at the choices nations have made in dealing with the past, and I will propose what should be done to heal victims and construct a democratic future after different kinds of dictatorship or war. The second part of the essay will look at how countries can actually carry out the right decisions and not be blocked by the continued power of those who committed crimes. In the last decade several exciting but controversial new strategies have emerged for overcoming the impunity that has long kept the past hovering in a vicious circle in many regions of the world.

Facing the Past: Making the Right Choice

A country's decisions about how to deal with its past should depend on many things: the type of dictatorship or war endured, the type of crimes committed, the level of societal complicity, the nation's political culture and history, the conditions necessary for dictatorship to reoccur, the abruptness of the transition, and the new democratic government's power and resources.

Different countries have chosen wildly different strategies to deal with the past. Spanish democrats after Franco's death, for example, chose to do nothing—no trials or purges. They gambled—successfully—that many faithful servants of dictatorship could learn to act like democrats. Also, Franco's most serious crimes had taken place so many years in the past that the desire for justice, or at least the political clout to achieve it, had faded. Greece, by contrast, prosecuted several dozen leaders of its military regime, including two former presidents. Some are still in prison more than two decades later.

The Czech Republic passed a law known as "lustration," which keeps anyone who appears on the old secret-police list of informants and many others who served the Communist government from high public positions. In Hungary, voters in 1994 elected

Gyula Horn as prime minister; Horn had been a minor participant in the Soviet-backed violence that suppressed a 1956 reformist uprising. Horn governed for four years in an odd coalition with the party of former dissidents. Hungary did pass a lustration law, but it was limited in scope and all but ignored.

After the military regime fell in Argentina in 1983, the new government held trials of nine of the top members of the junta, convicting five of serious crimes. In neighboring Chile, by 1999—twenty-six years after the coup—only one top commander of the Pinochet regime had yet been tried. He was former secret police chief Manual Contreras, and his trial was only due to pressure from Washington. He was convicted of participation in the car bombing of opposition leader Orlando Letelier and his American assistant, which took place in Washington, D.C. The arrest of General Pinochet, however, was embarassing judges into finally beginning to hold other military officers to account.

We will never really know which of these strategies work. Take the case of Argentina. Besides trying the top junta members, Argentina sought to prosecute lower-ranking military officers responsible for crimes. But when the military began to grumble in a country that had already seen eleven military coups in this century, President Raul Alfonsín blinked. He proposed laws setting a date for an end to indictments, and another law that gave amnesty to middle and junior officers on the grounds that they were following orders. His successor, Carlos Menem, even pardoned the junta members who had been convicted. Today, the Argentine military is a model—with a small budget, modern policies, and no interest in Argentine politics or internal affairs. Something worked—but what? The trials? Or the fact that they were cut off? Or was it simply the military's humiliation in the Falklands War that counted? So many different factors influence a country's political culture that it is impossible to determine the impact of a single policy.

We do know, however, what doesn't work. It may not be clear what effect trials of Pinochet and his fellow officers would have had on Chile, but it is clear what effect *not* trying them has had—Chile is not yet a full democracy. The limits of civilian power are defined by the military. The armed forces have an autonomous budget, a veto over civilian decisions should they choose to use it, undemocratic domination of the Senate, and, as the clamor of Chile's government to rescue Pinochet from trial in Spain showed, the continued ability to make the civilian government behave like an abused child cringing in fear of the next beating.

In my opinion, one of the most important rules for building a democratic political culture is that nations should use the principles that mark the democracies they hope to become, rather than the practices of politicized justice they have inherited from repressive regimes. Trials, for example, should follow strict standards of due process, including the prohibition on ex post facto justice, which criminalizes acts that were legal when committed. Administrative purges to keep members of the old regime out of the new government should be based on evidence of wrongdoing, not on membership in a party or appearance on a list. Amnesties should not be blanket amnesties covering the heinous crimes that every government has the international duty to punish.

Repressive governments have victimized their people in different ways and left behind different threats to the future. These regimes fall roughly into three categories: (1) right-wing military dictatorships, such as were found in Latin America, Greece, Nigeria, and, to a lesser extent, Indonesia and several other places; (2) Communist dictatorship; and (3) ethnic, tribal, or religious war—the wars that tore apart Bosnia, Rwanda, or Northern Ireland, for example. Apartheid South Africa shared some characteristics with each of the three categories.

These divisions, of course, are generalizations. Hungary and Turkmenistan were both Communist dictatorships, but in other ways the two countries were and are from two different parts of the galaxy. Argentina and Honduras were both anticommunist military dictatorships but otherwise resembled each other little. The same lack of resemblance applies to the ethnic wars in Rwanda and Bosnia. Yet the states in each category have enough in common that it is instructive to look at the kind of tyranny, the type of victimization, and the threats to the future that each category represents.

Latin American Dictatorships

LATIN AMERICA'S GENERALS ruled for one simple reason: They had guns. They had an anticommunist ideology, but they did not seek to impose it on the public. Instead, they tried to strip politics from public life. In Pinochet's Chile, where I lived for four years, the regime's good citizen went to work, came home, and played with his children. If his neighbor returned from a long absence with dead eyes and a shuffling gait, the good citizen noticed nothing. I knew several Chileans and Argentines who, upon finding out that a neighbor's child had been arrested in the middle of the night, decided that there must be a good reason and thought no more of it.

These regimes enforced the rules through violence, using murder, torture, and forced disappearance. In Guatemala, a truth commission found that more than 200,000 people, the vast majority Mayan Indian civilians, were killed during a thirty-six-year civil war in which the government's efforts to wipe out entire Mayan communities amounted to genocide. The government was responsible for 93 percent of the 200,000 deaths. El Salvador's war killed 75,000 people, most of them civilian campesinos, in a country of only 5 million—again, the vast majority of these people were killed by the government. In other countries, however, this intense repression was focused on a small group of the population—the sector that protested or that the government thought might protest. In Argentina, for example, most of the disappeared were journalists, psychologists (a profession considered subversive), and those who worked with the poor. In Chile, there were 3,000 dead or disappeared, in Argentina around 12,000, in Uruguay a few hundred, in Honduras 184.

These crimes, although sponsored by the state and often endorsed by the rich, were committed by a small number of specific people. In Uruguay, a country not much larger than its capital, Montevideo, political prisoners sometimes ran into their torturers on the street. Mothers of the disappeared in Argentina often knew the names of their children's kidnappers. The acts were also illegal when they were committed, which makes it legally possible to prosecute them.

What do Latin American victims need? As victims of serious violence committed by individual violators of existing laws, they need justice. They also need to know the truth, since many of the crimes, such as torture and disappearance, were committed in secrecy. "No one will ever know," says the torturer. The victim or family is not healed until people do know. But a quarter century after most of the disappearances in Chile, the vast majority of family members of the disappeared still do not know what happened to their loved ones. They may know in their hearts that their family members are dead, but until they see the body they will always wonder whether one day their loved one will walk through the door. The uncertainty long ago ceased to be hope. It is now simply a lack of closure that keeps these victims from rebuilding their lives.

The obstacle to truth and justice, of course, is that the militaries remain strong enough to thwart any attempts to try the perpetrators or even to persuade them to confess. The Latin American military dictatorships could arise because Latin American states have historically bent to the will of the wealthy and powerful, especially the military. Even after transitions to democracies, militaries retain their guns, the support of many in the upper class, and the feeling that civilians are running the country at their sufferance. The future threat to Latin American democracy is similar to the past threat—militaries unaccountable to their citizens.

Subordinating the armed forces to civilian laws is exactly what the continent needs to build real democracy. The same trials that can risk democracy in the short term are crucial to it in the long term. They are the only way to establish civilian control of the military and the primacy of law over force. Trials deter further crimes. And they demonstrate to countries that routinely solve their political disputes through violence that other ways exist. Justice expresses society's condemnation of violence and provides a marker to separate dictatorship from democracy.

To prevent further military coups, Latin American nations must strengthen their institutions, especially their judicial systems, which are underfinanced, weak, and subservient to power. After El Salvador's twelve-year civil war ended, the truth commission there recommended against trying anyone until the justice system was overhauled. The courts were so submissive that they had become part of the machine of repression.

There have been several attempts to prosecute powerful members of the military. In Honduras, human rights ombudsman Leo Valladares and several brave prosecutors indicted fifteen high-ranking military officers—including colonels in active service—for running a death squad in the early 1980s that killed or disappeared 184 people. The military has protected its own. The only defendant in custody is a man who was already in jail on drug charges. The rest are at large, and the army has supported them. The high command showed its displeasure with the indictment by sending tanks into the streets. The judge and several of those who brought the prosecutions have been threatened, and Valladares's bodyguard was shot to death.

Honduras's attempt to hold the military accountable is remarkable. Most countries do not try, and when they do, cases are dismissed for lack of evidence. Amnesty—either by law or by default—reigns. The Argentine prosecutions of junta members in 1985 could happen only because the military had been discredited by its humiliation in the Falklands War. And after officers staged three military rebellions, the trials were stopped and Alfonsin's successor, Menem, pardoned the junta leaders already convicted.

In part because impunity has reigned in Latin America, the new democracies have turned to truth commissions. The first well-known truth commission was in Argentina. When the Dirty War junta fell in 1983, President Alfonsín appointed a panel of distinguished citizens to form the National Commission on the Disappeared. They took testimony all over Argentina and in countries where Argentines were exiled and found that the military had produced, or rather not produced, at least 9,000 disappeared and probably many more. The report—called *Nunca Más*, or Never Again—described the torture and killing that had taken place in secret detention centers and told the stories of victims where it could. Since then Chile, El Salvador, Guatemala, and Haiti all established truth commissions. Unlike Argentina, they settled on truth commissions as consolation prizes, because the military was strong enough to block trials.

Truth commissions are crucial for two reasons. First, many of the crimes of the Latin American dictatorships took place in secret. Death squads are established precisely to allow the government to hide its crimes. Every day of secrecy marks another victory for the criminal. For the victims and for society, the full story must be known. "[Truth] does not bring the dead back to life," says José Zalaquett, a Chilean human rights lawyer and member of Chile's truth commission, "but it brings them out from silence." These reports, which are usually written by a group of people who span the political spectrum, may not establish the truth; but as historian and writer Michael Ignatieff says, they narrow the range of permissible lies. After their reports, militaries can no longer argue that they did not torture or kill, or that they did so in a war, or that the only victims were dangerous criminals. It is interesting that General Pinochet himself is the only person who continues to insist that he is innocent of the crimes for which Spain indicted him. Thanks to Chile's truth commission, virtually none of his defenders in Chile, even those on the far right, try to make that claim any more.

Truth commissions also allow the state to give official acknowledgment to the crimes it committed. On March 4, 1991, President Patricio Aylwin of Chile, Pinochet's democratic successor, went on television and presented the truth commission's report. In the name of the entire nation, Aylwin made a moving apology to the families of those murdered, his voice breaking as he spoke.

The Latin American truth commission reports were extremely important but greatly flawed. They did not have the power to compel the military to participate. In Chile, for example, the military refused to recognize the practice of forced disappearance, and so provided no information to the families of the disappeared. In Guatemala, the military had a policy of destroying every relevant document it could before the truth commission got hold of them. Because many of the victims feared reprisals, the commissions gathered their information in secret, which meant that the public could learn of the commission's findings only when the report came out.

In most cases these reports helped victims by identifying them and recognizing their suffering, but they did not name individual perpetrators. Most merely said, for example, that the victim was last seen in custody of the Third Infantry Brigade. The decision not to name names was made in part because of due process concerns, since truth commissions are not courts and their members felt they could not make accusations without trials. But the more important reason in most cases is that the military would not tolerate it.

Some Latin American countries were able to pay reparations to those tortured and to the families of those killed. Chile is probably doing the most of any nation. In early 1999, 5,746 relatives of those killed or disappeared were getting lifelong pensions, and good ones: The pension for a widow of one of these victims is three times the normal pension. More than 700 children are getting free tuition at any university in Chile. But in other places, victims have received nothing. In El Salvador, for example, where 75,000 people—the vast majority desperately poor civilians—were killed, no reparations were paid.

Communist Dictatorships

IN CONTRAST TO THE Latin American militaries, communism, at least since Stalin's death in 1953, relied mainly on coercive politics, not physical violence, to maintain power. Communist governments sought to politicize all aspects of life. They pronounced themselves the standard-bearers of a beautiful ideal and aimed for nothing less than the transformation of their citizens—the building of a "new socialist man." The good socialist citizen attended peace rallies, enrolled her children in Young Pioneers, and joined Marxist-Leninist scientific study groups at work. In the harsher police states, she denounced suspicious activity by her neighbors or colleagues. In the harshest states, such as Stalin's Soviet Union or Enver Hoxha's

Albania, there was no private life at all. Grumbling in a diary was cause for twenty years in a labor camp or for a death sentence.

Whereas Stalin used violence on a scale that would be unimaginable in Latin America—with 7 million executed, 5 million dead of government-induced famine, and 15 million sent to the gulag—communism in eastern Europe during those years was much less deadly. After Stalin's death, moreover, violence in the Soviet Union was rare. Communist regimes kept power mainly through corruption and coercion. The state kept citizens in line by rewarding good behavior with travel, good jobs, and the best schools for their children. Those who defied the state lost these things—a terrifying prospect.

Lothar Pawliczak, an East German who was active in dissident groups, was typical. He decided to work for the secret police by informing on a friend, a famous dissident, because he feared dropping out of the system—losing his job in a research institute; losing visits with his children, who lived with his former wife; and losing the right to publish academic papers. In a country where the government ran everything, living outside official lines was fearsome indeed. It was this fear, and not the threat of physical violence, that propped up communism. (Albania, still shooting poets in the 1970s, was the great exception.)

For most people under post-1953 communism, then, repression was far more diffuse than under the Latin American dictators—few were killed or tortured, but millions suffered terrible indignities. Virtually everyone endured shoddy goods, lack of privacy, shortages, inefficiency, mediocre health care and education, and infuriating lies by the government. Unlike what took place in Latin America, this repression was not illegal by existing laws. It was the very foundation of the system. It was also perpetrated not by an individual but by a whole bureaucracy.

And indeed, communism required the collaboration of virtually the whole population. Just as almost everyone was a victim of communism by virtue of living under it, almost everyone participated in some way in repression. Lines of complicity ran like veins and arteries inside the human body. It is hard for many people who lived under communism to recognize their own collaboration because it seemed normal to them—every other citizen behaved in the same way. But although those who taught socialist history or voted for the Party slate were victims of repression, they were also keeping the system going. "The question isn't what some 'they' did," said Jan Urban, a Czechoslovak journalist and dissident, "it's what *we* did." The evil of communism was in the sum of millions of non-evil parts.

So what do the victims of communism need? The ones who were tortured, unjustly imprisoned, or beaten, as well as the relatives of those killed, need real justice in a real court. There have been a few—far too few—examples of this kind of justice.

For instance, the four secret police agents who killed Father Jerzy Popieluszko, a Polish Solidarity activist, were convicted of murder in 1985, but two generals the men named as having given the orders were acquitted in 1994. The judge in the case said the secret police had removed evidence that could have pointed to the two men. During protests in the Polish city of Gdansk in 1970, at least forty-five people were killed when soldiers fired into the crowd. In June 1998, seven former officials were put on trial for ordering those shootings. In the Czech Republic, a special committee established to prosecute Communist criminals was able to get a few dozen convictions, mainly for the beating of student demonstrators on November 17, 1989. Miroslav Stepan, who had been the Communist boss of Prague, served a thirty-month term.

It is also possible to prosecute the very top leaders for some of these acts. Border guards in East Germany might not have been expected to question their orders to shoot fleeing citizens, for example, but East German leader Erich Honecker certainly knew that his order to shoot was unjust. In fact, Honecker was prosecuted for it, but the trial was stopped because of his terminal cancer.

Crimes like the killing of Father Popieluszko or the massacre of the citizens in Gdansk were specific acts of violence by people violating laws in effect at the time. But most people who lived under post-Stalinist communism are not angry about its sporadic physical violence. They are angry about the more widespread repression, and for these acts justice is elusive. The secret police and its collaborators—the mail-openers and phone-tappers, the designers of terrible automobiles and the teachers of lies in the guise of history —were obeying the law, and democracies do not prosecute people for acts that were not crimes when committed, except for acts, such as torture, that are so awful that any reasonable person should have considered them repugnant.

There are other problems with justice after communism. Trials are designed to prosecute individuals, and communism's crimes were more crimes of bureaucracies. If the Latin American military dictatorships were regimes of criminals, Communist dictatorships were criminal regimes. And there are too many victims to make justice practical, especially in countries where the judiciaries are degraded and weak. This is a bitter truth for many of the victims. "We expected justice, and we got the rule of law," Bärbel Bohley, one of the most important East German dissidents, told me.

Although some of the trials that have taken place in former Communist countries have been fair and appropriate, in many cases, nations that have tried their old leaders have bungled the job. The problem is the opposite of that in Latin America—in former Communist Europe the new leaders have too much power, and they follow in the Communist tradition of politicizing justice. In Albania, the worst offender, about forty members of the Communist elite were tried, and the process resembled the old-style Communist purges of the factions who lost power.

Surprisingly, another country that has misused trials is Germany, perhaps because the nation running the trials (the former West Germany) is not the nation of the defendants (the former East Germany). With Erich Mielke, the hated chief of the Stasi, or secret police, Germany seemed determined to try him for anything, like the marksman who shoots first and draws his targets later. Mielke was convicted of the 1931 murder of two policemen during a shoot-out between Nazis and Communist youth. The statute of limitations had long since expired, and the evidence against him had been gathered by the Nazis. There were indications that the confessions of some defendants had been gathered under torture. He got six years.

Germany also tried Markus Wolf, the head of the Stasi's foreign division (the equivalent of the CIA), for treason—although the West Germany he "betrayed" was not his country. Germany tried border guards for killing fleeing citizens. The guards' superiors, who gave the orders to shoot, sometimes testified at their trials. If the superiors were government employees at the time of the trials, they received a day's pay for their troubles. Then they left, free men.

Such trials have served only to make East Germans feel doubly victimized by West Germans. "Wessis feel they have won history and can do what they want," said one East German dissident, who under different circumstances would have favored trials. Political manipulation and abuse of power promote neither healing nor the rule of law; rather, they reinforce the habits conducive to new dictatorship.

One problem that unites practically every democracy shedding a tyrannical regime or a war is that their justices systems are too weak to do justice on a large scale. The former Communist countries were left with judges, prosecutors, and police accustomed to political justice. Replacing them will take years and will require new law schools, new police academies, plenty of money, and, most important, a genuine change in the society around them. The same is true with countries from El Salvador to Haiti to South Africa—nations with corrupt and incompetent law enforcement officers who protect the powerful. It is hard to undo habits built over decades or even centuries, and harder still when the courts are so starved of money that in some countries judges cannot buy pencil and paper, and court personnel are so poorly educated that they do not even understand the concept of writing down information and keeping everything related to a case in one file. Some court clerks in Haiti cannot even read. Even nations with the political power to bring the barons of the old regime to justice have found they can try only a handful of people. In the rest of the cases, victims get nothing—no justice, no truth, no acknowledgment of their suffering.

Reparations are also difficult under communism because victimhood was so widespread. The victims of real crimes—those unjustly jailed or tortured, for example—should get monetary compensation. Those unfairly jailed in Czechoslovakia now rightly receive higher pensions, although the amount is still negligible. Children denied schooling because of their parents' politics deserve affirmative action to right that wrong. But these reparations do not work for communism's average victims because there are simply too many of them. Paying virtually everyone would require taxing everyone, which would mean less money to improve health care, schools, and other programs—itself a form of reparation. Most property was expropriated years ago, so giving it back would mean paying the old by taxing the young.

One thing a new society *can* do for the victims of communism who suffered average repression is to uncover the truth—reveal the workings of the bureaucracy to acknowledge how they suffered. Such victims need to hear not only how the whole system worked, but also apologies and an acknowledgment of their suffering from anyone who hurt them personally—most importantly the colleagues and friends who spied on them. More than anything else, however, these victims need a new society that works better than the old. They need to be able to travel and have access to modern goods and decent education and private mail. They need fair courts and efficient government. The best redress for a miserable past for most of communism's victims is a better future.

To understand how former Communist countries can fulfill this obligation, it is necessary to look at how communism damaged political cultures. First, it created a world of arbitrary and absolute power, where law was twisted into political service. No institutions existed to check the power of the rulers—no free press, no opposition parties, no independent courts, no counterbalancing legislature. In Albania, even the practice of law was banned. The word "rights" had no meaning.

This world left its citizens unprepared for democracy in several ways. It created citizens who were unaccustomed to finding their own political views and values, who were used to accepting those supplied by the state. This habit of acceptance leaves people susceptible to the next demagogue to come along—such as Slobodan Milosevic in Serbia, Franjo Tudjman in Croatia, and, to a lesser extent, Vladimir Meciar in Slovakia or Sali Berisha in Albania. Such demagogues now most likely preach Europe's traditional pathology, ethnic nationalism. One of the reasons that East Germans slid so smoothly from dictatorship under Hitler to dictatorship under Stalin in just three years is that there was no de-Nazification, as in the Federal Republic. East Germans never had to examine the choices they made under the Third Reich. They were taught that those bad Germans were over there, in the west.

The second poisonous legacy of communism is a society with few checks on the leader. Unchecked power was necessary to maintain a Communist regime. But unchecked power can also be employed in the service of nationalism, or by autocrats whose only ideology is to keep themselves in office. It is common today throughout the former Soviet Union, and to a lesser degree in eastern Europe, that judges obey the phone call they receive, that newspapers either praise the government or risk being shuttered, that parliament simply ratifies the wishes of the supreme leader. The threat to democracy in former Communist countries comes from societies with passive citizens and leaders who can misuse their institutions.

Latin America's new leaders are too weak, whereas the leaders of former Communist nations are too strong. These countries desperately need the rule of law, as well as institutions that can check leaders before they become tyrants. They need citizenries who can have a full discussion of how communism worked, how it managed to lure normal people into bad acts. They must understand both why they failed to think for themselves in the past and the price society paid for this failure.

This understanding requires a public debate, and here truth commissions can help. Of the former Communist nations only Germany established one. The *Enquetekommission*, or Commission of Inquiry, held hearings all over East Germany and assigned 759 papers by specialists. In 1995 it produced a report of several thousand pages, which examined how the mechanisms of repression worked: How did communism persuade people to abandon their own search for values and adopt the ones coming out of the loudspeaker? What was the complicity of judges, journalists, teachers, clergy, the *nomenklatura*, politicians in the West? Truth commissions in former Communist nations are not only a way to uncover secret crimes and acknowledge the victims' suffering. They can help people adopt the habit of thinking for themselves—inoculation against future dictatorship.

The great flaw of the Enquetekommission, however, was that it reached mainly the victims, the only people interested. The challenge was to get the perpetrators, as well as victims, into the discussion. Germany unwittingly brought this about when it opened the secret-police files to the victims. Anyone can apply to the Gauck Authority—an independent agency with custody of the Stasi files, headed by the East German pastor Joachim Gauck—to see his or her own Stasi file. The Gauck Authority blacks over names of third parties who could be hurt, such as the neighbor whose drinking problem the file discusses. But the object of surveillance can see the rest.

For many people, their Stasi files have brought the past to life. They can now understand why they did not get the promotion at work. Gerd and Ulrike Poppe now understand the tensions in their family, since they now know that the Stasi sent men to seduce Ulrike and convinced the head of their son's school to turn the child against his parents. Asking for your Stasi file is a fateful decision. One woman, Vera Wollenberger, realized with horror that the informer "Donald," who gave the Stasi intimate details of her health and finances, could be none other than her husband. Some dissidents discovered that dozens of friends betrayed them. But others discovered that none did. The decision to open the files was a decision to treat citizens with respect, providing them with information that affected their lives. It has helped those victimized by the Stasi to put the past behind them.

The confessions of former informants have been a side effect of opening the files. Germany was the only country I visited where it was possible to find people who admitted to informing for the secret police. You couldn't turn on the TV in Germany without seeing some talk show discussion or interview with a Stasi informant.

The reason is that only in Germany do the spies know the game is up. The files are open; they will get caught. They come forward as damage control.

This situation has produced a torrent of discussion between the spies and their quarry—on television and around kitchen tables. The conversation is often frustrating. The victims want acknowledgment of their suffering; the spies want forgiveness. But the victims come to accuse, and the spies come to justify their behavior, and no one goes home happy. Since German television and newspapers pay for interviews, the same people who once found working for the Stasi to be good business later found they could make a tidy living repenting the Stasi on various stages and TV sets around Germany. These discussions often came to resemble the Oprah Winfrey show. "The lights, the TV cameras, you can't see if there is real shame here," said Werner Fischer, a former dissident who participated in or moderated many of these discussions. "It's a small thing to see, shame."

The German conversation may be unsatisfying, but that it exists at all is an achievement, one that helps the victims—if only because it gives them some control in a system where they had none. And the conversation has provoked a useful debate on the issue of collaboration.

In June 1997, the Czech files were opened to their victims, and Hungary followed three months later. But few people in Hungary have applied to see their archives, and many of those who did apply were disappointed, since a large percentage of the files had been shredded or not yet opened to the public. In 1998, Poland adopted laws opening its files to victims, but the files will not be ready for some time. Germany had an advantage—it could open the files because it is rich. The Gauck Authority hired thousands of people to handle the millions of requests for files. In other countries that open the files, people will have to wait for decades. But it is still worth doing, even if the requesters' names are simply entered into a drawing each month, with 100 people chosen. Sooner or later, people will see their files. And because of that, the spies will come forward.

The Social Democratic government that took power in the Czech Republic in July 1998 halted another method the country was using to deal with the past, the administrative purge, which has come to be known as lustration. In the Czech version, which is the best known, the secret-police files were kept by the Interior Ministry. Anyone applying for or holding a high post in government, a university, or a state-owned business had to contact the ministry, which searched the files. If the applicant's name was not on the list of secret-police informers, or on one of several other lists—such as the list of members of the People's Militia or of high Party functionaries—then he or she could have the job. Applicants on one of the lists, however, received a single letter—"B" was the designation for a secret agent, for example—and no other information. The only appeal was a lawsuit.

This law was passed in Czechoslovakia with the best of intentions. It was designed to keep people of low morals and Communist mentality out of the new government. In Vaclav Havel, the country had the world's most professionally moral head of state. Why staff the government with former spies?

But instead of fighting Communist habits, lustration ended up replicating them. Its supporters argued not that the secret-police lists were largely correct—which they undoubtedly were—but that they were perfect, which they certainly were not. Some of the people tarred were simply acquaintances of secret-police officials who had never informed, but had their names falsely used to meet a quota. Others signed an agreement to inform under duress but never did. Some were dissidents who inadvertently said something during an interrogation. One former dissident, Jirina Siklova, showed me her living room, a warren of hiding places, where the secret police found some bank receipts and accused her of being the banker for Charter 77, the dissident movement. She showed them her bank book and they went away, satisfied. What those who might read that record and accuse her of collaboration would not know, however, is that she really *was* the banker for Charter 77. The records the secret police saw were false. One of the hollowed-out books that remained undiscovered on her shelves held the organization's real records. "We are examining this question with no context," she said. "You know a person told the police something. It looks terrible. But I know that it's not important. I know what he *didn't* say."

Lustration gives citizens no information, allows them no appeal, treats them as guilty until proven innocent, and replicates the Communist mentality of the list. Communism is not a present danger for the Czech Republic and the rest of the east bloc. But Communist thinking is. On a small scale, lustration, like some of the former east bloc's trials, replicates communism's abuse of power.

The Czech Republic is now virtually finished with lustration. It was renewed in 1995 for four more years, but it now matters to people less and less, and both major Czech parties oppose extending it again after it expires in 2000. But several other countries have had their own versions of lustration.

In Germany, former Stasi employees can be barred from jobs but only after an examination of their whole file. The debate about Manfred Stolpe, the governor of Brandenburg state, is a good illustration. Under communism, Stolpe was the chief officer of East Germany's Protestant church. If he had been lustrated in the Czech Republic, he would have received a certificate with the single letter "B." But this was Germany, and the Gauck Authority's published report on Stolpe's activities was sixty-one pages long, plus annexes. It showed that he met with Stasi officials hundreds of times over three decades. Stolpe argued that he lessened persecution of the church. The debate over Stolpe's role was noisy and vicious—but it was exactly the debate lustration should produce. A public well informed about Stolpe's history debated the true complicity of those who talked to the Stasi. Shortly after, he won a landslide re-election as governor.

In its scope, however, German lustration is more unjust than the Czech version. Whereas Czech lustration applies to high-ranking officials, in some parts of the former East Germany, women who had dished out mashed potatoes in the Stasi cafeteria would be ineligible even to sweep streets. Most other eastern European nations have tried some form of lustration. Poland's 1997 law is typical— public officials who admit having collaborated with the secret police are not barred from public life. Those who lie or conceal it, however, will be banned for ten years. These laws have often been overturned or simply ignored when left-wing parties have won power.

President Havel, who initially opposed the lustration law but ended up signing it, had originally proposed that people could be barred from jobs only after the state had proven they harmed others. This idea, which was rejected by parliament, is the proper way to keep the guilty out of the government. Other countries have used it successfully. After El Salvador's civil war, for example, a commission made a thorough, impartial, and individual investigation of the records of military officials and named more than 100 of them who were credibly accused of serious crimes, including the defense minister. All left the armed forces, although some went so slowly that they completed their service and retired with full honors and pensions. This purge has helped to transform El Salvador's military, which is now half its former size and has reformed more than any other institution since the war. These kind of purges can rid the state of those complicit in repression, without turning into a Cultural Revolution.

Ethnic War

ETHNIC WAR IS THE THIRD, and probably most intractable, kind of disease plaguing societies. Wars between people of differing religions, races, tribes, or ethnicities are particularly hard to end, since people who feel they are fighting for their very survival are not amenable to compromise. From Northern Ireland, to the Basque separatist movement in Spain, to Rwanda, to Bosnia, to Chechnya, ethnic hostility needs three things to spill over into violence.

First, there must be a history of repression or violence strong enough so that a group can use fear to motivate its members to kill others. There has never been an ethnic war where people, even those responsible for the bulk of the crimes, did not consider themselves victims and what they did justifiable for their own cultural or physical survival.

Second, the political situation must provoke resentment or fear. Catholic Republicans in Northern Ireland, for instance, felt they had been discriminated against for decades. But the biggest risk of violence comes when there is a change in the political situation that inspires new fear. For example, the breakup of Yugoslavia into ethnic states made Serbs, who had been the dominant ethnic group, afraid that they would be mistreated in new states where they were minorities, such as Croatia or Bosnia.

Third, and most important, ethnic warfare requires a psychopath with a television station willing to exploit people's fear. Without Slobodan Milosevic broadcasting propaganda about how Muslims were eating Serb babies and taking Serb women for harems, Serbs would not have turned so brutally on their neighbors. The same was true in Rwanda, where radio programs broadcast false reports of Tutsi plots to kill Hutu and encouraged Hutu to massacre Tutsi.

Not only are the violent emotions of ethnic conflict hard to change; even more difficult to confront are the vast numbers of terrible crimes such as murder, rape, or torture that are committed in the course of an ethnic war. To someone convinced that all Muslims or Tutsi or Albanians are dangerous enemies, there is no such thing as a civilian. Propaganda can turn a terrifyingly large number of otherwise ordinary people into vicious killers in these neighbor-versus-neighbor wars.

Justice is necessary. Trials are crucial for the families of the victims and for these nations' future. Trials (or even indictments) can break the control that the instigators of ethnic violence continue to enjoy. Even though Radovan Karadzic, the Bosnian Serb leader, has not been pursued by NATO, his indictment by the Yugoslav tribunal put him into hiding and removed his political influence. Trials can help break the cycle of revenge that has kept these wars recurring. They can personalize crimes so that victims hold responsible individual Hutu and not the entire group. The Kosovo Albanian who watched his family murdered would be less likely to try to avenge that killing if he knew Belgrade would find the killers, try them, and put them in jail.

Trials can also provoke a dialogue in society that can crack through victimization myths, helping people to see those from other ethnic groups as human beings who have also suffered. A Serb policeman I met in the Serb Republic town of Prijedor was absolutely typical. When I asked questions about the Serb slaughter of Muslims in local concentration camps, he answered by talking about Serb children killed in World War II. Serb children were indeed slaughtered in World War II—but mainly by Croats and

Germans, not Muslims, and even if Muslims had been the killers, that is no justification for killing other innocents. Such responses infuriate victims, who need to hear the guilty parties acknowledge that others suffered as well and that their own people committed crimes.

The abandonment of the justifications of victimization is also crucial for healing a political culture so that ethnic conflict does not return. Grudges fester and grow as each generation avenges the past generation's suffering or commits crimes out of fear that past slaughter will be repeated. In Rwanda, Hutu massacred Tutsis in part because they remembered five Tutsi massacres of Hutu that had taken place in neighboring Burundi since the 1960s. In the Balkans, these cycles have been going on for thousands of years and have been brought to the surface by unscrupulous leaders in uncertain times. Slobodan Milosevic began his nationalist campaign in Kosovo by invoking the defeat of Serb Prince Lazar at the hands of the Turks in 1389. The force of these victimization myths encourages the popularity of the very leaders most apt to exploit them, such as Milosevic. These societies need a dialogue on victimization, and they need to be exposed to how leaders manipulate the myths to keep power.

For trials to have this effect, however, they must be not only fair but also transparent and accessible enough to the population to overcome propaganda that will paint them as one-sided. The violations of civil rights routine in Britain's antiterrorism courts—people charged with terrorism can be held for seven days before being charged, and in Northern Ireland's special courts there is no right to a jury trial—were an excellent recruiting tool for the Irish Republican Army.

But although justice is crucial after ethnic mass murder, it is also impossible. International tribunals such as those for Bosnia and

Rwanda are useful, but they are not the full solution. They are hugely expensive: The Bosnia tribunal had a 1999 budget of $94 million—and that was *before* Kosovo exploded. Tribunals can try only a small group of perpetrators, and that group should be composed of those at the very top. Justice must necessarily be extremely selective in countries with tens of thousands, hundreds of thousands of cases. Except for Spain and Britain, most nations riven by ethnic conflict are underdeveloped, with weak courts. In Rwanda, Hutu killers specifically targeted judges to ensure justice could never occur. Furthermore, judges are just as susceptible to ethnic biases as anyone else, and it may be impossible to get unprejudiced trials.

These broken societies must find other ways, then, to bring the benefits of justice to the victims and to the political culture. A truth commission can help. The idea of a truth commission in Bosnia—first proposed by an American group, the U.S. Institute of Peace—is gaining strength among Bosnians. It would assemble a commission of respected Muslims, Croats, and Serbs to try to write a common history of the war. If it can take testimony in public in a way credible to all groups, it can help to convince people that their own ethnic brethren were not the only ones who had grievances or who suffered. The Institute of Peace recommends that the commission seek out witnesses who can testify about cross-ethnic acts of kindness they experienced.

South Africa

APARTHEID SOUTH AFRICA HAD characteristics from all three kinds of regimes I have described above. It had the ethnic divisions—not just black–white but also the part political, part ethnic violence between the African National Congress and the largely Zulu Inkatha Freedom Party—that has led to cycles of killings and revenge. Like communism, apartheid counted on an extensive spy network and ruined the lives of large numbers of people. It also had the widespread societal complicity of communism, since apartheid was a bureaucratic endeavor that required the cooperation of everyone from grade-school teachers to generals. In addition, it had the targeted physical violence of the Latin American military dictatorships.

As elsewhere, South Africa's victims of serious crimes need real justice and an acknowledgment of what happened, preferably from the perpetrators themselves. As under communism, they also need affirmative action and reparations. Finally, South Africa must improve its institutions so that the next generation can get the decent education, health care, housing and other services that blacks were long denied.

Acknowledgment, preferably from the mouths of perpetrators, is also important to combat racism in South Africa and to build a common political future. Many white South Africans closed their eyes to the crimes apartheid was committing in their names. Helping them to understand how blacks have suffered can improve race relations and the support for affirmative action. Openness about anti-apartheid terror actions will have the same results.

The future danger to South Africa is not a resurgence of apartheid. Like communism, apartheid was shot in the heart and is not coming back. The danger is a highly polarized society or one that falls into African-style dictatorship. Apartheid left South Africa with a legacy of abuse of power, corrupt police, and unfair courts. The rebellion against apartheid left South Africa with one-party domination. South Africa will not always have leaders with the restraint and wisdom of Nelson Mandela. Without stronger institutions, South Africa could someday become another Zimbabwe, with a capricious, corrupt, and autocratic ruler who permits little dissent.

All these factors make South Africa's Truth and Reconciliation Commission an exciting new development. South Africa had a very different political equation from the Latin American nations with truth commissions. The incoming Mandela government did not have complete power over the old apartheid leaders, but it had much more power than the Latin democrats. It could order the apartheid leaders to testify, and it had a court system with the power to try them. The victims of apartheid were less afraid of reprisals for speaking out. The new government's clout allowed it to solve many of the problems that hampered truth commissions in Chile or El Salvador.

First, it could hold its hearings in public. The truth commission did publish a 3,500-page report, but few will read it. That does not matter, because its public proceedings were carried live on radio and appeared on the television news and in the newspapers every day. Some black newspapers carried stories on virtually every person's testimony, and even Afrikaans papers covered the commission in depth. No one living in South Africa could escape the truth commission or fail to see the human stories of repression.

Second—and this was probably due to the legal structures South Africa did have in place (although they dispensed justice only for whites)—the truth commission also managed to name names while largely adhering to the due process of law. This fairness was important for a South Africa that wished to avoid repeating the abuses of power that characterized the apartheid regime and most of its neighbors.

In an attempt to ensure due process, the commission interviewed in advance the victims who were planning to testify in public. Everyone the victims planned to accuse was notified and given the right to come to the same hearing and reply. Amnesty-seekers who did not have lawyers were given them. Everyone the commission was planning to name in its final report as a gross violator of human rights was told in advance what the commission was planning to say and on what basis. They then had the right to tell their side of events to the commission before it wrote the final report.

The third accomplishment of South Africa's truth commission was that it produced not just an official acknowledgment of crimes from a head of state but confessions from the perpetrators. The truth commission offered a trade-off: Anyone who confessed in full to a political crime from the apartheid era had a good chance of getting amnesty. This was not a blanket amnesty that hid the truth and furthered a culture of impunity. This amnesty brought out the truth in hundreds of cases where it would otherwise have been hidden; and it also contributed to some trials because the government was able to learn information from the amnesty-seekers that it could use to try those who had not applied. Although the truth commission was attacked for its amnesty provisions by the family members of some high-profile victims—for example, the wife of Steve Biko (whose killers were later denied amnesty)—it made an important contribution in democratizing healing for the less famous victims.

Although South Africa, unlike Latin America, had the political power to put apartheid leaders on trial, it had, and still has, a feeble justice system. Many of the police are from the old regime and are doing what they can to sabotage justice. None of the police, old or new, can investigate crimes effectively—many, for example, cannot even drive. The justice system is overwhelmed by crime. South Africa has been able to try only a handful of apartheid's leaders, and several of those, such as Defense Minister Magnus Malan, were acquitted. Even absent the truth commission, a few such trials is probably all the country would have accomplished. The rest of the victims would have been shut out.

The truth commission—even with all the limits Meredith describes—at least gave them something. Many were able to hear their victimizers confess on national television. They got to hear the policeman say, if not that he was sorry, at least that, yes, their loved one was beaten to death and did not, as previously advertised, suddenly go wild in police custody and bang his head. They could be sure that the policeman's family, friends, and colleagues heard this confession. This is something. Moreover, anyone who wanted to could go before an auditorium full of people and television cameras to tell his or her own story.

Although other nations cannot duplicate South Africa's truth commission—in Chile the military would simply have laughed if told its soldiers had to confess or risk prosecution—all countries trying to overcome atrocities of the past must face the fact that they will likely be able to hold only symbolic trials of a few leaders. Thus finding alternatives to traditional trials that still preserve citizens' rights is the task of every nation that recognizes the limits of its ability to deal with the past.

FACING THE PAST: MAKING IT WORK

So FAR I HAVE LAID OUT my views on what different types of new democracies should do to help heal the victims of war or tyranny and create a healthier political culture to keep such plagues from returning. A few governments, like that of South Africa, have been able to carry out the best policies we know so far. Most have not. In a few cases, such as some former Communist countries whose leaders retain the habit of abusing their power, the new government has simply chosen not to respect the rule of law. In the vast majority of cases, however, the problem is impunity—those guilty of crimes retain the power to elude trial and defy efforts to get to the truth. I now turn to how countries marked by centuries of impunity for the powerful can begin to hold their old leaders accountable.

If there is one lesson to be drawn from the experiences of all the nations that have tried to deal with the past, it is that begging is useless. Changing the balance of power is the only way to make a previously powerful person stand trial or confess his or her crimes. The new state must be strong enough to bring perpetrators to trial, or it must create a situation where they choose to do the right thing because the alternative is worse. In South Africa, police came forward to tell the truth because they feared trial if they didn't. In Germany, former spies confessed to their victims because they knew they would be caught, and they wanted to put out their version of events first.

The long-term solution is for nations to create working justice systems that can try even the wealthy or members of the military. This long term is too far away for many nations to be of much use today. Fortunately, in the last decade, a new player has emerged that can both help countries strengthen their judicial systems and alter the calculus of dealing with the past. That new player is called, in an infelicitous phrase, the international community.

The Nuremberg tribunals had important flaws. They used the concept of collective guilt; they hung Julius Streicher, a Nazi newspaper publisher, purely for speech crimes; and they were, above all, victors' justice. But the Nuremberg and Far East tribunals after World War II marked a high point in the international community's efforts to deal with a repressive past. In the euphoria of the late 1940s, which saw the creation of the United Nations and the adoption of the Geneva conventions, the Universal Declaration of Human Rights, and conventions against genocide and torture, many had high hopes for the creation of a permanent world court to enforce these conventions and try international criminals.

But the cold war got in the way. The United States and the Soviet Union could not agree on the definition of aggression—one of the crimes tried at Nuremberg, then considered a core crime for any international court. Plans for the permanent court were shelved, and few serious efforts at international justice took place for fifty years.

Now the cold war is over, and international institutions are no longer the subject of the old struggles between the superpowers. There is also a new consensus on the desirability of democracy, human rights, and the rule of law. Since the late 1980s, these two factors have produced several new international attempts to hold serious criminals accountable.

The Americas have an international infrastructure for protecting human rights, the Inter-American Court of Human Rights and its related commission. In 1988, the court issued its first decisions, two judgments holding the Honduran government responsible for the forced disappearance of two of its citizens. Honduras paid the families of each man more than a quarter million dollars. In other cases, the court has prodded national courts to take justice seriously. Under threat of an Inter-American Court judgment, for example, Guatemala in 1993 took the unprecedented step of trying and sentencing two former civil patrol officials for killing two human rights workers in the village of Chunimá; the officials were sentenced to twenty years in jail each.

A better-known advance in the international community's treatment of crimes was the creation in 1993 of the International Criminal Tribunal for Yugoslavia, and in 1994 of its sister tribunal for Rwanda. In mid-1999, the United Nations was also working on the structure of a new mixed court to try leaders of the Khmer Rouge regime, with participation from both the international community and Cambodians.

In July 1998, 120 nations signed a treaty that will establish an International Criminal Court to try genocide, crimes against humanity, and war crimes. And there is a growing recognition that some crimes are so heinous that they can be prosecuted anywhere, by any nation. Although this law has been around for decades, it is starting to be used, with the arrest of General Pinochet as the most controversial example.

These international developments are important in three different ways. First, they have modernized the law itself. Rape, sexual slavery, and other sex crimes are now firmly considered crimes against humanity and, in some cases, can be part of genocide. An appeals court of the Yugoslavia tribunal ruled in the court's first case that crimes against humanity can be committed in peacetime. After the creation of the International Criminal Court statute, no state can now claim that serious crimes committed internally are its own business; they can be judged in international courts. The Inter-American Commission on Human Rights released a ruling in 1999 that El Salvador's blanket amnesty of 1993 was illegal, since it covered heinous crimes every state has a duty to punish.

Second, these new international efforts at justice are putting teeth into international law for the first time since Nuremberg. Until the establishment of the Yugoslavia tribunal, the world was like a city with strong laws but no police, courts, or jails to enforce them. The prosecutions of the Yugoslavia and Rwanda tribunals are still limited and largely symbolic; they cannot do justice on a grand scale. But the Rwanda tribunal has convicted some of the most important men behind the genocide, including former prime minister Jean Kabanda, who got a life sentence after pleading guilty. The Yugoslavia tribunal has hooked no big fish because NATO is unwilling to arrest the most powerful of the indicted, such as Bosnian Serb leader Radovan Karadzic. Nonetheless, in September 1999 it has thirty of the sixty-five publicly accused individuals in custody including some important Bosnian Serbs, and among those on trial in mid-1999 were people like Tihomir Blaskic, who was the commander of the Bosnian Croat army—an upper-medium fish at least. And its prosecutions have a ripple effect. The court is scaring people. Throughout the Serb Republic of Bosnia, people who participated in the genocide are afraid of being nabbed, especially because recent indictments are sealed, so no one knows who is on the list. Many have left public life and gone into hiding.

The International Criminal Court will be established when sixty nations have ratified the treaty they signed. This court will be weaker than the Yugoslavia and Rwanda tribunals, since the countries who met to draw up the rules were very conscious that their own citizens could become defendants. The court's biggest flaw is that in most cases it can try people for war crimes or crimes against humanity only with the consent of either the country where the crimes were committed or the country to which perpetrators belong. This means that for internal conflicts—which make up the vast majority of wars today—the court will be extremely limited. A future Saddam Hussein (the court will not be retrospective) can only be prosecuted for crimes against his own people if he gives his consent! This will allow dictators in his situation to travel freely.

But the court is still a major advance. It will allow prosecutors to gather information on cases of genocide, war crimes, and crimes against humanity, bringing them to international attention. When these crimes are committed in international wars, or when they involve matters where the UN Security Council gets involved, criminals will be tried. It is enough of an advance that the United States became one of seven nations that voted against its creation, terrified of the remote possibility that an American soldier might be tried. Washington did everything possible to weaken the court— even threatening to withdraw American troops from Germany if Bonn voted for rules that would make the court more effective.

The other development—the growing acceptance of universal

jurisdiction, where any nation can try the worst international crimes because they are an affront to all humanity—is not new law at all. Grave breaches of the 1949 Geneva conventions have always been prosecutable in any nation, but until now, no one has chosen to do so. Now, for the first time, countries are taking the idea of universal jurisdiction seriously. The United States signaled its approval of this principle when it sought to have Pol Pot tried in Canada or Denmark. Those countries do not have citizens among the Khmer Rouge victims, but they do have laws allowing them to try foreigners for genocide. The United States has such laws for torture but not genocide—an oversight that should be remedied.

Since the early 1990s, it has been legally possible to bring criminal prosecutions for torture in American courts, even when both the defendants and the victims are foreigners. No such prosecution has yet taken place. But these acts are being litigated in civil trials in American courts. Some trials have ended in large damage judgments, although ones unlikely to be collected. Guatemala's General Héctor Gramajo, for example, who studied at Harvard's Kennedy School of Government after retiring from the military, was slapped with a $47.5 million judgment in American court for abuses against eight Guatemalans and an American nun while he was in power. Bosnian Serb leader Karadzic is being sued in a New York court for mass rapes of Bosnians allegedly carried out on his watch.

The expansion of universal jurisdiction took place largely outside the public eye until the dramatic arrest of General Pinochet in October 1998. Technically, Spain is not using only universal jurisdiction to charge Mr. Pinochet, since he is accused of torture, kidnapping, and terrorist acts against not only Chileans but some Spanish citizens who were living in Chile. But his arrest has provoked a worldwide discussion of the issue. In mid-1999 the case was still winding through a labyrinthine legal process, but Britain seemed to have concluded that the general must stand trial in Spain. Other dictators are already becoming cautious. Before Laurent Kabila traveled to Belgium for a meeting last November, he checked to ensure there was no warrant for his arrest. The world may soon see new efforts to indict Pinochet's colleagues, perhaps General Efraín Ríos Montt, who presided over the most intense genocide, or so Guatemala's truth commission has implied. Fidel Castro, as potent a symbol as Pinochet, could also be indicted.

The fear, of course, is that a prosecution such as Spain's could imperil transitions to democracy in the native country of the person under trial, although this is not a serious concern in Chile. In fact, Chile offers an example of how such foreign prosecutions can contribute to transitions. If the Chilean government attempted to try Pinochet—one of its promises in its efforts to get him back from London—the military would likely make trouble, since officers know they could pressure the government into backing down. The military has no such leverage over Britain or Spain or over an international criminal court. Misbehavior would simply make them look like thugs, which would not help their case.

The more troubling question is whether dictators would ever leave power if they could not clinch an immunity deal. British law provides sovereign immunity to sitting heads of state. The law is dangerous, since it gives dictators incentive to stay in power. But no such law exists in many other places. The International Criminal Court statute grants no immunity to sitting heads of state. Nor do the tribunals for Yugoslavia and Rwanda—as was dramatically illustrated by the May 1999 indictment of Slobodan Milosevic, Yugoslavia's president. Heads of state are specifically *included* under the genocide convention, as they have the greatest complicity.

If other countries followed Britain and postponed prosecutions until a dictator had left power, it could indeed complicate some negotiated transitions, especially those that end a war that has essentially been stalemated. Some dictators would be more inclined to cling to power. Most, however, would be unable. Dictators such as Pinochet leave power not because they choose to but because they have to—because the forces that propped them up, be they the Politburo in Moscow or a military junta and the support of a wealthy elite, are dissolving. Dictators go because they lose control.

Whatever incentive the fear of trials could give to a dictator to stay in power, however, could be balanced, at least in part, by the fact that new accountability would discourage crimes to begin with. Such discouragement would not occur immediately—it is unrealistic to think that Turkish police would stop torturing because Pinochet got nabbed; but if several Pinochets did, and people began to take it as a serious possibility, then we would indeed see fewer crimes.

The other issue raised by the Pinochet case is that of sovereignty. Spain chose not to prosecute the criminals who worked with its own Pinochet, General Franco. How can it then decide that the bargain Chileans made to get their country back is suddenly illegitimate?

Part of the answer to this question lies in a change of context. The international climate was very different in the time of Franco, and even at the time of his death. Today, there is wide recognition that the crimes Pinochet is accused of cannot be hidden behind sovereignty—one example of that consensus is the International Criminal Court's statute, signed by the vast majority of the world's nations, that serious crimes committed in internal wars are subject to international prosecution.

Moreover, part of the question of sovereignty must be the issue of how "sovereign" a decision Pinochet's amnesty was. It was not a decision of Chile's people. He issued it for himself. The amnesty was also clearly illegitimate, since these types of crimes against humanity can never receive a blanket amnesty. The democratic governments of Patricio Aylwin and Eduardo Frei kept the deal in part because Pinochet left behind a congress packed with appointed senators that ensured his followers would have an undemocratic veto. Because of that, the democratic forces lack the votes to overturn the amnesty.

The other reason the government protects the amnesty is fear, not fear of a military coup—anything that killed Chile's steady economic growth would have no popular support. But the very cautious government is afraid of any kind of insubordination or show of strength by the military.

Spain's challenge to Chile's sovereignty is also unlikely to throw international diplomacy into chaos. For better or worse, few countries will prosecute other nations' leaders for crimes that are muddied with political decisions or whose prohibition under international law is not clear—for example, civilian deaths in an aerial bombing, which is not illegal unless the civilian casualties are disproportionate to the military objective. In addition, no country is apt to hold a visiting leader or former leader, as Britain did for Spain, unless the country requesting him or her has a trustworthy judicial system and can show good evidence. Libya may wish to indict Ronald Reagan for the 1986 bombing of Tripoli, but no country has an extradition treaty with Libya. Politically motivated prosecutions will receive little support. It is likely that the only people who need fear arrest and prosecution are those who committed the most heinous crimes.

Finally, any debate about whether to establish a new international accountability for such crimes must consider the cost of not doing so. We cannot forget that the current system lets dictators kill innocents with impunity. Surely changing this is worth a little diplomatic uproar. Pinochet is like a man who has killed a few members of a household and taken the others hostage. No nation would simply agree to let him walk free because he can create havoc. Murder is wrong and must be punished.

In addition to modernizing law generally and putting the sort of teeth into international law that were displayed in the Pinochet case, the third reason that international progress on punishing serious crimes is important is that it changes the climate for everyone. If a consensus grows internationally that countries must punish serious criminals, then nations are less likely to issue amnesties. International pressure can be an effective counterweight to the threats of the military.

Chile is a good example. Pinochet's capture has lifted the silence blanketing the killings of his coup. International embarassment has emboldened judges, who are forcing the military to confront its crimes. Twenty-five officers have been arrested on charges of murder, torture and kidnapping—although not Pinochet, who as Senator-for-life still enjoys parliamentary immunity. In August, talks began between military officers and human rights lawyers.

International trials should not become substitutes for national trials but should be done in a way to encourage national justice. To make the largest contribution toward healing victims and building a culture of justice, trials should be held in the country concerned. So far they have not been. Rwanda's tribunal is in Arusha, Tanzania, and Yugoslavia's is in The Hague, Netherlands. So people in the affected countries cannot follow the proceedings and can only hear them reported on highly propagandistic local radio and TV. Most people in Serbia and the Serb Republic of Bosnia believe the local reports, which paint the Yugoslavia tribunal as anti-Serb. The distance also keeps the tribunals from providing a visible example of fair trials. The trials at the international tribunal for Rwanda contrast sharply and favorably with the appalling domestic trials

Rwanda itself is holding for genocide. It would take Rwanda 500 years to try everyone held in jails there. Most will wait for years and never go to trial, and those that do run a high risk of being executed after only a summary trial. This kind of "justice" only contributes to resentment.

The greatest value that international prosecutions provide for national justice, however, is as cudgel. They change the balance of power. As with South Africa's truth commission or the opening of Germany's files, international prosecutions' existence can help persuade perpetrators to do things they would not otherwise do—come forward with the truth, for example, or submit to national justice. The International Criminal Court, for example, will only prosecute when national courts are unable or unwilling.

This leverage does not yet exist, since international justice is not yet applied consistently enough. Such leverage requires both an international criminal court in full operation and wide acceptance of the Pinochet precedent. With these two things in place, the international community could greatly help the cause of accountability by guaranteeing that it will step in and prosecute those most responsible for genocide, war crimes, and crimes against humanity if the countries that harbor the perpetrators fail to do so. To ensure that the certainty of justice does not provide incentive for tyrants to cling to power, there should be no immunity for sitting heads of state.

The idea of a system of international guarantees of justice is just beginning to be a subject of serious discussion. Paul van Zyl, who was the executive secretary of South Africa's truth commission, is one of those who has most advanced the debate. Different people have different ideas of how to do it. The following would be my plan.

A system of international guarantees would have to take into account the reasons why a particular nation has not done justice. I can think of four such reasons, and each needs a different solution. Some nations—Haiti, for example—simply can not try people because their judicial systems are broken and investigators and judges lack the skills they need. In these cases, requiring prosecutions would be silly. It would bankrupt already feeble justice systems and would encourage injustice, since countries would resort to unfair summary trials.

The solution here is to concentrate on the big fish and to try to use their trials as an opportunity to strengthen a weak judicial system. International jurists would work with local courts and investigators to collect evidence and hold trials, demonstrating good practices along the way. Such trials would in a sense be training for locals, and the money would come from the international community. If that could not work or the country was unwilling to hold a local trial, then the most important accused would be tried in the International Criminal Court, an ad hoc tribunal, or a foreign nation.

The second case occurs when a country chooses, through democratic means—a referendum or approval by an elected parliament—to use a South Africa–style truth commission, granting amnesty to those who tell the full truth. The international community should encourage these arrangements by, if necessary, providing the courts that would prosecute those who do not apply for amnesty or those who don't get it. This would give even countries with weak judicial systems the leverage they need to encourage the full truth.

Third are cases where those considered most responsible for serious crimes are not prosecuted because the new government is afraid such trials would destabilize delicate transitions, such as in Chile. Here, the international community would step in if countries were afraid to prosecute. That threat might give new governments the power that would enable them to try people at home. If a government still thinks that such trials would be too dangerous, then an international court would try them. Its prosecutions would not be destabilizing because the criminals who could derail a national trial with their threats would have no such power over an international trial.

Fourth, there are some situations when even an international prosecution could genuinely upset a transition and cause a resumption of war or dictatorship. This happens when individuals who have been involved in state terror or guerrilla terror renounce such tactics, lead their movements into peace negotiations, and have now become relative moderates, trying to keep a harder-line wing in check. Palestinian leader Yasir Arafat is one example. Sinn Fein leader Gerry Adams is another. It is hard to think about prosecuting someone who gets, or could have gotten, the Nobel Peace Prize.

These cases will be infrequent, since these kinds of leaders are seldom those with the most responsibility for crimes—Gerry Adams, for example, would not likely have the level of guilt to make him an international target. Yasir Arafat is more of a question mark. In a case like this, the world cannot ask a nation to commit suicide. But these exceptions must be few, and there must be a very good case that prosecution would indeed lead directly to a resumption of war, terror, or dictatorship.

Changing the balance of power that a new, democratic government enjoys when dealing with the crimes of the past would produce more justice and more truth. What it might not produce is more people who feel satisfied with the job their new democracies have done. All over the world, from Cape Town to Vladivostok, from Jakarta to Tierra del Fuego, bitterness reigns. The vast majority of people who lived through war or tyranny will tell you that their hopes for the future went unfulfilled.

One reason that hopes have been unfulfilled is that they were unrealistically high. Walter Momper, the former mayor of Berlin, told me that with the trial of former East German leader Erich Honecker, people thought they could get rid of the past. Citizens of Communist countries dreamed of the system's fall for decades. Many believed that democracy and capitalism—especially as embodied in the rich societies they saw in the movies—would emerge, gleaming, when communism was chipped away. But in any nation, the new society will function with much the same customs and ways of thinking as the old.

Czechs who supported lustration, for example, were horrified to see that the old Communists simply went into business—money being the new currency of power—and did quite well. They had contacts, good education, managerial experience, and, most important, they were the operators who manage to come out on top in any system. This situation is not easy to change. Governments come and go, but the habits of a lifetime remain.

This fact is devastating to many people who had dreamed of, and deserved, better. For them, the most effective way to deal with the past may be to concentrate on creating a better present and future. Putting a few generals on trial is of limited use if the justice system continues to be submissive and corrupt. Scholarships for children are worth little if the schools they can attend have no books. A high-profile trial from the past can focus a nation's attention on flaws in the justice system and encourage their repair. But it can also drain a large part of the money that could otherwise go to improving peoples' lives today.

The conviction of Eugene de Kock, the infamous South African hit-squad commander known as Prime Evil, for example, helped ensure that others feared conviction enough to confess to the truth commission. It showed that the democratic government could and would punish heinous crimes. It may deter future de Kocks. But the cost was huge. The state called over 100 witnesses—some of whom needed to be put in witness protection programs abroad—and paid the cost of defending de Kock, which alone came to 1 million dollars. Was that the best use of money in a country desperately in need of housing, water, police, hospitals, and schools?

On an international scale, dealing with the past can, and at times has, become a politically palatable substitute for actions that could prevent or cut short atrocities as they are happening. The West supported the tribunals for Yugoslavia and Rwanda, for example, out of guilt over having done nothing to prevent the genocide. In Kosovo, NATO did intervene while the atrocities were occurring. But it did so only from high in the air, a strategy designed to avoid risk to NATO's soldiers and therefore to keep support for the war high in NATO countries. The people who lost out were the Kosovo Albanians, thousands of whom were being slaughtered on the ground. And Kosovo is the *best* example of an international intervention to stop genocide. The chances of something similar happening in Africa are remote.

Stopping atrocities should be more urgent than punishing those who have committed them. Trials and truth are not an end in themselves. They are desirable because they help people and societies to heal, and they thus make it less likely that future generations will suffer. They should be used only in service of those goals and not as a way to divert international pressure from more difficult but necessary work.

INDEX

PublicAffairs is a new nonfiction publishing house and a tribute to the standards, values, and flair of three persons who have served as mentors to countless reporters, writers, editors, and book people of all kinds, including me.

I.F. Stone, proprietor of *I. F. Stone's Weekly*, combined a commitment to the First Amendment with entrepreneurial zeal and reporting skill and became one of the great independent journalists in American history. At the age of eighty, Izzy published *The Trial of Socrates*, which was a national bestseller. He wrote the book after he taught himself ancient Greek.

Benjamin C. Bradlee was for nearly thirty years the charismatic editorial leader of *The Washington Post*. It was Ben who gave the *Post* the range and courage to pursue such historic issues as Watergate. He supported his reporters with a tenacity that made them fearless, and it is no accident that so many became authors of influential, best-selling books.

Robert L. Bernstein, the chief executive of Random House for more than a quarter century, guided one of the nation's premier publishing houses. Bob was personally responsible for many books of political dissent and argument that challenged tyranny around the globe. He is also the founder and was the longtime chair of Human Rights Watch, one of the most respected human rights organizations in the world.

·　　·　　·

For fifty years, the banner of Public Affairs Press was carried by its owner Morris B. Schnapper, who published Gandhi, Nasser, Toynbee, Truman, and about 1,500 other authors. In 1983 Schnapper was described by *The Washington Post* as "a redoubtable gadfly." His legacy will endure in the books to come.

Peter Osnos, *Publisher*